Data Cleaning with Power BI

The definitive guide to transforming dirty data into
actionable insights

Gus Frazer

Data Cleaning with Power BI

Group Product Manager: Kaustubh Manglurkar

Publishing Product Manager: Deepesh Patel

Book Project Manager: Hemangi Lotlikar

Senior Editor: Rohit Singh

Technical Editor: Yash Bhanushali

Copy Editor: Safis Editing

Proofreader: Safis Editing

Indexer: Subalakshmi Govindhan

Production Designer: Alishon Mendonca

Developer Relations Marketing Executive: Nivedita Singh

First published: February 2024

Production reference: 1270224

Published by Packt Publishing Ltd.

Grosvenor House

11 St Paul's Square

Birmingham

B3 1RB, UK.

ISBN 978-1-80512-640-9

www.packtpub.com

To my incredible wife, whose unwavering support and love sustained me throughout the writing of this book, even as we welcomed our son, Maximus, into the world. I am grateful for your patience and encouragement.

Also, to the skilled team at Packt for their guidance and expertise in shaping this book.

– Gus Frazer

Contributors

About the author

Gus Frazer is a seasoned analytics consultant who focuses on business intelligence solutions. With over eight years of experience working for the two market-leading platforms, Power BI (Microsoft) and Tableau, he has amassed a wealth of knowledge and expertise.

He also has experience in helping hundreds of customers to drive their digital and data transformations, scope data requirements, drive actionable insights, and most important of all, clean data ready for analysis.

I want to thank the people who have been close to me and supported me during the journey of writing this book.

About the reviewer

Rajendra Ongole is a BI specialist/consultant and Power BI trainer. He likes to share his knowledge of different Microsoft technologies on Power Platform, such as Power BI, Power Apps, Power Automate, and Power Virtual Agents. He has more than 13 years of experience in software development in different domains, such as telecom, manufacturing, industrial automation, and a project management office. Every day, he uploads a new video on Power Platform to share his knowledge with his subscribers!

Table of Contents

Preface   xv

Part 1 – Introduction and Fundamentals

1

Introduction to Power BI Data Cleaning   3

Technical requirements   3   Where do we begin with data?   9
Cleaning your data in Power BI   4   Summary   9
Understanding Power Query   5   Questions   9
Understanding DAX   6

2

Understanding Data Quality and Why Data Cleaning is Important   11

What is data quality?   12   Early detection of issues   14
Where do data quality issues come   Continuous improvement and learning 14
from?   12   Empowerment and collaboration   15
The role of data cleaning in   Best practices for data quality overall 15
improving data quality   13   Establishing data quality standards 15
Data integrity and accuracy   14
Decision-making and business outcomes 14 Summary   16
Data ownership and accountability   14   Questions   17
A holistic view of the data ecosystem 14

3

Data Cleaning Fundamentals and Principles   19

Defining data cleaning	20	Data transformations	24
Who's responsible for cleaning data?	20	Data quality assurance	24
Building a process for cleaning data	22	Documentation	25
Data assessment	23	**Understanding quality over quantity in data cleaning**	**25**
Data profiling	23		
Data validation	24	**Summary**	**26**
Data cleaning strategies	24	**Questions**	**26**

4

The Most Common Data Cleaning Operations   29

Technical requirements	29	Creating calculated columns versus measures	41
Removing duplicates	30		
Removing missing data	33	Calculated columns	41
Splitting columns	36	Measures	42
Merging columns	38	Calculation group	43
Replacing values	38	Considerations	44
		Summary	**45**
		Questions	**45**

Part 2 – Data Import and Query Editor

5

Importing Data into Power BI   51

Technical requirements	51	Assessing data relevance	55
Understanding data completeness	52	Assessing data formatting	56
Understanding data accuracy	54	Assessing data normalization, denormalization, and star schemas	61
Understanding data consistency	54		

Dimension modeling and star schema   63

Denormalized data in dimension tables   65

Summary   67

Questions   67

6

Cleaning Data with Query Editor   69

Technical requirements   69

Understanding the
Query Editor interface   69

Data cleaning techniques
and functions   73

Adding columns   73

Data type conversions   74

Date/time   75

Rounding   75

Pivot/unpivot columns   75

Merge queries   76

Using Query Editor versus DAX
for transformation   76

Power Query Editor   77

Data Analysis Expressions (DAX)   78

Workflow   78

Summary   79

Questions   79

Further reading   80

7

Transforming Data with the M Language   81

Technical requirements   81

Understanding the M language   82

Structure of M   82

Common use cases of M   86

Filtering and sorting data with M   87

Transforming data with M   88

Working with data sources in M   90

Creating parameters and variables   90

Summary   104

Questions   104

8

Using Data Profiling for Exploratory Data Analysis (EDA)   107

Understanding EDA   107

Exploring data profiling features
in Power BI   108

Reviewing column quality,
distribution, and profile   109

Column distribution   109

Column quality   110

Column profile   111

Turning data profiles into
high-quality data   113

Recommended actions on column distribution 113   Summary   115

Value distribution   113   Questions   116

Part 3 – Advanced Data Cleaning and Optimizations

9

Advanced Data Cleaning Techniques   121

Technical requirements   121

Using Power Query Editor from within Dataflow Gen1 – fuzzy matching and fill down   122

Fuzzy matching   122

Fill down   126

Best practices for using fuzzy matching and fill down   127

Using R and Python scripts   128

Benefits of using R or Python scripts   129

Getting started with using R or Python scripts in Power BI   129

Using ML to clean data   133

Data cleaning with anomaly detection   134

Data preparation with AutoML   134

Data enhancement with AI Insights   146

Summary   149

Questions   150

10

Creating Custom Functions in Power Query   153

Planning for your custom function   153

Defining the problem   154

Identifying parameters   154

Setting clear objectives   154

Using parameters   154

Types of parameters   154

Defining parameters   155

Best practices for using parameters   163

Creating custom functions   163

Defining the function structure   163

Writing M code   164

Testing and debugging   164

Documentation   164

Summary   171

Questions   171

11

M Query Optimization — 173

Technical requirements   174
Creating custom functions   174
Filtering and reducing data   176
Using native M functions   183
Optimizing memory usage   184

Parallel query execution   185
Using Table.Buffer and Table.Split   187
Summary   194
Questions   194
Further reading   195

12

Data Modeling and Managing Relationships — 197

Understanding the basics of
data modeling   198
Importing versus DirectQuery   198
Dimensional modeling   200
Snowflake schema   201
Intermediate tables   203
Calendars and date tables   204
Role-playing dimensions   205
Aggregating tables   207
Incremental refreshes   207

Using bidirectional cross-filtering 209
What is bidirectional cross-filtering? 210
Best practices for bidirectional
cross-filtering   213

Understanding what's the
right cardinality   214

Understanding cardinality   215
Why cardinality matters   216
Choosing the right cardinality   216

Handling large and
complex datasets   218
Understanding big data   218
Challenges of working with big data
in Power BI   218
Best practices for handling big data 218

Avoiding circular references   220
Understanding circular references   220
Best practices for avoiding circular references 222

Summary   223
Questions   224
Further reading   226

Part 4 – Paginated Reports, Automations, and OpenAI

13

Preparing Data for Paginated Reporting   231

Technical requirements	232	Filters	241
Understanding the importance of		Parameters	242
paginated reports	232	Creating a dataset example	243
Connecting to data sources within		**Using filters and parameters**	**246**
Power BI Report Builder	235	**Using row groups/column groups**	**250**
Data preparation	239	Organizing and structuring data	250
Query	240	Enhancing readability and presentation	251
Fields	241	**Summary**	**257**
Options	241	**Questions**	**257**

14

Automating Data Cleaning Tasks with Power Automate   259

Technical requirements	260	Power Automate	274
Handling triggers for automation	260	Summary	275
Automating notifications	261	Questions	276
Automating refreshing of data	264	Further reading	276
Creating snapshots (temporary tables) of			
cleaned data	267		
Best practices with			

15

Making Life Easier with OpenAI   279

Optimizing efficiency with OpenAI, ChatGPT, and DAX   280

Using OpenAI for M queries   283

Using Microsoft Copilot   288

Tackling challenges with AI   294

Summary   296

Questions   296

Further reading   297

Putting it together   297

Assessments   299

Chapter 1 – Introduction to Power BI Data Cleaning   299

Chapter 2 – Understanding Data Quality and Why Data Cleaning is Important   299

Chapter 3 – Data Cleaning Fundamentals and Principles   299

Chapter 4 – The Most Common Data Cleaning Operations   300

Chapter 5 – Importing Data into Power BI   301

Chapter 6 – Cleaning Data with Query Editor   301

Chapter 7 – Transforming Data with the M Language   302

Chapter 8 – Using Data Profiling for Exploratory Data Analysis (EDA)   302

Chapter 9 – Advanced Data Cleaning Techniques   303

Chapter 10 – Creating Custom Functions in Power Query   304

Chapter 11 – M Query Optimization   304

Chapter 12 – Data Modeling and Managing Relationships   304

Chapter 13 – Preparing Data for Paginated Reporting   305

Chapter 14 – Automating Data Cleaning Tasks with Power Automate   305

Chapter 15 – Making Life Easier with OpenAI   306

Index   307

Other Books You May Enjoy   316

Preface

In the ever-evolving landscape of data-driven decision-making, Microsoft Power BI stands as a stalwart, offering a suite of robust tools to harness the potential hidden within raw data. However, amid the plethora of features, the process of data cleaning often becomes a daunting hurdle for many users. In this transformative guide, we delve into the heart of data cleaning with Power BI, demystifying the complexities that often leave users perplexed and frustrated.

Despite the wealth of capabilities that Power BI provides, countless individuals find themselves grappling with the intricacies of preparing their data effectively. This book aims to bridge the gap between the potential of Power BI and the stumbling blocks that impede users from harnessing its full capabilities. The journey begins with an exploration of data quality and the pivotal role of data cleaning, unraveling the mysteries that make this process seem formidable. It navigates through the fundamentals, addressing common challenges with clarity and offering practical insights to streamline your data preparation journey.

As we guide you through the intricacies of Query Editor, the M language, and data modeling, you will discover the simplicity beneath the surface complexities. The book not only equips you with essential skills but also empowers you to establish relationships within your data, transforming it into a cohesive foundation for insightful analysis. Furthermore, our exploration of best practices and the integration of Power Automate will elevate your proficiency, enabling you to automate tasks seamlessly.

This book is not just a manual; it is a roadmap to demystify the art of data cleaning in Power BI. It goes beyond the technicalities, instilling confidence in you to embark on your data-cleaning journey with assurance. In an era where data reigns supreme, this guide is not just about learning the tools; it's about conquering the challenges that often stifle progress. By the time you reach the final chapters, the synergy of your newfound knowledge and the innovative collaboration with OpenAI and ChatGPT will redefine your approach to data cleaning, making it an intuitive and empowering experience.

Who this book is for

This book would be useful for data analysts, business intelligence professionals, business analysts, data scientists, and anyone else who needs to work with data regularly. Additionally, the book would be helpful for anyone who wants to gain a deeper understanding of data quality issues and best practices for data cleaning in Power BI.

Ideally, if you have a basic knowledge of BI tools and concepts, then this book will help you advance your skills in Power BI.

What this book covers

Chapter 1, Introduction to Power BI Data Cleaning, provides an introduction and overview of the Power BI tools available. This will form the fundamental knowledge of the tools used in this book and will be critical during the cleaning process.

Chapter 2, Understanding Data Quality and Why Data Cleaning is Important, gives you an overview of why data quality is important, what affects data quality, and how quality data is crucial.

Chapter 3, Data Cleaning Fundamentals and Principles, provides an understanding of what to think about before jumping into the platform to start cleaning data. It helps to stage and set a mindset when looking at the data that you are preparing. You will leave this chapter with insight into how to frame your data challenge, where it might be coming from, how best to tackle it, and more.

Chapter 4, The Most Common Data Cleaning Operations, teaches you how to identify and tackle the most common data challenges/corrections. You will get hands-on as you walk through examples of carrying out the cleaning steps.

Chapter 5, Importing Data into Power BI, explores the six main considerations when importing data for analysis in Power BI, which include metrics that matter the most when identifying how clean your data is.

Chapter 6, Cleaning Data with Query Editor, presents hands-on experience of working with one of the most powerful aspects of the platform, Power Query Editor. It will help you build your knowledge on how to use this tool efficiently and with confidence.

Chapter 7, Transforming Data with the M Language, helps you understand and learn how to use M for filtering, sorting, transforming, aggregating, and connecting to data sources. You will learn about the syntax and capabilities of M, as well as how to apply its functions and operators to perform different tasks. The chapter includes examples of using M to clean and preprocess data, create custom functions, and summarize and group data.

Chapter 8, Using Data Profiling for Exploratory Data Analysis (EDA), introduces you to what data profiling is and why it's important. It also covers some of the benefits of using data profiling tools within Power BI, such as identifying data quality issues and improving data accuracy.

Chapter 9, Advanced Data Cleaning Techniques, provides an overview of the range of advanced techniques to shape and clean your data. This chapter also provides some context of what techniques you can use within Power BI.

Chapter 10, Creating Custom Functions in Power Query, covers the planning process, parameters, and the actual creation of the functions in Power Query. The planning process includes understanding data requirements and defining the functions' purpose and expected output. The parameters section covers different types of parameters and how to use them to make functions more flexible and reusable. Finally, the creation section will teach you step by step how to write M language functions and how to test and debug them. Overall, this chapter will provide you with a comprehensive guide to creating custom functions in Power BI.

Chapter 11, M Query Optimization, builds upon the knowledge learned in *Chapter 10* by providing you with insight into how you can optimize the queries created for optimal performance. You will leave this chapter with four examples of how to optimize their queries.

Chapter 12, Data Modeling and Managing Relationships, explains how to manage data relationships in Power BI and how to use them to prepare your data. Often, dirty data can be a repercussion of bad data models, so this chapter will provide you with the knowledge to ensure you have set the model up for success.

Chapter 13, Preparing Data for Paginated Reporting, provides you with a hands-on crash course into the world of paginated reports. It will guide you through examples of how you can prepare your data for use in Power BI Report Builder.

Chapter 14, Automating Data Cleaning Tasks with Power Automate, gives an overview of Power Automate, which is often seen as a great tool and ally in the Power tools kitbag to Power BI. With more and more Power BI analysts and Microsoft customers beginning to use the other features of the Microsoft Power tools, this chapter gives you an understanding of how you might use Power Automate to help with the cleaning of your data.

Chapter 15, Making Life Easier with OpenAI, provides insight into how OpenAI and tools such as ChatGPT and Copilot are improving the way we work with data. It also provides context and examples of how you can potentially use these technologies to get ahead.

To get the most out of this book

This hands-on guide provides you with a strong foundation of best practices and practical tips for data cleaning in Power BI. With each chapter, you can follow along with real-world examples using a test dataset, gaining hands-on skills and building confidence in your ability to use DAX, Power Query, and other key tools.

Here are the key software that you will need through the book:

Software/hardware covered in the book	Operating system requirements
Power BI Desktop	Windows or macOS
Power BI Report Builder	
Power BI Service	
Power Automate	
R	
Python	

Further instructions on installing R or Python are available in the chapters covering those topics.

If you are using the digital version of this book, we advise you to type the code yourself or access the code from the book's GitHub repository (a link is available in the next section). Doing so will help you avoid any potential errors related to the copying and pasting of code.

Download the example code files

You can download the example code files for this book from GitHub at `https://github.com/PacktPublishing/Data-Cleaning-with-Power-BI`. If there's an update to the code, it will be updated in the GitHub repository.

We also have other code bundles from our rich catalog of books and videos available at `https://github.com/PacktPublishing/`. Check them out!

Conventions used

There are a number of text conventions used throughout this book.

`Code in text`: Indicates code words in text, database table names, folder names, filenames, file extensions, pathnames, dummy URLs, user input, and Twitter handles. Here is an example: "For example, the commonly used `CALCULATE` function in DAX is a super-charged version of the `SUM-IF` Excel function."

A block of code is set as follows:

```
Total Sales by Category =
CALCULATE(
    SUM('Sales'[Sales Amount]),
    ALLEXCEPT('Sales', 'Sales'[Product Category])
)
```

Any command-line input or output is written as follows:

```
py -m pip install --user matplotlib
py -m pip install --user pandas
```

Bold: Indicates a new term, an important word, or words that you see on screen. For instance, words in menus or dialog boxes appear in **bold**. Here is an example: "Connect to this CSV using Power BI Desktop by selecting **Get data** in the toolbar and then **Text/CSV**."

> **Tips or important notes**
> Appear like this.

Get in touch

Feedback from our readers is always welcome.

General feedback: If you have questions about any aspect of this book, email us at `customercare@packtpub.com` and mention the book title in the subject of your message.

Errata: Although we have taken every care to ensure the accuracy of our content, mistakes do happen. If you have found a mistake in this book, we would be grateful if you would report this to us. Please visit `www.packtpub.com/support/errata` and fill in the form.

Piracy: If you come across any illegal copies of our works in any form on the internet, we would be grateful if you would provide us with the location address or website name. Please contact us at `copyright@packt.com` with a link to the material.

If you are interested in becoming an author: If there is a topic that you have expertise in and you are interested in either writing or contributing to a book, please visit `authors.packtpub.com`.

Share Your Thoughts

Once you've read *Data Cleaning with Power BI*, we'd love to hear your thoughts! Scan the QR code below to go straight to the Amazon review page for this book and share your feedback.

`https://packt.link/r/1-805-12640-7`

Your review is important to us and the tech community and will help us make sure we're delivering excellent quality content.

Download a free PDF copy of this book

Thanks for purchasing this book!

Do you like to read on the go but are unable to carry your print books everywhere?

Is your eBook purchase not compatible with the device of your choice?

Don't worry, now with every Packt book you get a DRM-free PDF version of that book at no cost.

Read anywhere, any place, on any device. Search, copy, and paste code from your favorite technical books directly into your application.

The perks don't stop there, you can get exclusive access to discounts, newsletters, and great free content in your inbox daily

Follow these simple steps to get the benefits:

1. Scan the QR code or visit the link below

https://packt.link/free-ebook/9781805126409

2. Submit your proof of purchase

3. That's it! We'll send your free PDF and other benefits to your email directly

Part 1 – Introduction and Fundamentals

In this introductory part, you will embark on a foundational exploration of Power BI data cleaning, discovering the essential tools, understanding the significance of data quality, and grasping fundamental principles for effective data cleaning. You will gain hands-on experience in identifying and tackling common data challenges, setting the stage for a robust understanding of Power BI's data cleaning processes.

This part has the following chapters:

- *Chapter 1, Introduction to Power BI Data Cleaning*
- *Chapter 2, Understanding Data Quality and Why Data Cleaning is Important*
- *Chapter 3, Data Cleaning Fundamentals and Principles*
- *Chapter 4, The Most Common Data Cleaning Operations*

1

Introduction to Power BI Data Cleaning

Although not definitive, it's generally accepted that when creating data visualizations, cleaning and preparing data can often account for as much as 50-80% of the overall time spent on a data visualization project. Power BI provides you with some great tools to carry this out and so we will dive deeper into what is available during this chapter.

In this chapter, we're going to cover the following main topics:

- Cleaning your data in Power BI
- Understanding Power Query
- Understanding **Data Analysis Expressions (DAX)**
- Where do we begin with data?

After this chapter, you will understand with confidence which tools are available within Power BI to help prepare your data for analysis, how to navigate around Power Query, and then what to consider when getting started with preparing your data for analysis.

Technical requirements

Please ensure you have installed Power BI Desktop on your device so that you can follow along with the instructions and navigation provided in the chapter.

Follow this link to install Power BI Desktop: `https://www.microsoft.com/en-us/download/details.aspx?id=58494`.

Cleaning your data in Power BI

Data preparation typically involves cleaning, transforming, and structuring data into a format that is suitable for analysis. Power BI offers several tools to help with this process, including the Power Query Editor, data modeling, and DAX formulas. In the later chapters of this book, you will dive deeper into each of these tools. Here is an example of the Power Query Editor window accessed from within the Power BI Desktop application:

Figure 1.1 – User interface (UI)/toolbar of the Power Query Editor

The **Power Query Editor** is a powerful tool that allows you to clean and transform data. It provides a user-friendly interface to perform various data transformation tasks, such as splitting columns, merging tables, filtering data, and removing duplicates. It also has several built-in functions to help you transform your data, such as date and text transformations.

Data modeling is another important aspect of Power BI, empowering users to forge meaningful connections between tables and establish hierarchies that provide a structured view of their data. By creating relationships, you enhance the cohesion of your datasets, fostering a comprehensive understanding of the underlying information. These relationships enable you to draw valuable insights, facilitating a more insightful analysis of your data. Moreover, defining hierarchies adds an extra layer of organization, allowing for seamless navigation through your data and enhancing both accessibility and user experience.

Furthermore, the creation of measures through data modeling serves as a powerful tool for performing intricate calculations on your datasets. Whether it's aggregating data, deriving **key performance indicators** (**KPIs**), or conducting complex analyses, measures provide a dynamic way to extract actionable insights from your information. This capability is instrumental in making informed business decisions, as it allows for the extraction of relevant metrics and performance indicators. In essence, data modeling not only aids in structuring your data but also acts as a catalyst for extracting maximum value from your Power BI reports, optimizing their performance and usability.

DAX is a formula language used in Power BI to create custom calculations and measures. It provides a powerful set of functions to perform complex calculations on your data. DAX formulas can be used to create calculated columns, calculated tables, and measures. For illustration purposes, the following screenshot provides an example of a new measure being created with a DAX function to pull the current date/time:

Figure 1.2 – UI of new measure being created with DAX

With the aforementioned techniques, you have various options to clean data; however, in the next section, we will explore Power Query in further detail as it's likely where you will get started.

Understanding Power Query

As mentioned, Power Query is a powerful data transformation and preparation tool within Microsoft Power BI. It allows users to **extract, transform, and load** (more commonly known in the industry as **ETL**) data from various sources, enabling efficient data cleaning, shaping, and integration for analysis and reporting. In this chapter, we will delve into the details of Power Query, exploring its functionality, features, and UI.

Rather than a query language as such, Power Query is primarily accessed and used through the Power Query Editor UI. An example of this view is shown next:

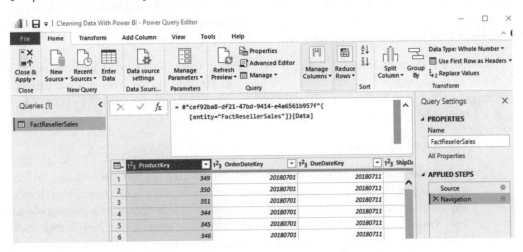

Figure 1.3 – UI of the Power Query Editor

This UI is the hub for cleaning and preparing data within Power BI. It allows users such as yourself to connect to a wide range of data sources and apply transformations within the UI. As you begin to clean and prepare data, Power Query then tracks the steps of your cleaning process.

The actual language applied when carrying out cleaning steps is a language called *M code*. When interacting with the UI within Power Query, Power BI creates code in the M language to do transformations. We will dive deeper into how you can use this language directly using the Advanced Editor later.

It's important to know that there are two ways to access Power Query from within Power BI. The first is through online experiences such as *dataflows*, and the second is within the Power BI Desktop application. It's important to note, though, that the techniques learned in this book will allow you to use Power Query within tools such as Excel, Power Apps, Power Automate, Azure Data Factory, **SQL Server Integration Services** (**SSIS**), **SQL Server Analysis Services** (**SSAS**), and Customer Insights.

Understanding DAX

DAX is a formula and query language that plays a pivotal role in Power BI, helping users of Power BI to perform complex calculations and analysis on their data. It's a language created by Microsoft for their suite of products and was first introduced in 2009 along with Power Pivot for Excel, something that was then also incorporated into Power BI. Helping to create and define custom calculations and formulas goes beyond the capabilities of traditional Excel functions.

Interestingly, it originated from the need to bridge the gap between *relational database systems* and *traditional spreadsheet tools* to help lower the barrier for professionals by providing a formula language that was more user-friendly for business analysts who may not be SQL experts, hence why DAX has been designed to work with tabular data models. Microsoft recognized the limitations of Excel at handling large sets of data and complex calculations, and this then led them to develop DAX, which could handle this in similar spreadsheet-like expressions. For example, the commonly used CALCULATE function in DAX is a super-charged version of the SUM-IF Excel function.

As mentioned at the start of this section, DAX is unique in that it serves a dual purpose, acting as both a formula language and a query language within the context of Microsoft's **business intelligence** (**BI**) tools such as Power BI, Power Pivot, and **SSAS**. Here's an explanation of why DAX is considered both a formula and a query language:

- DAX as a **formula language**:

  - **Calculation and transformation**: DAX is extensively used as a formula language to define calculations and transformations on data within a tabular or relational data model. Users leverage DAX formulas to create measures, calculated columns, and tables that express complex business logic. The syntax and functions in DAX are designed to be user-friendly, resembling Excel formulas, making it accessible to business analysts and users familiar with spreadsheet-style calculations.

  - **Single-row computations**: In its formula-language role, DAX operates at the level of individual rows or records, allowing users to define calculations based on the values within a single record. This makes it suitable for deriving new values, aggregating data, and performing calculations at a granular level.

- DAX as a **query language**:

  - **Data retrieval and shaping**: DAX also functions as a query language, enabling users to retrieve and shape data within a data model. While traditional query languages such as SQL are often associated with relational databases, DAX, in its query language role, is tailored for working with tabular data models. Users can construct queries to retrieve specific sets of data, apply filters, and organize the results.

  - **Set-based operations**: In the query language role, DAX operates at a set level, allowing users to perform set-based operations on tables or columns. This includes filtering data, creating relationships between tables, and specifying conditions for data retrieval.

DAX's dual role is particularly significant in the context of Microsoft's BI tools. Its integration with Power BI and other tools means that users can seamlessly transition between creating complex calculations (formula language) and shaping data for analysis (query language) within a unified environment. In summary, DAX's versatility as both a formula and a query language makes it a powerful tool for users working with tabular data models. Whether defining calculations at the row level or shaping data at the set level, DAX provides a unified language for comprehensive data analysis and BI.

The following is a summary of some of the key reasons customers of Power BI leverage DAX on a daily basis:

- **Custom calculations**: DAX allows users to create measures and/or calculated columns based on data in multiple tables. DAX facilitates the creation of intricate business logic, leveraging relationships between tables and enabling users to express complex analytical requirements that go beyond standard aggregations. Whether performing advanced calculations, handling **Time Intelligence (TI)**, or developing tailored metrics, DAX provides a user-friendly and powerful framework for expressing the intricacies of business data in a way that is intuitive and efficient.

- **Aggregations and summarizations**: DAX provides powerful functions that we will review later in the book to help users carry out analysis at different levels of granularity and level of detail. Such examples are SUMX, AVERAGEX, and COUNTX. These functions enable users to conduct analyses at various levels of granularity and detail within Power BI's highly efficient data model. The underlying architecture of Power BI excels at handling substantial volumes of data, making it exceptionally proficient in aggregating and summarizing even very large datasets. This efficiency ensures that users can perform complex analyses seamlessly, delivering swift and responsive results, even when dealing with extensive and intricate datasets.

- **Time analytics**: It includes built-in functions for handling time-based calculations such as **Year to Date (YTD)**, **Month to Date (MTD)**, and rolling averages. This feature simplifies the analysis and also calculations by having these pre-built functions. We will review later in this book how to use these to improve performance.

DAX is a hugely powerful tool in the kitbag of an analyst or developer using Power BI. That being said, though, there are vast amounts of publications and memes online about difficulties with DAX. As with any formula or query language, it requires time and practice to develop best practices on how to ensure you achieve accurate data.

Leading on from this, DAX can often have strong implications on the performance of your reports depending on how well you've used it, especially if the model contains very large amounts of data. Later in this book, you will learn techniques on how to optimize this on real-world examples for optimal performance.

DAX expressions are built using a combination of functions, operators, and references to columns or tables within your Power BI data model. These expressions are then used to create calculated columns, measures, and even tables. Next is a summary of how these key ingredients are used to create DAX expressions:

- **Functions**: Built-in to help you carry out calculations and are often categorized into different types such as mathematical, statistical, text, and TI functions.

- **Operators**: Similar to functions, there are a number of operators used within common expressions to combine values, such as **arithmetic operators** (+, -, *, /), **comparison operations** (=, <, >, <>, >=, >=), **logical operators** (AND, OR, NOT), and more.

- **Column, measure, and table references**: Your expressions will often call on/refer to data within your data model. You can identify these as columns. Measures are referenced using square brackets ([ ]) and tables are referenced using single quotes (' ') with their table name.

> **Tip**
> Adhering to best practices, it is recommended to include the table name when referencing columns but omit it when referencing measures in your Power BI data model. While Power BI does not enforce these conventions, incorporating the table name when referencing columns enhances clarity and reduces ambiguity in your formulas. This practice helps distinguish between columns and measures, contributing to a more maintainable and comprehensible data model. Be proactive in implementing these conventions for a streamlined and effective Power BI development experience.

You will be learning a number of different common DAX calculations within this book, but the following example code (title `Total Sales by Category`) demonstrates the aforementioned scenario well.

Let's consider a scenario where we wanted to create a calculated column in Power BI that calculates the total sales amount per product category. We'll assume that we have a table called `Sales` with columns such as `Product Category` and `Sales Amount`.

We would use the following expression to get the desired results with total sales by category:

```
Total Sales by Category =
CALCULATE(
    SUM('Sales'[Sales Amount]),
    ALLEXCEPT('Sales', 'Sales'[Product Category])
)
```

We will dive deeper into what these functions do later in the book as both `CALCULATE` and `ALLEXCEPT` are key functions to learn. However, you can see the preceding code includes functions, operators, and table references.

Where do we begin with data?

As you progress through this book, you will learn how to use these technologies together to clean and prepare your data for performant data visualization. However, before diving into some examples and learning how to actually carry out these transformations, it's important you pick up a few best practices on what you should consider before getting started.

Key elements to consider here are what is meant when we say *data quality*, why it is important (outside of the obvious reasons), who's responsible for it, and how to plan for this data preparation.

Summary

In summary, Power BI provides several tools to help with cleaning and preparing your data. The Query Editor allows you to clean and transform data, data modeling helps you to organize your data, and DAX formulas allow you to create custom calculations and measures. By using these tools, you can ensure that your data is ready for analysis and that your reports provide accurate and meaningful insights.

In this chapter, we have shone a light on the aforementioned technologies and provided an example of how to structure your DAX expressions.

The following chapters will provide you with a deeper understanding of why you should cleanse data in Power BI and key considerations in this planning. This is crucial learning because it will help you later down the line when it comes to implementing changes and managing the who/why/where of the data being cleansed.

Questions

1. What percentage of time is generally spent on data cleaning and preparation in a data visualization project?

    A. 20-30%

    B. 50-80%

    C. 10-20%

    D. 80-100%

2. Name three tools provided by Power BI for data preparation.

    A. Power Extract, data integration, data expressions

    B. Power Query, data modeling, SQL queries

C.   Data analytics, Query Editor, data mining

D.   Power Query, data modeling, DAX formulas

3.   What is the primary function of Power Query in Power BI?

A.   Creating visualizations

B.   Writing SQL queries

C.   Data transformation and preparation

D.   Building relationships between tables

4.   What is DAX, and how is it used in Power BI?

A.   As a data visualization tool

B.   As a programming language

C.   As a formula language for creating calculations and measures

D.   As a data storage format

5.   Why was DAX created, and what problem did it aim to solve?

A.   To create charts and graphs

B.   To bridge the gap between relational databases and spreadsheet tools

C.   To replace SQL queries

D.   To handle big data efficiently

6.   Explain the dual role of DAX as a formula language and a query language.

A.   It can perform calculations only

B.   It can retrieve and shape data

C.   It is used for data visualization

D.   It can be used for both calculations and querying within Power BI

7.   Why is it recommended to include the table name when referencing columns in DAX expressions?

A.   It is not recommended

B.   It enhances clarity and reduces ambiguity

C.   It improves performance

D.   It is a mandatory requirement

2

Understanding Data Quality and Why Data Cleaning is Important

Data is all around us, and so subsequently, data quality is also all around us. Now, if you work in the data space, then you have definitely encountered data quality.

In the world of data analysis and **business intelligence** (**BI**), data is the foundation upon which insights and decisions are made. However, the quality of the data we work with can greatly impact the accuracy and reliability of our analyses.

In this chapter, we will explore factors that affect data quality and delve into why data cleaning is a crucial step in the data preparation process. You will learn key concepts to ensure the data you work with is clean and accurate for the analysis you're looking to carry out. In addition to this, you will also learn best practices that you can implement within your own business.

We'll cover the following topics in this chapter:

- What is data quality?
- Where do data quality issues come from?
- The role of data cleaning in improving data quality
- Best practices for data quality overall

After completing this chapter, you will understand with confidence the factors that contribute to data quality issues. This is critical for those just starting on their data journey but equally important to review if you've been working with data for many years. These factors will also be referenced in later chapters, such as *Chapter 8, Using Data Profiling for Exploratory Data Analysis (EDA).*

What is data quality?

Firstly, before diving into how you can leverage Power BI to clean your data, it's important to understand some key basics of what will affect your data quality.

Data quality is essential for accurate analysis, informed decision-making, and successful business outcomes. Understanding factors that affect data quality and recognizing the importance of data cleaning are crucial steps in the data preparation process.

In general, several factors describe and make up the quality of a dataset for analysis, which we will dive into further in the following list:

- **Data accuracy**: Data accuracy means the extent to which data represents the true values and attributes it is intended to capture, indicating the degree to which it aligns with the true, real-world information it seeks to represent. Factors such as human errors during data entry, system glitches, or outdated information can compromise data accuracy.

- **Data completeness**: This describes the degree to which all required data elements are present in a dataset. Missing or incomplete data can occur due to data collection errors, system limitations, or data integration challenges.

- **Data consistency**: The uniformity and coherence of data across different sources or datasets. Inconsistencies may arise from variations in data formats, naming conventions, or conflicting data definitions.

- **Data validity**: Refers to the extent to which data conforms to defined rules, constraints, or standards. Invalid data can result from data entry errors, data integration issues, or changes in business rules.

- **Data timeliness**: The relevance and currency of data in relation to the analysis or reporting timeframe. Outdated or stale data can lead to inaccurate insights and hinder decision-making.

Now you have an understanding of important attributes that affect data quality, we can begin to learn about where these data quality issues come from. In the next section, we will dive deeper into the source of these data inequalities. This will help you when trying to understand how you can improve data cleanliness from the source itself.

Where do data quality issues come from?

Data quality issues can arise from various sources throughout the data life cycle. Some common origins of data quality issues include the following:

- **Data entry errors**: Mistakes made during manual data entry processes can introduce errors such as typos, misspellings, or incorrect values. Human error, lack of training, or inadequate validation mechanisms can contribute to data entry issues.

- **Incomplete or missing data**: Data may be incomplete or have missing values due to various reasons, such as data collection processes that fail to capture all required information, data entry omissions, or system limitations that prevent data collection.

- **Data integration challenges**: When combining data from multiple sources or systems, inconsistencies can arise due to differences in data formats, naming conventions, or data structures. Mismatched or incompatible data elements can lead to data quality issues.

- **Data transformation and manipulation**: Data transformations, such as aggregations, calculations, or data conversions, can introduce errors if not implemented correctly. Issues can arise from improper formulas, incorrect assumptions, or errors in the data manipulation process.

- **Data storage and transfer**: Unreliable storage systems may lead to data corruption, loss, or unauthorized access, impacting data quality. Events such as hardware failures or system crashes can result in data loss, affecting completeness and accuracy. Delays in data transfer may lead to latency issues, with outdated or stale data impacting the accuracy of analyses. Lastly, incompatibility between systems during data transfer can cause format mismatches and structural issues, introducing inaccuracies.

- **Data governance and documentation**: Inadequate data governance practices, including a lack of data standards, data definitions, or metadata documentation, can lead to misunderstandings or misinterpretations of data, resulting in data quality problems. Poor documentation of data lineage makes it challenging to trace the origin of quality issues and prevent future problems.

- **Data changes and updates**: As data evolves over time, changes in business rules, system updates, or modifications to data sources can impact data quality. Data may become outdated, inconsistent, or no longer aligned with the intended use.

- **External data sources**: When incorporating data from external sources, such as third-party providers or open datasets, data quality issues may arise. Inaccurate or unreliable data from external sources can affect the overall data quality.

It is important to identify the specific sources of data quality issues to effectively implement data cleaning and quality improvement strategies. By addressing the root causes of these issues, organizations can enhance data quality and ensure the reliability and accuracy of their analyses and reports.

The role of data cleaning in improving data quality

In the era of data-driven decision-making, the quality and reliability of data are paramount for organizations. While data cleaning is often seen as a task for data professionals or analysts, the responsibility for ensuring clean data extends beyond a specific team or department. In this section, we will explore the importance of data cleaning and why it should be considered a shared responsibility within a company, involving stakeholders from all levels and functions.

Data integrity and accuracy

Data cleaning plays a vital role in maintaining data integrity and accuracy. Inaccurate or inconsistent data can lead to flawed analysis, flawed decision-making, and potential business risks. By recognizing data cleaning as a shared responsibility, all individuals working with data can contribute to maintaining the integrity of the data they generate, use, or interact with.

Decision-making and business outcomes

Data serves as the foundation for informed decision-making. When data quality is compromised, the decisions made based on that data are also compromised. By acknowledging the impact of data quality on business outcomes, individuals across the organization can understand the importance of data cleaning in facilitating accurate insights and driving successful outcomes.

Data ownership and accountability

Every individual who interacts with data, regardless of their role, possesses a level of data ownership and accountability. By considering data cleaning as part of this ownership, employees become active participants in maintaining data quality. When employees take responsibility for the accuracy and cleanliness of the data they work with, a culture of data stewardship is fostered within the organization.

A holistic view of the data ecosystem

Data flows across departments, systems, and processes within an organization. Each touchpoint introduces the potential for data quality issues. Recognizing data cleaning as everyone's responsibility encourages individuals to consider the broader data ecosystem and how their actions impact the quality of data used by others. This holistic view promotes collaboration and communication to address data quality concerns.

Early detection of issues

Data cleaning is not just about rectifying existing issues; it also involves proactively identifying and addressing data quality issues. Employees on the front lines of data collection, entry, and analysis are often the first to notice anomalies or inconsistencies. By encouraging a culture where data issues are shared and addressed promptly, organizations can mitigate the impact of poor data quality before it cascades into larger problems.

Continuous improvement and learning

Data cleaning presents opportunities for continuous improvement and learning. When individuals actively participate in data cleaning, they gain insights into data patterns, common errors, and areas for improvement. This knowledge can be shared, leading to enhanced data collection processes, better data entry practices, and improved data quality over time.

Empowerment and collaboration

Recognizing the shared responsibility of data cleaning empowers employees to take ownership of the data they work with. It fosters a sense of collaboration and accountability, as individuals understand that their actions impact the overall data quality and, consequently, the success of the organization. By leveraging the collective expertise and commitment of employees, organizations can effectively address data quality challenges.

Best practices for data quality overall

Of course, this book will delve deep into how you can actually clean your data with Power BI, but it wouldn't be responsible for us to not provide some insight into implementing best practices to prevent dirty data.

As we discussed previously, dirty data can have a significant impact on business operations, decision-making, and overall success. To combat the challenges posed by dirty data, organizations must establish robust data cleaning practices. In this segment of the chapter, we will explore best practices that businesses can implement to effectively tackle dirty data and ensure data quality throughout their operations.

Establishing data quality standards

Define clear data quality standards that align with your organization's goals and objectives. These standards should include criteria for accuracy, completeness, consistency, validity, and timeliness, as discussed next:

- **Developing a data governance framework**: Develop a comprehensive data governance framework that outlines roles, responsibilities, and processes for data management. Establish data stewardship roles to oversee data quality initiatives and enforce data governance policies. This framework will help create a structured approach to data cleaning and ensure accountability across the organization.

- **Implementing data validation and verification techniques**: Apply data validation and verification techniques to identify and resolve inconsistencies, errors, and outliers. Use automated validation rules, data profiling tools, and statistical analysis to check data against predefined rules and validate its accuracy. Implement regular data audits to identify data quality issues and take corrective actions.

- **Standardizing data entry processes**: Standardize data entry processes to minimize human errors and ensure consistent data formats. Implement data entry controls, such as drop-down menus, data validation lists, and input masks, to guide data entry and prevent incorrect or inconsistent data. Provide training and guidelines to employees on proper data entry practices.

- **Leveraging data cleaning tools and technologies**: Utilize data cleaning tools and technologies, such as Power Query in Power BI, to automate the data cleaning process. These tools can help identify and correct data errors, remove duplicates, handle missing values, and perform various data transformations. Invest in appropriate data cleaning solutions based on your specific requirements.

- **Collaborating across departments**: Data cleaning is a collaborative effort that involves various departments within an organization. Foster collaboration and communication between departments to address data quality issues holistically. Encourage cross-functional teams to share insights, exchange knowledge, and work collectively toward data cleaning goals.

- **Continuous data monitoring**: Implement mechanisms for ongoing data monitoring to proactively identify and resolve data quality issues. Establish data quality metrics, set up alerts and notifications for data anomalies, and regularly monitor data quality dashboards. Continuously monitor data sources, data pipelines, and data integration processes to maintain high data quality standards.

- **Data education and training**: Provide data education and training programs to equip employees with the necessary skills and knowledge to understand and address data quality issues. Offer training on data cleaning techniques, data entry best practices, data validation methods, and the importance of data quality. This education will empower employees to take ownership of data quality and contribute to the battle against dirty data.

Ensure that all stakeholders understand and adhere to these standards, fostering a shared commitment to data quality.

Summary

In this chapter, we explored factors that affect data quality and why data cleaning is crucial in the data preparation process. We discussed the importance of understanding data quality standards and the impact of data accuracy, completeness, consistency, validity, and timeliness on analyses and decision-making. We also identified common sources of data quality issues, such as data entry errors, incomplete or missing data, data integration challenges, data transformation and manipulation, data storage and transfer issues, data governance and documentation gaps, data changes and updates, and external data sources.

Furthermore, we delved into why data cleaning is everyone's responsibility within a company. By recognizing data cleaning as a shared responsibility, individuals can contribute to data integrity, decision-making, and a holistic view of the data ecosystem. We highlighted the benefits of the early detection of data issues, continuous improvement, empowerment, collaboration, and the role of data ownership and accountability.

Finally, we discussed best practices for implementing data cleaning in a business. These practices include establishing data quality standards, developing a data governance framework, implementing data validation and verification techniques, standardizing data entry processes, leveraging data cleaning tools and technologies, fostering collaboration across departments, implementing continuous data monitoring, and providing data education and training.

By implementing these best practices, organizations can effectively tackle dirty data, ensure data quality, and drive better business outcomes through accurate insights and informed decision-making.

In the next chapter, we will cover fundamental concepts and key principles that form the backbone of effective data cleaning practices. You will learn essential knowledge and processes to confidently tackle the challenges of dirty data and transform it into reliable, accurate, and actionable information.

Questions

1. What does data accuracy refer to in the context of data quality?

    A. The extent to which data represents true values and attributes

    B. The relevance and currency of data

    C. The completeness of required data elements

    D. Data consistency

2. What factor can compromise data accuracy?

    A. Data completeness

    B. Data consistency

    C. Data timeliness

    D. Human errors during data entry

3. What describes the degree to which all required data elements are present in a dataset?

    A. Data accuracy

    B. Data completeness

    C. Data consistency

    D. Data validity

4. Why is data cleaning considered a shared responsibility within a company?

    A. It is solely the responsibility of data professionals

    B. It helps maintain data integrity and accuracy

    C. It is a task for analysts only

    D. It does not impact decision-making

5. What does recognizing data cleaning as everyone's responsibility encourage within an organization?

    A. Isolation of data-related tasks

    B. A culture of data stewardship

    C. Dependency on data professionals

    D. Ignoring data quality concerns

6. What does data cleaning involve beyond rectifying existing issues?

    A. Proactively identifying and addressing data quality issues

    B. Ignoring data quality issues

    C. Avoiding data cleaning altogether

    D. Isolating data issues

7. What does the establishment of data quality standards include?

    A. Criteria for data transformation

    B. Criteria for data governance

    C. Criteria for data accuracy, completeness, consistency, validity, and timeliness

    D. Criteria for data storage

8. What is the significance of standardized data entry processes?

    A. Minimizing human errors

    B. Encouraging inconsistent data formats

    C. Increasing data integration challenges

    D. Preventing data validation issues

9. What role do data cleaning tools and technologies play in the data cleaning process?

    A. They complicate the process

    B. They automate the data cleaning process

    C. They introduce errors

    D. They are irrelevant for data cleaning

3

Data Cleaning Fundamentals and Principles

In this chapter, we will delve into the fundamental concepts and key principles that form the backbone of effective data cleaning practices, with the aim of sharing essential knowledge and processes to confidently tackle the challenges of dirty data and transform it into reliable, accurate, and actionable information.

As the previous chapter introduced, poor data quality can lead to people like yourself needing to clean data ready for it to be analyzed. Data cleaning is an indispensable step in the data preparation process, ensuring that the data we work with is trustworthy, consistent, and fit for analysis. It involves identifying and rectifying errors, inconsistencies, duplicates, missing values, and other data anomalies that can hinder the reliability and validity of our analyses. By implementing sound data cleaning practices, you can enhance data quality, improve decision-making, and unlock the full potential of your data.

Throughout this chapter, we will uncover the core principles that guide successful data cleaning efforts. We will explore the importance of understanding data context, establishing data quality criteria, implementing robust data validation techniques, and adopting a systematic and iterative approach to cleaning data. By internalizing these principles, you will develop a strong foundation for effectively cleaning and preparing data for analysis.

We will be covering the following topics in this chapter:

- Definition of data cleaning
- Who's responsible for cleaning data?
- Building a process for cleaning data
- Understanding quality over quantity in data cleaning

By the end of this chapter, you will have developed a better understanding of the key roles, responsibilities, and processes involved in creating a strong process for cleaning data within your business for analysis.

Defining data cleaning

Data cleaning and preparation is the methodical and strategic process of identifying, rectifying, and mitigating inaccuracies, inconsistencies, and imperfections in your dataset. It is the essential step that bridges the gap between raw data and meaningful insights. Just as a skilled artisan refines raw materials to create a masterpiece, data cleaning transforms your dataset into a polished and reliable foundation for analysis.

Recognizing the inevitability of data imperfections, the task at hand is to establish a framework and adhere to principles that guide your data cleaning efforts. This framework is crucial for preventing the cycle of perpetual data cleaning, analysis, and the subsequent return to data cleaning due to oversights in the initial iteration. Without a structured approach, the process becomes cyclical and may lead to inefficiencies, compromising the effectiveness of your analyses.

In the following section, you will begin to learn about the different roles and responsibilities linked to the process of cleaning data within your business.

Who's responsible for cleaning data?

Businesses rely on data to inform strategies, make informed decisions, and gain a competitive edge. However, the process of ensuring data cleanliness is not automatic; it requires a well-defined strategy and a team of individuals with specific roles. In this section, we will explore the key roles responsible for cleaning data within a business and shed light on the importance of each position:

- **Data steward**: At the forefront of data cleaning responsibilities is the data steward. This role involves overseeing the overall quality and integrity of data within the organization. Data stewards act as guardians of data, ensuring that it aligns with established standards and complies with regulations. They play a crucial role in developing and implementing data quality policies, monitoring data health, and addressing issues promptly.

- **Data analysts**: They are instrumental in the hands-on work of cleaning and preparing data for analysis. Their responsibilities include identifying discrepancies, inconsistencies, and errors in datasets. With various tools and techniques, data analysts transform raw data into a clean, usable format. They collaborate closely with data stewards to implement data quality standards effectively.

- **IT professionals**: IT professionals, including database administrators and system architects, are essential for maintaining the infrastructure that houses the data. They play a critical role in ensuring the accessibility, security, and efficiency of databases. Collaborating with data stewards and analysts, IT professionals help design systems that facilitate data cleaning processes and maintain the integrity of the overall data architecture.

- **Business users and subject matter experts**: They bring a unique perspective to the data cleaning process. Their intimate knowledge of business processes and domain expertise is invaluable for identifying anomalies in the data that might go unnoticed by others. By actively participating in data validation and verification, these individuals contribute to a more accurate representation of business realities.

- **Data quality manager**: In larger organizations, the role of a data quality manager may be established to oversee the comprehensive data quality strategy. This manager is responsible for coordinating efforts across various teams, setting priorities, and ensuring that data quality initiatives align with organizational objectives. They act as a bridge between business stakeholders and technical teams, fostering collaboration to enhance overall data quality.

Establishing clear responsibilities for cleaning data within a business is essential for maintaining the trustworthiness and reliability of information. Each role mentioned here plays a unique and crucial part in this process, contributing to the collective effort to ensure data integrity.

Outside of these roles, leadership roles such as management and C-suite executives also play a pivotal role in ensuring the cleanliness of the data within a business. Here's a view of some of the leadership roles and their responsibilities:

- **Analytics (BI) managers**: They are responsible for the overall strategy and implementation of **Business Intelligence** (**BI**) initiatives. They play a crucial role in aligning data cleaning efforts with broader business goals and objectives.

  They also allocate resources, including personnel and technology, to ensure effective data cleaning processes. They are responsible for prioritizing data quality initiatives based on organizational needs and allocating budgets accordingly. They ensure that data stewardship, analytics, IT, and business units work cohesively to maintain high data quality standards.

  Lastly, BI managers oversee the training and development of staff involved in data-related tasks. They ensure that teams have the necessary skills to clean, analyze, and interpret data accurately.

- **C-suite executives**: Executives, including the **Chief Executive Officer** (**CEO**) and **Chief Information Officer** (**CIO**), set the organizational tone for prioritizing data quality. Their commitment to data integrity influences the entire company culture.

  C-suite executives align data quality initiatives with broader business strategies. They ensure that clean data supports decision-making processes at the highest level, contributing to the organization's success. This, in turn, means they typically oversee investments in technology infrastructure that supports data quality. This includes approving budgets for advanced data cleaning tools, ensuring the availability of skilled personnel, and staying abreast of technological advancements.

Let's go through a breakdown of how the different C-suite leadership positions play important roles in ensuring data cleanliness within a business:

- **Chief Data Officer (CDO)**: The CDO oversees data governance policies and frameworks, ensuring that they align with industry standards and regulations. They play a key role in establishing and enforcing data quality standards across the organization.

  In addition to governance, by collaborating with other executives and departments, the CDO ensures that data-related initiatives are integrated into broader organizational strategies. They work to create a unified approach to data management.

- **Chief Information Security Officer (CISO)**: The CISO is responsible for ensuring the security of data assets. In the context of data cleaning, they play a crucial role in implementing measures to protect sensitive information and maintaining data privacy during the cleaning process.

- **Chief Analytics Officer (CAO) or chief data scientist**: For organizations heavily invested in advanced analytics, the CAO or chief data scientist ensures that data cleaning processes support the requirements of complex analytical models. They may guide the development of sophisticated algorithms for more accurate data cleaning.

- **Chief Technology Officer (CTO)**: The CTO oversees the technological infrastructure supporting data cleaning processes. They ensure that the organization has the necessary hardware, software, and cloud solutions to facilitate efficient and effective data cleaning.

- **Chief Risk Officer (CRO)**: The CRO assesses risks associated with data quality issues, including potential financial, legal, or reputational risks. They work with other leaders to develop risk mitigation strategies related to data cleaning.

- **Chief Compliance Officer (CCO)**: The CCO ensures that data cleaning practices adhere to industry regulations and compliance standards. They play a critical role in mitigating legal risks associated with data quality issues.

- **Chief Financial Officer (CFO)**: The CFO oversees budgeting and resource allocation for data-related initiatives, including data cleaning. They ensure that necessary financial resources are allocated to support data quality improvement efforts.

By recognizing the importance of these roles and fostering collaboration among team members, businesses can build a robust framework for effective data cleaning and, consequently, achieve more informed and sustained success.

In the next section of this chapter, you will learn how to go about building a process for cleaning data within your business.

Building a process for cleaning data

The process of cleaning data involves several key steps that help to form a systematic approach to ensure comprehensive data cleaning.

While the specific steps may vary depending on the nature of the data and the organization's requirements, the following general process provides a framework for effective data cleaning.

The effective steps to cleaning data follow this flow:

1. Data assessment
2. Data profiling
3. Data validation
4. Data cleaning strategies
5. Data transformation
6. Data quality assurance
7. Documentation

Let's go through these effective steps in detail next.

Data assessment

First of all, it's imperative to assess the quality of data before we get started with cleaning the data. This may sound obvious; however, tracking this information will help you later down the line to ensure you have not missed any data transformations.

Equally, in the world of data analysis, it is always critical to ensure we're showing our worth and work. As such, by having built a data assessment before and after cleaning, you will be able to demonstrate the impact.

An example of this would be a data analyst conducting an assessment of the data to identify issues. Then, a data steward within your business would collaborate with that analyst to define and establish standards that would help to monitor that data's health moving forward or, at the very least, address the issues promptly. Linking back to business objectives, a data steward or data quality manager might also be responsible for linking the assessment of data with organizational objectives.

Additionally, you might look to include database administrators in this step to help you verify and ensure that the database structure aligns with the data quality standard being introduced.

Data profiling

Data profiling, sometimes referred to as **Exploratory Data Analysis** (**EDA**), helps provide us with a deeper understanding of the data we're working with by analyzing its structure and content. This again can often be carried out by the team members in the data analyst role to understand the data structure and content.

This step involves examining the data for patterns, distributions, outliers, and just missing data. Profiling helps identify potential quality issues and guides the cleaning effort that you will need to do later in this process.

Depending on the size of your teams, it can also be beneficial to include any machine learning engineers within this step to assess how you might be able to use machine learning techniques to recognize patterns that affect data quality.

Data validation

In the validation phase, you generally implement techniques to validate the data against a predefined use case or business requirement. This step will ensure that the data you're working with adheres to the correct rules and will be able to achieve the desired business outcomes for the analysis. Examples of this would be to carry out range checks, format checks, referential integrity checks, or other validation methods tailored to the specific data attributes and business rules. The most common examples we see of this would be predefined formats used in previous business reports that will require the data to be transformed.

Like the previous examples, this responsibility will tend to lie with the data analysts as they implement data cleaning strategies and business analysts as they collaborate to ensure that the data aligns with the business objectives. If you have a data steward, then they might also define the validation steps, scenarios, and testing processes to ensure fair and accurate validation.

Data cleaning strategies

Data cleaning strategies include designing and implementing approaches to address specific data issues identified during the assessment and profiling stages. Now, it goes without saying that the roles mentioned in the previous three steps will be involved in carrying out the data cleaning strategies. However, here, you might have additional leadership roles such as management or department heads, depending on the size of the business, overseeing the strategy and implementation of these data cleaning strategies. This oversight is important, especially as you begin to look at allocating resources, budget, or technology to these efforts.

Data transformations

This phase generally refers to the process of applying operations and functions to clean and enhance the data. This step involves aggregating data, deriving new variables, performing calculations, or applying data conversions. Transformations are performed to align the data with the desired format, structure, or analysis requirements.

Data quality assurance

Quality assurance ensures that the cleaned data meets the defined quality standards and is fit for its intended purpose. Generally, this phase would involve you carrying out data integrity checks, comparing the cleaned data with its original source data, and verifying its accuracy. This becomes very important when you start building out more complex data models in Power BI, which may improve performance but could impact the data integrity.

Collaboration across roles is key in this particular step as processes are established, governed, and maintained. If you have a data governance manager within your team, then they might help to establish and enforce policies in this step for the overall assurance of the data.

Additionally, CDOs can help by overseeing these policies and frameworks to ensure they align with industry standards, while also ensuring that these are visible across the organization and not just within a data team. This would logically form part of their data strategy and vision for the business so they have a vested interest in this step.

Documentation

Gone are the days when people could just build or develop without documenting what changes were being made. This causes companies huge pains later down the line as others in the business won't know what changes have been made to the data and thus are required to start fresh.

Documenting the data cleaning journey is a crucial aspect for this reason. This involves recording the steps taken, decisions made, and any assumptions or transformations applied to the data during the cleaning. This can often be seen as heavy admin on top of the already lengthy data cleaning process, but this proves invaluable when faced with future analyses of similar data, audits on your data, and lastly, data governance tracking.

Ensuring you have proper documentation is just the first hurdle. In the next section, you will learn more about understanding why it's important to have good data, not lots of data.

Understanding quality over quantity in data cleaning

When it comes to data cleaning, quality should always take precedence over quantity. While large datasets may initially seem enticing, the real value resides in the precision, dependability, and uniformity of the data. Imagine having a vast pool of data that is riddled with errors, duplications, and inconsistencies – the potential insights gleaned from such a dataset would be marred by inaccuracies and inefficiencies.

To illustrate this, consider a scenario where a retail company aims to analyze customer purchasing behavior to optimize its marketing strategies. If the data used for analysis contains duplicate entries, outdated information, or inaccuracies in customer preferences, the resulting insights could lead to misguided marketing campaigns, resulting in wasted resources and missed opportunities. In this context, the quality of data directly correlates with the reliability and accuracy of the conclusions drawn from the analysis. In the context of data quantity, though, bringing in data that has no correlation to a customer's behavior just because it's available will not add value to the analysis and could cause unnecessary performance issues.

Moreover, a meticulous approach to data cleaning ensures that the information adheres to data regulations, mitigating the risks associated with non-compliance. For instance, in industries with stringent privacy regulations such as healthcare or finance, relying on high-quality data is not only a best practice but also a legal requirement. A healthcare organization analyzing patient data must ensure the accuracy and privacy of the information to comply with data protection laws and maintain the trust of patients.

By focusing on data quality, organizations fortify their analytical endeavors, fostering a more robust and reliable basis for strategic decision-making. Consider a financial institution that relies on data to assess credit risk. If the data used in this process is of low quality, contains errors in financial histories, or is missing crucial information, the institution could make flawed assessments, leading to poor lending decisions and financial repercussions.

In essence, the objective of data cleaning is not simply to accumulate copious amounts of data within a model; rather, it revolves around cultivating a reservoir of high-quality data that serves as the driving force behind actionable and impactful results. Understanding the paramount importance of data quality empowers organizations to make informed decisions, optimize processes, and stay ahead in an increasingly data-driven landscape.

Summary

In this chapter, we delved into the fundamentals of data cleaning and explored key principles to consider when cleaning data. Data cleaning is a crucial step in the data preparation process, as the quality of the data greatly impacts the accuracy and reliability of analyses and decision-making.

You learned about seven key principles when it comes to planning and preparing to clean your data, which not only provide best practices but also document the impact you've had on that data or the business.

In the next chapter, we will dive into the practical aspect of data cleaning using Power BI. You will be following along as we go through the most common data cleaning steps within Power BI, providing hands-on experience to clean and transform data for improved quality and usability.

Questions

1. What is the aim of data cleaning in the data preparation process?

    A. Accumulating raw data

    B. Transforming data into a masterpiece

    C. Ensuring data is dirty for analysis

    D. Focusing on data quantity over quality

2. Why is it essential to establish a framework and principles for data cleaning efforts?

    A. To speed up the data cleaning process

    B. To prevent a cycle of perpetual data cleaning

    C. To add additional steps in the process of data cleaning

    D. To create more documentation of data

3. What does the process for cleaning data involve?

   A. Data visualization

   B. Data assessment, data profiling, data validation, data cleaning strategies, data transformation, data quality assurance, and documentation

   C. Data storage

   D. Data generation

4. What does data profiling help identify in the data cleaning process?

   A. Patterns, distributions, and outliers

   B. Data storage mechanisms

   C. Data generation techniques

   D. Data transformation errors

5. What is the significance of documenting the data cleaning journey?

   A. It demonstrates the importance of the data team

   B. It helps you get a raise

   C. It is crucial for tracking data governance and changes made to the data

   D. It minimizes the need for data governance tools

6. What does the principle of "quality over quantity" emphasize in data cleaning?

   A. Prioritizing data where every field has a value

   B. Reducing storage costs of large data

   C. Focusing on getting a small set of data that shows the desired outcome

   D. Prioritizing the accuracy, reliability, and consistency of data

4

The Most Common Data Cleaning Operations

Now that you've built a strong knowledge of data quality and the importance of assessing and documenting your data cleaning process, it's time to roll your sleeves up and get stuck into some data.

In this chapter, you will be learning how to deal with the most common data cleaning steps within Power BI, as listed next. For each of these example topics, you will find a step-by-step walk-through on how to carry out these transformations yourself.

We will cover the following specific topics:

- Removing duplicates
- Removing missing data
- Splitting columns
- Merging columns
- Replacing outliers
- Creating calculated columns versus measures

By the end of the chapter, you will have built a strong base of foundational knowledge on how to tackle some of the most common and simplest transformations that we often see needing to be done when connecting to data in Power BI.

Technical requirements

You will find the uncleaned dataset to be used during this chapter at the following link: `https://github.com/PacktPublishing/Data-Cleaning-with-Power-BI`.

Removing duplicates

In many cases, as we start working with data, there will often be duplicates within the data. As we discussed in *Chapter 2, Understanding Data Quality and Why Data Cleaning is Important*, there are a number of reasons why the values in your data may have been duplicated. For example, say we're a retailer and we accidentally entered two product items for the same product. We don't want to have inaccurate numbers for that product by leaving the duplicate data in, so it's key that we remove it before we get started with our analysis.

So, let's get started. In the following example, we will find, select, and remove the duplicate in the data:

1. Download the `Products.xlsx` dataset from the given GitHub repository.

2. Connect to this CSV using Power BI Desktop by selecting **Get data** in the toolbar (as shown) and then selecting **Excel workbook**:

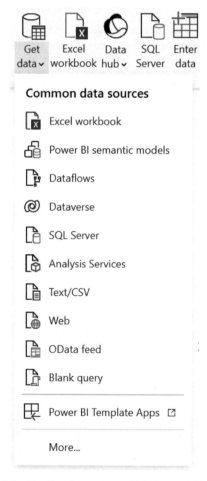

Figure 4.1 – The Get data menu within Power BI Desktop

3. Select the `Products.xlsx` file and then select the sheet you would like to connect to. In this case, it's the sheet labeled **Products**.

4. Now select **Load data**, which will then take you directly to Power BI. If you were to select **Transform data**, then you would be taken directly to the Power Query Editor, where you might transform the data.

Now that you have loaded the data into Power BI, we can begin to look at our data.

To do this, select **Table view** on the navigation bar on the far left side of Power BI Desktop, as shown in the following figure. By default, Power BI likely left you in **Report view** after you loaded your data as this is the default view when you open Power BI Desktop.

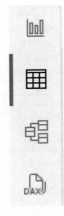

Figure 4.2 – The view navigation from within Power BI Desktop

As we can see in *Figure 4.3*, the data we have loaded might be the start of our data model because it resembles a table that we'd use as a dimension table. It's important to note, though, that you might not always start with a dimension table, as you may choose to begin with a fact table.

In Power BI, dimension tables contain descriptive attributes such as customer names or product categories, providing context to the numerical data in fact tables, which store quantitative measures such as sales revenue or quantities sold. This separation of descriptive and numerical data enhances efficiency, scalability, and flexibility in data analysis. Together, they form a star or snowflake schema, optimizing storage, retrieval, and analytical capabilities in BI applications. We will go into more detail on this later in *Chapter 12, Data Modeling and Managing Relationships*.

Product_ID	Product_Name	Product_Category	Product_Cost	Product_Price
1	Action Figure	Toys	$9.99	$15.99
2	Animal Figures	Toys	$9.99	$12.99
3	Barrel O' Slime	Art & Crafts	$1.99	$3.99
4	Chutes & Ladders	Games	$9.99	$12.99
5	Classic Dominoes	Games	$7.99	$9.99
6	Colorbuds	Electronics	$6.99	$14.99
7	Dart Gun	Sports & Outdoors	$11.99	$15.99
8	Deck Of Cards	Games	$3.99	$6.99
9	Dino Egg	Toys	$9.99	$10.99
10	Dinosaur Figures	Toys	$10.99	$14.99
11	Etch A Sketch	Art & Crafts	$10.99	$20.99
12	Foam Disk Launcher	Sports & Outdoors	$8.99	$11.99
13	Gamer Headphones	Electronics	$14.99	$20.99
14	Glass Marbles	Games	$5.99	$10.99
15	Hot Wheels 5-Pack	Toys	$3.99	$5.99
16	Jenga	Games	$2.99	$9.99
17	Kids Makeup Kit	Art & Crafts	$13.99	$19.99
18	Lego Bricks	Toys	$34.99	$39.99
19	Magic Sand	Art & Crafts	$13.99	$15.99
20	Mini Basketball Hoop	Sports & Outdoors	$8.99	$24.99
21	Mini Ping Pong Set	Sports & Outdoors	$6.99	$9.99
22	Mono poly	Games	$13.99	$19.99
23	Mr. Potatohead	Toys	$4.99	$9.99
24	Nerf Gun	Sports & Outdoors	$14.99	$19.99
25	PlayDoh Can	Art & Crafts	$1.99	$2.99
26	PlayDoh Playset	Art & Crafts	$20.99	$24.99
27	PlayDoh Toolkit	Art & Crafts	$3.99	$4.99
28	Playfoam	Art & Crafts	$3.99	$10.99
29	Plush Pony	Toys	$8.99	$19.99
30	Rubik's Cube	Games	$17.99	$19.99
31	Splash Balls	Sports & Outdoors	$7.99	$8.99
32	Supersoaker Water Gun	Sports & Outdoors	$11.99	$14.99
33	Teddy Bear	Toys	$10.99	$12.99
34	Toy Robot	Electronics	$20.99	$25.99
35	Uno Card Game	Games	$3.99	$7.99
36	Jenga	Games	$2.99	$9.99
37			0	0

Figure 4.3 – The products table imported into Power BI

As you can see on rows 16 and 36 in the data in the previous screenshot, there is a duplicate for the Jenga product. We must look to remove this duplicate as, when it comes to building our model, it could end up causing our facts to return inflated since Power BI will count the values of [Price] and [Cost] incorrectly due to them being there twice.

There are a number of ways you could do this, but the simplest way is through the Power Query UI. So, in order to reach this page, you will need to carry out the following steps:

1. Provided you are in **Report**, **Table**, or **Model view**, navigate to the **Home** tab in the toolbar and then select **Transform Data** to access the Power Query Editor.

2. Now select the column in which the main identifier and duplicate is located. In this case, we want to select Product_Name.

3. With that column selected, you can now select **Remove Rows** within the toolbar and select **Remove Duplicates**, as shown:

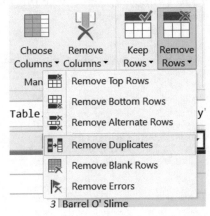

Figure 4.4 – The Remove Rows menu within the toolbar

> **Important note**
>
> Avoid using columns that could result in an error. For example, if you were to select Cost or Price, then this could result in the wrong data being pulled through. This is because Power Query will focus on the values within that specific column with this method of removing duplicates, resulting in other products valued at a similar price to Jenga also being deleted.

> **Important note**
>
> In the previous example, we ended up removing the row with the duplicate, which had the product ID 36. Be cautious of this in the future as this ID might be used later down the line when you try to connect this dimension to a fact table, as the fact table might reference the product ID we just removed.

Removing missing data

Next, we have the very common issue of missing data or, as most people would recognize, null values. In *Chapter 2, Understanding Data Quality and Why Data Cleaning is Important*, we understood the reasons why this might happen – for example, due to the type of join between two tables, which might cause many null values to show.

These null values can often either ruin the look of your reporting or potentially skew the numbers being used or analyzed, so it's often best we look to remove these.

In the example of our products table, we can see that we have a row with blank or 0 values shown in *Figure 4.5*. If you were viewing this from within the Power Query Editor, then the blank values would be showing as null. While this would otherwise be acceptable as we won't necessarily see the null product within a visualization, there is a price and cost value against the null product with the 0 value. This could affect the analysis, particularly if we were trying to calculate the average product price, as it would bring the average product price down.

Product_ID	Product_Name	Product_Category	Product_Cost	Product_Price
1	Action Figure	Toys	$9.99	$15.99
2	Animal Figures	Toys	$9.99	$12.99
3	Barrel O' Slime	Art & Crafts	$1.99	$3.99
4	Chutes & Ladders	Games	$9.99	$12.99
5	Classic Dominoes	Games	$7.99	$9.99
6	Colorbuds	Electronics	$6.99	$14.99
7	Dart Gun	Sports & Outdoors	$11.99	$15.99
8	Deck Of Cards	Games	$3.99	$6.99
9	Dino Egg	Toys	$9.99	$10.99
10	Dinosaur Figures	Toys	$10.99	$14.99
11	Etch A Sketch	Art & Crafts	$10.99	$20.99
12	Foam Disk Launcher	Sports & Outdoors	$8.99	$11.99
13	Gamer Headphones	Electronics	$14.99	$20.99
14	Glass Marbles	Games	$5.99	$10.99
15	Hot Wheels 5-Pack	Toys	$3.99	$5.99
16	Jenga	Games	$2.99	$9.99
17	Kids Makeup Kit	Art & Crafts	$13.99	$19.99
18	Lego Bricks	Toys	$34.99	$39.99
19	Magic Sand	Art & Crafts	$13.99	$15.99
20	Mini Basketball Hoop	Sports & Outdoors	$8.99	$24.99
21	Mini Ping Pong Set	Sports & Outdoors	$6.99	$9.99
22	Monopoly	Games	$13.99	$19.99
23	Mr. Potatohead	Toys	$4.99	$9.99
24	Nerf Gun	Sports & Outdoors	$14.99	$19.99
25	PlayDoh Can	Art & Crafts	$1.99	$2.99
26	PlayDoh Playset	Art & Crafts	$20.99	$24.99
27	PlayDoh Toolkit	Art & Crafts	$3.99	$4.99
28	Playfoam	Art & Crafts	$3.99	$10.99
29	Plush Pony	Toys	$8.99	$19.99
30	Rubik's Cube	Games	$17.99	$19.99
31	Splash Balls	Sports & Outdoors	$7.99	$8.99
32	Supersoaker Water Gun	Sports & Outdoors	$11.99	$14.99
33	Teddy Bear	Toys	$10.99	$12.99
34	Toy Robot	Electronics	$20.99	$25.99
35	Uno Card Game	Games	$3.99	$7.99
36	Jenga	Games	$2.99	$9.99
37			0	0

Figure 4.5 – The products table within Power BI highlighting a specific column called Product_Price

There are a couple of ways in which you can remove blank rows, using the prebuilt functions shown in *Figure 4.6*. For most scenarios, if you have an entire row with `null` values, then you can resolve this by selecting **Remove Blank Rows**.

Figure 4.6 – The drop-down menu when selecting Remove Rows from within Power Query

In this particular example, though, removing blank rows will not be suitable as there is a value for `Product_ID` labeled 37. So, in this example, the simplest solution would be to use **Remove Bottom Rows** to remove the data we do not need:

Remove Bottom Rows

Specify how many rows to remove from the bottom.

Number of rows

Figure 4.7 – The UI for the Remove Bottom Rows function within Power Query

> **Important tip**
>
> While it is the simplest solution for this example, it might not be the best solution in other datasets. This is because there could be multiple blank rows and they might not necessarily all be located at the bottom of the table.

If you are following along, here are the steps to remove the error from the products table:

1. Click on **Remove Bottom Rows**.

2. Select the number of rows to remove – in this example, we need to remove one row.

3. Check whether the data is showing correctly. Then, select **Close & Apply**.

This example is simple as the null value is located on the last row of the table. Later in this book, you will learn how you can use an advanced editor for more specific customer scenarios.

Splitting columns

When working with data, particularly data extracted directly from source systems, there often comes a time when we will need to split columns to gain the desired dimensions for our analysis. This might be because the software or database of that source system might store that data in a particular format/encoding/arrangement. The most common example of this could be splitting a Date field in order to extract dimensions for [Day], [Month], and [Year].

In this example, we will connect and open the calendar.xlsx file. This Excel table includes one column of dates (as shown in *Figure 4.8*) and is to be used as a date table within Power BI. In this example, we might need to extract the individual date components for our analysis. Once connected, select **Transform data** to enter Power Query once again.

	ABC 123 Date
1	01/01/2015
2	01/02/2015
3	01/03/2015
4	01/04/2015
5	01/05/2015
6	01/06/2015
7	01/07/2015
8	01/08/2015
9	01/09/2015
10	01/10/2015
11	01/11/2015
12	01/12/2015

Figure 4.8 – The Date column within the date table in Power BI

In order to split the columns, we will use the prebuilt function for splitting columns shown in *Figure 4.9*. Given the format of the data, it's best to split the columns using **By Delimiter**. This is because using the delimiter is the simplest way to split this column.

There are many other options to split columns, such as using the number of characters. This would be great for an example where we need to extract the first letters of a product code, for example.

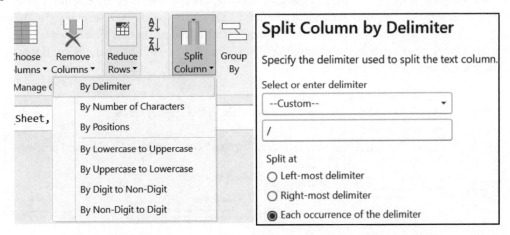

Figure 4.9 – The drop-down menu above the split column function (left) and a
close-up of the UI for the Split Column by Delimiter function (right)

Power BI has the smart capability to recommend what delimiter to use based on the data in the columns you have selected. Selecting **OK** will then split the column into the following format:

123 Date.1	123 Date.2	123 Date.3
1	1	1	2015
2	1	2	2015
3	1	3	2015
4	1	4	2015

Figure 4.10 – The date table with the columns now split into three columns

It's recommended to then rename the columns to the appropriate fields, as shown. This can be done by right-clicking on the column headers and selecting **Rename**.

123 Month	123 Day	123 Year
1	1	1	2015
2	1	2	2015
3	1	3	2015
4	1	4	2015

Figure 4.11 – The date table with the three columns renamed Month, Day, and Year

Here, we have learned how to split columns using the functions within Power Query. Next in this chapter, we will look at how to do the opposite and merge columns.

Merging columns

Just like the previous scenario, there are often situations where you need to merge columns to achieve the desired format. For example, depending how date data is stored, you may need to merge the [Day], [Month], and [Year] columns to achieve a singular Date column. In the following figure, we can see an example description and configuration of how you might do this using the prebuilt function of **Merge Columns** in Power Query:

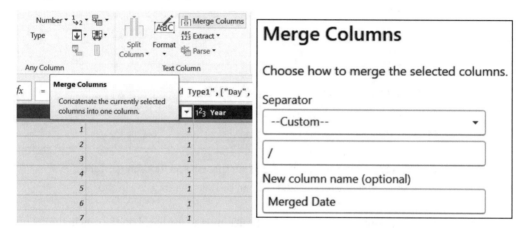

Figure 4.12 – The drop-down menu above the Merge Columns function (left)
and a close-up of the UI for the Merge Columns function (right)

To use the **Merge Columns** function, follow these steps:

1. Select the columns you would like to merge.

2. Select the **Merge Columns** function, which can be located on the **Home** or **Transform** tab in the ribbon toolbar.

3. In the **Merge Columns** configuration window, you can select a separator to sit between the merged values. As we are working with dates, we can select **Custom** and add / as the custom separator.

4. Select **OK** and check whether the values have returned correctly.

Replacing values

When connecting to and analyzing data, there are often times when we might find outliers within the data. If we identify that there are values skewing the data or showing incorrectly, it's important for us to be able to replace the data with the correct values.

There are many scenarios where you might need to do this in Power BI. Here are just some example scenarios:

- Replacing variations of **N/A** or **Not Applicable** with a consistent value such as **Unknown**.

- You may need to rename or reclassify certain values in your dataset to align with your reporting needs or to create meaningful categories. For instance, you can replace abbreviations or acronyms with their full names or group similar values together.

- You can replace numeric code with descriptive labels or convert coded values into meaningful text representations.

- In cases where your data contains missing or `null` values, you can use the **Replace Values** function to replace them with a specific value or marker that suits your analysis or reporting requirements.

- When dealing with inconsistent formats, such as different date formats or variations in capitalization, you can utilize the **Replace Values** function to standardize and unify the format across the dataset.

- If you're working with multilingual data, you can use the **Replace Values** function to translate certain values from one language to another. This can be useful when generating localized reports or visuals.

Going back to our product dataset, we can use the **Replace Values** function to fix an error in the product names/categories. In the data, we have a product name that has been extracted with a misspelling. Row 22 should read **Monopoly**, so we need to replace the value with the correct value to ensure our analysis and reporting show the correct data:

| 22 | Mono poly | Games | $13.99 | $19.99 |

Figure 4.13 – The row mentioned in the example should read
"Monopoly" but currently reads as "Mono poly"

To replace this value, please follow these steps:

1. Open Power Query to transform data.
2. Locate the data in the data view that needs to be replaced.
3. Then, you have two ways of accessing the replace function:
    - You can right-click on the value that needs replacing, as shown, and select **Replace Values…**:

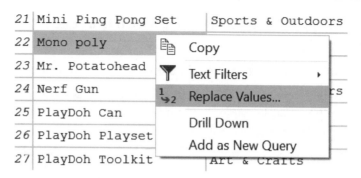

Figure 4.14 – The drop-down menu when right-clicking on the value that needs to be replaced

- Alternatively, click on the **Replace Values…** function at the top of the toolbar.

4. Regardless of the step you choose, you will have the option to then select the new value you'd like this to be replaced with:

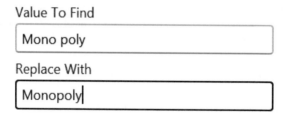

Replace Values

Replace one value with another in the selected columns.

Value To Find

Mono poly

Replace With

Monopoly

▷ Advanced options

Figure 4.15 – The UI for the Replace Values function within Power Query

> **Important note**
> Although we can make these transformations in Power Query, ideally, these types of data quality issues should be corrected at the source system. Performing multiple such spelling corrections within Power Query is generally a very bad practice. This is because it is difficult to govern and doesn't scale well when there are many corrections required.

Having learned how to replace values within our data using the functions within Power Query, let's look at how to create calculated columns versus creating measures within Power BI.

Creating calculated columns versus measures

When preparing data for analysis in Power BI, we often need to add additional data to the model (often derived from existing data). This can often come in the form of using DAX to either create a measure or an additional column. This could be for a new value we need or a new dimension. Before understanding which option is best, it's important to understand what the difference is between a calculated column and a measure within Power BI.

The best way to add a new measure or column is to first navigate to **Table view** on the far-left toolbar.

The view will automatically jump to the **Table tools** tab along the top toolbar, which will then present you with the following options for calculations: **New measure**, **Quick measure**, **New column**, and **New table**, as shown:

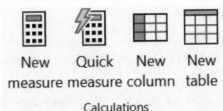

Figure 4.16 – The Calculations section within the Table view of Power BI

It's important to note that if you are working from **Model view** within Power BI Desktop, this will look slightly different with the latest introduction of **Calculation group**, as you can see in the following figure – this is described later in the chapter:

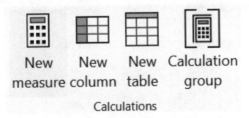

Figure 4.17 – The Calculations section within the Model view of Power BI

Calculated columns

A calculated column is a column that you add to a table in the Power BI data model. It uses a formula that calculates a value for each row in the table. The calculation is performed during the data loading process, and the resulting values are stored in the column.

The calculated column becomes a part of your data model and can be used in visuals and calculations.

In the example of our products table, we could add a column to the data model, which would look like the following:

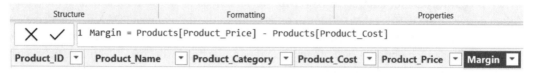

Figure 4.18 – The products table within Power BI with a specific column selected named Margin

Measures

A measure is a calculation performed on the fly, usually aggregating or summarizing data, based on the context of the visual or calculation.

Measures are typically used in calculations that involve aggregations such as sums, averages, counts, or ratios. Measures are defined using DAX and can be created within Power BI using the **New measure** feature.

Similar to the calculated columns example, if you select **New measure**, you can add a similar DAX expression to calculate the margin, but this will not add a column with the margin data to the data model. The following screenshot shows an example of this being added as a measure:

Figure 4.19 – DAX calculation to add a measure named Margin (measure)

You can then see the difference between the two values on the right-hand side:

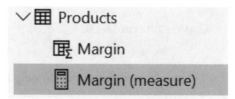

Figure 4.20 – The new measure has been added to the products table within the Power BI service

Measures can be identified with the calculator logo and calculated columns can be identified with the table logo to the left of the value.

Calculation group

Calculation groups were introduced in Power BI to tackle the challenges associated with managing a large number of repetitive measures and to simplify the logic applied in diverse calculations. Functioning as a container for a set of calculation items, **Calculation groups** empower users to apply variations of measures based on specific conditions. Essentially, they allow users to define and apply calculation logic dynamically, eliminating the need for numerous similar measures with slight variations.

Consider a real-world scenario where a fact table contains various metrics such as sales amount, sales quantity, costs, discount, profit, and more. Traditionally, offering additional insights about these metrics, such as the previous month/quarter/year or year-to-date comparisons, required the creation of separate measures for each metric and time intelligence. This approach resulted in a significant number of measures with duplicated logic, posing challenges in maintenance.

Calculation groups present a more efficient solution. Instead of generating multiple redundant measures, you can utilize a placeholder measure and define calculation items to be applied to it. This concept will be explored further through a straightforward example.

Prior to Microsoft's latest release, where they added the ability to create calculation groups within the product, Power BI users would typically need to use third-party tools such as **Tabular Editor**. There is much to be said, though, for why many users still look to leverage the immense power of tools such as Tabular Editor. Here are just a few examples:

- **Advanced functionality and control**: Third-party tools often provide more advanced features and greater control over the data model compared to native Power BI tools. Tabular Editor, for instance, offers a rich set of functionalities for model development, scripting, and managing calculations.

- **Efficiency and productivity**: Some users find third-party tools to be more efficient and productive for certain tasks. These tools may have optimized workflows and shortcuts that make it faster to perform specific actions, especially for users who are familiar with those tools.

- **Scripting and automation**: Tabular Editor and other third-party tools often provide scripting capabilities, allowing users to automate certain tasks or apply changes across multiple objects simultaneously. This can be particularly useful for large and complex data models.

- **Version control and source code management**: Third-party tools may offer better support for version control and source code management. This can be crucial for teams working collaboratively on data models, allowing them to track changes, roll back to previous versions, and manage the development life cycle more effectively.

It's worth noting that the decision to use third-party tools alongside Power BI depends on individual preferences, specific project requirements, and the level of expertise of the users involved. Some people may find that the native Power BI tools, including calculation groups, meet all their needs, while others may prefer the additional capabilities provided by third-party tools.

Considerations

There are some considerations you should make when deciding which to use:

- Calculated columns are best suited for calculations that require row-level context or depend on the relationships between tables.

- Measures are ideal for performing aggregations and calculations on your data.

- Calculated columns can consume more memory and storage as the calculated values are stored for each row in the table.

- Simple calculated columns such as the previous *Margin* example can also be added with Power Query instead of DAX. It's often seen as best practice to add such columns with Power Query; however, of course, the best solution would be if these columns were created upstream in the source systems or database.

- Measures are memory-efficient as they are not precalculated and don't consume additional storage.

- Avoid creating too many calculated columns as they can increase the complexity and size of your data model.

- Measures are calculated dynamically based on the filters and slicers that impact visual contexts. They respond to user interactions and provide accurate results.

- Visual context, specifically, relates to the filters and conditions applied to a visual or a set of visuals on a report canvas. Contexts influence how data is presented and can be summarized as follows:

  - **Row context**: Occurs at the individual row level when iterating through the data table. Established within formulas and calculations row by row.

  - **Filter context**: Set of filters applied to a particular visual element on the report canvas. This comes from slicers, cross-filters, highlighting, and so on.

  - **Page context**: Refers to filters applied at the entire page level affecting all visuals on a page.

  - **Drill-through context**: Established when users drill through from one page to another, passing the context from the source page to the target page.

- Use calculated columns when the calculated value needs to be used across multiple visuals or calculations consistently.

- Use measures when you need to calculate values based on the summarized data displayed in a visual.

These considerations will help you make the correct decisions when it comes to cleaning your data with measures or adding new columns to the data.

Summary

In this chapter, you began your journey into the practical aspects of data cleaning within Power BI. You covered some of the most common data cleaning steps in Power BI, including removing duplicates, handling missing data, splitting columns, merging tables, dealing with date formats, replacing values, and creating calculated columns versus measures.

The chapter also highlighted the importance of replacing values in your data. Outliers, incorrect values, or inconsistent formats can hinder analysis. You learned about various scenarios where replacing values is necessary and used the **Replace Values** function in Power Query to fix errors and standardize data.

Lastly, the chapter explored the difference between calculated columns and measures in Power BI and explained when to use each option and their respective benefits. Calculated columns are best suited for row-level calculations, while measures are ideal for aggregations and calculations based on visual context. The chapter concluded by emphasizing the considerations when deciding between calculated columns and measures and providing guidelines to help you make informed choices based on factors such as memory usage, storage, and the complexity of your data model.

Now that you have a strong understanding of data quality and the importance of documenting your data cleaning process, it's time to roll up your sleeves and start working with real data. You have gained practical knowledge and hands-on experience in performing common data cleaning tasks within Power BI. This sets the foundation for the next chapter, which focuses on importing data into Power BI and further refining your data for analysis.

Questions

1. Why is it important to remove duplicates from your data before building a model in Power BI?

    A. To increase file size

    B. To enhance data accuracy in the analysis

    C. To speed up data loading

    D. To add complexity to the data model

2. In the provided example with the products table, which column is selected for removing duplicates, and why is it crucial to choose the right column?

    A. `Product ID`, for simplicity

    B. `Cost`, for accurate financial analysis

    C. `Product Name`, as the main identifier

    D. `Date`, for chronological precision

3. How can missing data, represented as `null` values, impact the analysis of your dataset?

   A. Enhances visual appeal

   B. Distorts analysis results

   C. Speeds up data processing

   D. Reduces data complexity

4. When might you need to split columns in Power BI, and what example is given in the chapter?

   A. To increase data complexity – for example, splitting product codes

   B. To enhance visual appeal – for example, splitting financial data

   C. To gain desired dimensions for analysis – for example, splitting a date field

   D. To decrease file size – for example, splitting customer names

5. In the Date table example, which function was used to split the columns, and why was it chosen?

   A. **Merge Columns**, for simplicity

   B. **Split Columns by Number of Characters**, for precision

   C. **Split Columns by Delimiter**, based on data format

   D. **Remove Columns**, for data reduction

6. In which of the following scenarios is merging columns in Power BI necessary.

   A. Merging columns is never necessary

   B. Merging columns to increase file size

   C. Merging columns to format date data

   D. Merging columns for visual appeal

7. What steps are involved in using the **Merge Columns** function, as outlined in the chapter?

   A. Select the columns, click **Merge Columns**, choose a separator, and select **Close & Apply**

   B. Click **Split Columns | Merge Columns**, rename the columns, and save changes

   C. Click **Merge Columns | Split Columns**, choose a separator, and apply changes

   D. Select the columns, click **Remove Columns | Merge Columns**, and save changes

8. Why is it important to replace values in your dataset, and what scenarios are mentioned where this might be necessary?

    A. To complicate data analysis; scenarios include increasing file size

    B. To standardize and correct data; scenarios include fixing errors and standardizing formats

    C. To add variability to data; scenarios include introducing outliers

    D. To slow down data processing; scenarios include replacing data with random values

9. In the provided example with the product names, how is the incorrect value `Mono poly` corrected?

    A. Using the **Remove Values** function

    B. Using the **Merge Values** function

    C. Using the **Replace Values** function

    D. Using the **Delete Values** function

10. What is the fundamental difference between calculated columns and measures in Power BI?

    A. Both perform row-level calculations

    B. Measures are dynamic, columns are precalculated row by row

    C. Measures are best for row-level context

    D. Calculated columns are memory-efficient

11. When is it advisable to use calculated columns, and when should measures be preferred, according to the considerations mentioned in the chapter?

    A. Calculated columns for aggregations; measures for row-level context

    B. Calculated columns for memory efficiency; measures for file size reduction

    C. Calculated columns for dynamic calculations; measures for static calculations

    D. Calculated columns for row-level context; measures for aggregations

Part 2 – Data Import and Query Editor

This part will delve into the intricacies of data import and the potent Query Editor. You will learn about the key aspects that need to be considered when importing data and build confidence in working with the Query Editor. You will also explore the M language, unraveling its syntax and capabilities for transforming data, before being introduced to data profiling for exploratory data analysis, thus enhancing data accuracy within Power BI.

This part has the following chapters:

- *Chapter 5, Importing Data into Power BI*
- *Chapter 6, Cleaning Data with Query Editor*
- *Chapter 7, Transforming Data with the M Language*
- *Chapter 8, Using Data Profiling for Exploratory Data Analysis (EDA)*

5

Importing Data into Power BI

Now that we understand the importance of cleaning data and even how to tackle some of the most common data-cleaning operations, it's time to start bringing some data into Power BI.

When it comes to importing data into Power BI, there are six main topics, as listed next, to consider. Most importantly, for the top three, there are metrics that help us identify how clean data is prior to us working on it. In this chapter, you will learn about these topics and how you can use the Power BI platform to assess these metrics within your own data.

Specifically, we will be going through the following topics:

- Understanding data completeness
- Understanding data accuracy
- Understanding data consistency
- Assessing data relevance
- Assessing data formatting
- Assessing data normalization, denormalization, and star schemas

By the end of this chapter, you will be able to confidently assess how clean the data you've imported is and also how to use Power BI to assess it.

Technical requirements

You will find the uncleaned dataset to be used during this chapter at the following link: `https://github.com/PacktPublishing/Data-Cleaning-with-Power-BI`.

Understanding data completeness

When importing data into Power BI, one of the primary concerns is ensuring data completeness.

Before diving into the technical aspects of importing data, it is essential to understand the context in which data completeness becomes a critical factor. Incomplete data can lead to skewed analyses, erroneous visualizations, and misleading business insights. Therefore, in this section, we will explore the significance of data completeness and how it forms the foundation for accurate and reliable reporting in Power BI.

To assess data completeness in Power BI, we can employ various techniques. For instance, we can use data profiling to identify the percentage of missing values for each column. Power BI's built-in data profiling capabilities help us visualize the completeness of data across different fields in our dataset.

By analyzing these visualizations, we can pinpoint columns with high percentages of missing values, indicating areas that require attention.

Additionally, Power BI provides filtering options to exclude records with missing values, allowing us to observe how data visualizations and summaries change based on the data's completeness.

Let's jump into our dataset to understand how complete the data is. For this analysis, we will connect to the CSV file labeled `AdventureWorks_Products (unclean).csv` with the help of the following steps:

1. Open Power BI and select **Get Data** from the toolbar.
2. Then, select **Text/CSV** as the data connector.
3. Select `AdventureWorks_Products (unclean).csv`.
4. Select **Transform Data**, which in turn will open the Power Query Editor screen, as shown in *Figure 5.1*.

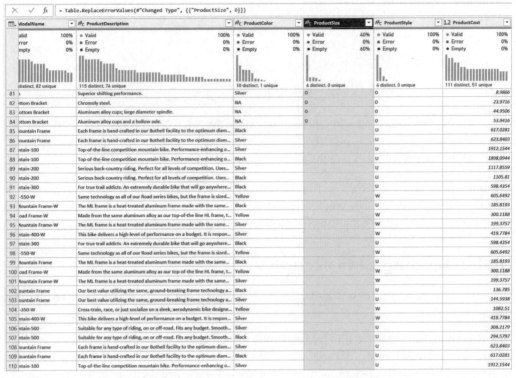

Figure 5.1 – The view within Power Query for the Products table

---

Important note

The previous view shows column quality and column distribution metrics. To activate this, you will need to navigate to the **View** tab within the Power Query Editor ribbon. In the **Data Preview** group, you can then select the **Column Quality** and **Column Distribution** checkboxes to see them.

---

5. As we assess the data preview in the Power Query Editor, we can then see there is a gap in the data for the **ProductSize** column, as shown in *Figure 5.1*.

We can see in this figure that 60% of the data for **ProductSize** is empty, and as such, the completeness of the data is impacted.

Note

If you are not seeing a percentage, then it's likely because Power Query has added an additional step called **Changed Type** to your query. Power Query may automatically attempt to set the data type of columns when importing from CSV. In this example, it has likely tried to change the type of the **ProductSize** column from **Text** to **Whole Number**. Simply remove the **Changed Type** step by selecting the **X** symbol next to the step in the query settings pane, as illustrated in the following screenshot:

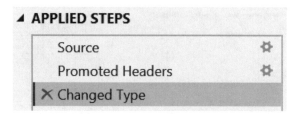

Figure 5.2 – The applied steps within the Power Query Editor

6.   Select **Close & Apply** to save the work done in Power Query.

Ensuring data completeness in Power BI is paramount for accurate analyses and reliable reporting. By utilizing techniques such as data profiling and visualizing missing values, we can identify and address areas of concern, ultimately enhancing the quality and integrity of our insights.

Understanding data accuracy

Understanding the context in which data accuracy matters is crucial for data analysts and business professionals alike.

In this section, we will delve into two methods to validate data accuracy and detect errors or inconsistencies. By addressing data accuracy during the data import process, you will gain confidence in the integrity of your datasets, enabling you to make well-informed decisions based on trustworthy insights from Power BI.

Power BI provides several tools to assess data accuracy. One such tool is conditional formatting, where we can define rules to highlight data points that fall outside predefined accuracy ranges or thresholds. For example, we can set rules to flag unusually high or low values in our dataset.

Additionally, Power BI offers data profiling functionalities to examine data distributions and identify potential outliers. By identifying and addressing inaccurate data points, users can ensure that their visualizations and analyses are based on reliable information. You will learn more about these tools and techniques to assess and profile data accuracy in *Chapter 8, Using Data Profiling for Exploratory Data Analysis (EDA)*.

In the pursuit of data-driven decision-making, embracing these tools fosters a data environment where accuracy is not just a goal but a consistent reality.

Understanding data consistency

Data consistency is the key to unlocking the full potential of Power BI as a powerful data analysis and visualization tool. However, achieving data consistency can be challenging, especially when dealing with multiple data sources and diverse data formats.

In this section, we will focus on understanding data consistency and its impact on Power BI reports and dashboards. By addressing data consistency proactively, you will be better equipped to harmonize and integrate disparate data, enabling you to create coherent and impactful visualizations in Power BI.

Power BI's data modeling capabilities play a crucial role in assessing and ensuring data consistency. By creating relationships between tables and using data modeling best practices, such as defining proper data types and data categories, users can ensure that the data aligns seamlessly, leading to accurate and consistent analyses. You will learn more about this later in the book in *Chapter 12, Data Modeling and Managing Relationships*.

Furthermore, Power BI's **Data Analysis Expressions** (**DAX**) language allows users to create calculated columns and measures that adhere to consistent data rules and business logic, further enhancing data consistency across the reports.

Embracing these data consistency practices ensures that your Power BI environment becomes a reliable foundation for data-driven insights, thus fostering a culture of trust in decision-making processes.

Assessing data relevance

Data is only valuable when it is relevant to the questions we seek to answer and the goals we want to achieve. Irrelevant or extraneous data can clutter reports and hinder the decision-making process.

Therefore, it is crucial to consider data relevance during the data import stage. In this section, we will emphasize the importance of evaluating data relevance and ensuring that only pertinent data is imported into Power BI. By filtering and transforming data thoughtfully, you will gain a deeper understanding of your business objectives and derive meaningful insights from their Power BI visualizations.

Power BI's data transformation capabilities allow users to filter out irrelevant data during the import process. For example, when importing sales data, users can filter the data to include only the relevant product categories, time periods, or regions that align with the analysis objectives. Moreover, Power BI's query editor provides a wide range of transformation options, such as removing duplicates, aggregating data, and combining datasets, thus enabling users to create clean and focused datasets that directly address their business questions.

In this example, we will assess the relevance of the data we need using the same dataset we connected to earlier in this chapter. A simple example of this would be to understand which columns are necessary and which are not. This dataset is pretty small, but as you start to work with larger datasets, performing this check will help keep performance strong and make it a positive experience working with that data/report.

Let's assume we're carrying out an analysis of product data. Would we really need the lengthy product description in the data? Likely not, so here we could decide to remove this column.

To remove the column from within the Power Query Editor (the window that pops up when you select **Transform Data**), you need to do the following:

1. Select the irrelevant column you would like to remove. You can select multiple columns one by one by holding down *Ctrl*, or alternatively select a range of columns by holding down *Shift* when selecting columns.

2. Then select **Remove columns** from the toolbar.

3. Lastly, select **Remove Columns** from the menu shown:

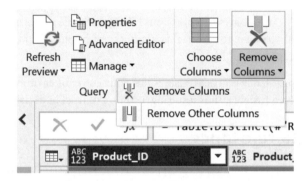

Figure 5.3 – The Remove Columns function within Power Query

This will then remove the column and thus reduce the size of your data model.

Assessing data formatting

Effective data visualization heavily relies on appropriate data formatting. Raw data may not be suitable for direct visualization, and thus, appropriate data formatting becomes essential for clarity. Mastering data formatting enhances the visual appeal, improving the user experience and their understanding of complex datasets.

Power BI's formatting options allow you to control how data is displayed in visuals such as charts, tables, and maps. Users can customize color schemes, font styles, and axis labels to create visually engaging and informative visuals. Conditional formatting features enable dynamic changes based on data values, highlighting important data points. Leveraging these capabilities transforms raw data into compelling visualizations, effectively communicating key insights to stakeholders.

This can most commonly happen when connecting to and working with revenue data. Particularly if this data needs to be formatted with a particular currency and so on.

In the following example, let's prepare the data to format the currency based on the relevant fields:

1. Let's prepare some data in the Power Query Editor before we begin. Select **Transform Data** from within the **Report**, **Table**, or **Model** views to then open the Power Query Editor.

2. We can see the data contains two columns labeled [ProductPrice] and [ProductCost], with {Text} data types, which in some cases have 3-4 decimal places. In order to ensure this data shows correctly on our visuals, we need to format these columns as currency.

3. Change the type of the [ProductPrice] and [ProductCost] columns to {Fixed Decimal Number}. This is a preset type used mainly for currency values. Do this by selecting the type icon next to the column header.

4. Now we would ideally like to add a margin to this data. So, let's do this by adding a column using the Subtract function. Select the **Add Columns** tab in the Power Query Editor.

5. To ensure we are subtracting the data correctly and to prevent us from seeing a negative number, we need to reorder the columns in the data. Otherwise, the Subtract function would subtract [ProductPrice] from [ProductCost]. To do this, select [ProductCost] and drag this into the position left of the [ProductCost] column.

6. Select the two columns [ProductPrice] and [ProductCost], then select **Subtract** from the drop-down menu under **Standard** in the **From Number** ribbon group, as shown. This will add a new column called **Subtraction**, which represents our margin value.

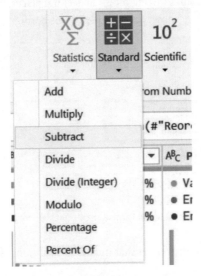

Figure 5.4 – The Subtract function within the Power Query Editor

7. Now, we need to rename the column Subtraction. There are two ways we could do this. One option would be to right-click on the column header and select **Rename**, which would then create a new step. Or we can simply adjust the query from the previous step:

    I. To do this, select the **Subtraction** function. We can then see the M query used to add the new column in the formula bar. Here's an example:

```
= Table.AddColumn(#"Reordered Columns", "Subtraction", each
[ProductPrice] - [ProductCost], Currency.Type)
```

II.   The query automatically labels the new column Subtraction. So, if you simply edit this to ProductMargin, the new column will be labeled ProductMargin, saving you from needing to add additional steps when you add columns. The query should read as follows:

```
= Table.AddColumn(#"Reordered Columns", "ProductMargin", each
[ProductPrice] - [ProductCost], Currency.Type)
```

8. Select the **Home** tab in the ribbon and then select **Close & Apply** to save the transformations made in the Power Query Editor. This should take you back to the **Table** view in Power BI. If it doesn't, then simply navigate to the **Table** view.

9. Here we can see that although the newly created ProductMargin column was set to the {Fixed Decimal Number} type, there are values with multiple decimal places showing.

10. Select the ProductMargin column. This will then open a new tab labeled **Column tools** on the toolbar, where we can see the formatting options to transform that data.

11. Select how many decimal numbers you would like to format this value to, which in this example will be 2. Notice **Auto** is still showing multiple decimal places, which isn't normal for a currency value. The following figure shows an example of this configuration:

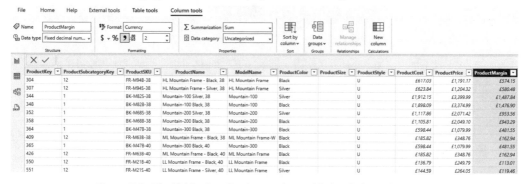

Figure 5.5 – The Table view for the product table loaded into Power BI

12. Now let's create a table in the report that includes conditional formatting. Select **Report View** in the navigation ribbon.

13. Let's create a table visual. Select **Table** from **Visual types**, as shown in *Figure 5.5*. This will create a table template on your report page.

14. With that table selected, add the following data to the table by either selecting the checkboxes next to these columns or dragging these into the box under **Visual types** that says **+Add data**, as highlighted in the following screenshot:

- **ProductColor**

- **ProductMargin**

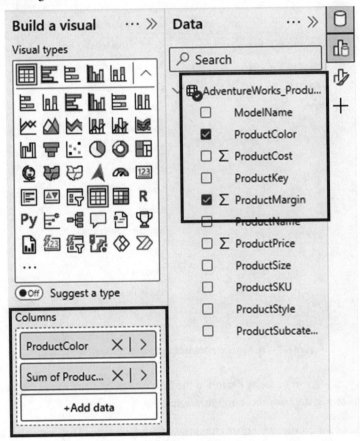

Figure 5.6 – Visual types and Columns selected in Power BI

15. By default, Power BI will have aggregated our numeric field to **SUM**, which for this example is fine. Now, to add conditional formatting to this visual, we can right-click on the field labeled **[Sum of ProductMargin]**.

16. Then, select **Conditional formatting**, and finally, let's select **Background color**, as shown. This will open the configuration window for the background color.

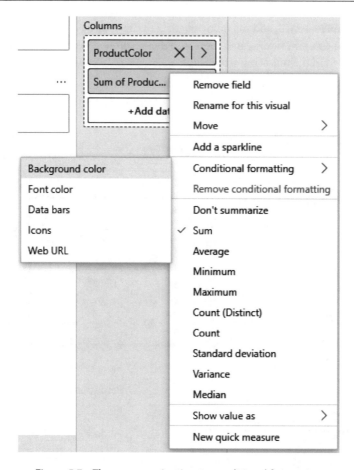

Figure 5.7 – The menu navigating to conditional formatting

17. The configuration will be set by default to the field we selected and the aggregation it had. Carry out the following steps for this configuration:

I.   Adjust the configuration by changing **Maximum** from **Highest value** to **Custom** and inputting 1 as the custom value.

II. Check the **Add a middle color** box. Then, adjust the configuration by changing **Center** from **Middle value** to **Custom** and inputting 0 as the custom value.

III. Change the colors to the following:

- Light red for **Minimum**

- Light yellow for **Center**

- White for **Maximum**

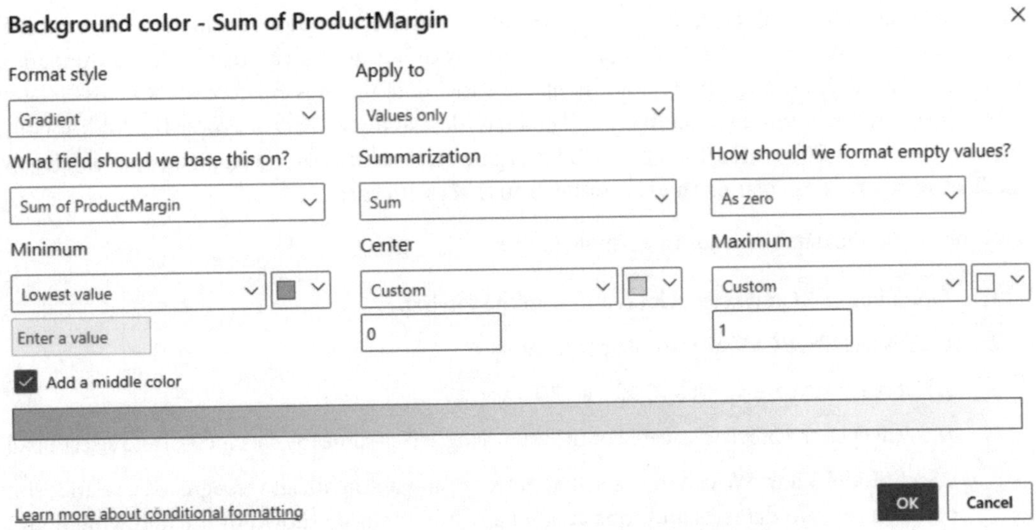

Background color - Sum of ProductMargin   ✕

Format style   Apply to

| Gradient   ⌄ | | Values only   ⌄ |

What field should we base this on?   Summarization   How should we format empty values?

| Sum of ProductMargin   ⌄ | | Sum   ⌄ | | As zero   ⌄ |

Minimum   Center   Maximum

| Lowest value   ⌄ | | ■ ⌄ | | Custom   ⌄ | | ▢ ⌄ | | Custom   ⌄ | | ☐ ⌄ |

| Enter a value | | 0 | | 1 |

☑ Add a middle color

Learn more about conditional formatting   **OK**   Cancel

Figure 5.8 – Background color/conditional formatting configuration

18. Select **OK** to complete the configuration.

We can now see that the conditional formatting has been applied and is highlighting negative margins with products that are available in cream and gray colors. In this example, preparing data for formatting currency is essential, particularly when working with revenue data. By following the steps outlined, you can ensure accurate representation and enhance the clarity of financial information.

Mastering these formatting techniques in Power BI not only refines the visual appeal of your reports but also elevates the precision and impact of the insights conveyed to your audience.

Assessing data normalization, denormalization, and star schemas

Data normalization is a fundamental concept in database design, and it holds equal importance in the realm of data preparation for Power BI. In this section, you will explore the context in which data normalization becomes necessary, especially when dealing with denormalized or redundant datasets. By understanding the principles of data normalization and applying them judiciously, you will be able to structure your data efficiently, leading to improved data organization and optimal performance of Power BI reports and dashboards.

Power BI's data modeling capabilities support data normalization by enabling users to establish relationships between tables based on common keys. By doing so, you can reduce data redundancy, which not only saves storage space but also ensures that data updates are consistent across related tables. This results in more streamlined and efficient data analyses within Power BI. Additionally, the use of DAX in Power BI allows users to aggregate and summarize normalized data efficiently, facilitating complex calculations and cross-table analyses with ease.

Let's jump into the data to create an example of this:

1. Open Power BI and select **Get Data** from the toolbar.

2. Then select **Text/CSV** as the data connector.

3. Select `AdventureWorks_Sales_2017.csv`.

4. This will open the preview screen. For the time being, let's assume the data is clean and select **Load**.

5. Select **Model View**. We can then see that Power BI has automatically recognized a relationship between the two datasets and thus created a relationship, as shown in the following figure, forming the first branch of our star schema.

6. To adjust this relationship further, simply select **Manage relationships**, which then opens the following window:

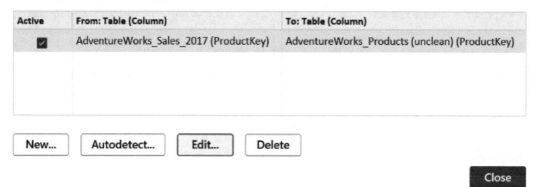

Figure 5.9 – The Manage relationships window within Power BI

7. By selecting **Edit**, we can then adjust the columns selected for this particular relationship:

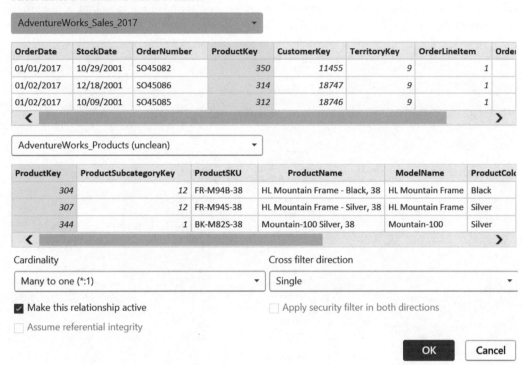

Figure 5.10 – The Edit relationship window within Power BI

In this example, Power BI has selected the correct columns for this relationship, so we won't need to make any adjustments here. It does this by using a feature called **relationship autodetect**. This is where Power BI attempts to create a relationship between two tables you're loading at the same time. Defining the cardinality and cross-filter direction makes the relationship active by using the column names in the tables you have selected to identify potential relationships. If it doesn't identify any similarities with high confidence, then it doesn't create a relationship.

Dimension modeling and star schema

At this stage, it's important we introduce the concepts of dimension modeling and star schemas. Dimension modeling involves organizing data into dimension and fact tables. Dimension tables store descriptive attributes and fact tables store numerical measures.

These dimension and fact tables are then connected with relationships usually in the form of a star schema. The term star is used because you usually start with a fact table in the middle and create relationships to dimension tables around the fact table, like points of a star, as highlighted in the following example:

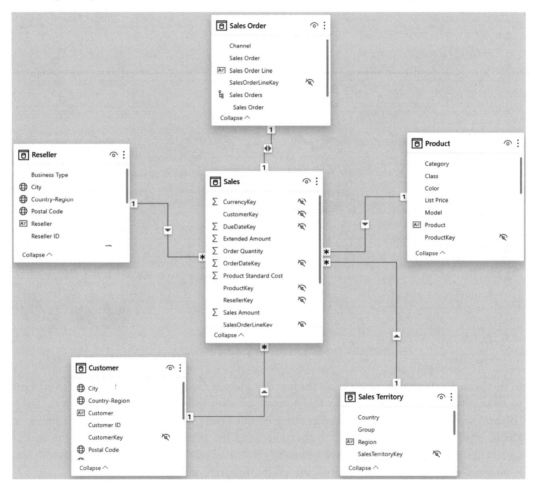

Figure 5.11 – Screenshot of the edit relationships window within Power BI

For those not familiar with star schemas, they are specialized data models that are typically used when designing data warehouses. This is where you might be introduced to concepts such as the Kimball method, which are often referred to in this space. Ralph Kimball is known for his book on the data warehouse toolkit. If you're interested in learning more about this, then I'd definitely recommend looking into the Kimball method.

Now, there's a lot of documentation on what happens underneath the hood of Power BI when it's working with star schemas, but here is a high-level summary of the benefits of using this type of model versus just importing one large flat file/table with all your data:

- **Usability**: Star schemas make it simpler to navigate within the fields pane as fields are grouped by their dimension tables and fact tables. However, if you imported this as a flat file, you would see it all within that one table. Granted there is the capability to create display folders within your fields pane to group your data.

- **Simpler DAX**: If you have a nice, clean star schema, then your DAX is typically much cleaner and more performant as you need to write fewer lines of code to achieve the same result. The result is usually easier to read.

- **Performance**: Star schemas are great to ensure scale. If you're working with small sets of data (for example, under 100,000 rows of data), then generally it might perform the same as a flat table, but as you start to scale, you will often see the queries vastly improve in performance. For example, the query ran in the background when using your new DAX measure might take 29 seconds to run on a flat table with 7 million rows versus 7 seconds if that same amount of data was presented in a star schema.

- **Faster refreshes**: Flat tables won't have a date table, for example, and as such, Power BI by default automatically creates auto date/time intelligence table in the background, which slows down your refreshes. That, in combination with the refresh on the much larger table, will result in a slower refresh. There are some good blogs that go into more detail on this topic, such as Phil Seamark on DAX, which discusses how you can visualize the performance of a Power BI refresh. There are example Power BI files within the GitHub repo that include a star schema and a flat table for you to compare. These have the following names:

  - `Adventure Works Sales Data (Flat Table)`
  - `Adventure Works Sales Data (Clean Star Schema)`

Denormalized data in dimension tables

We have briefly covered normalization and the use of star schemas when importing your data into Power BI; however, it's important to mention that Power BI can and will also work with denormalized data.

To clarify, denormalization within dimension tables involves incorporating aggregated values or pre-calculated metrics to improve query performance. Here's an example to help describe how this might be used.

Consider a `Products` dimension table in the context of a retail dataset. Here's the original normalized `Products` table:

ProductID	ProductName	Category	Manufacturer
101	Laptop	Electronics	ABC Electronics
102	Refrigerator	Appliances	XYZ Appliances
103	Chair	Furniture	PQR Furnishings

Figure 5.12 – Example of a normalized products table

In a normalized form, the `Products` table contains only descriptive attributes. To retrieve the total sales and average price for each product, one would typically join this table with the `Sales` fact table, which might be resource-intensive for large datasets.

Now, let's denormalize the `Products` table by incorporating aggregated values:

ProductID	ProductName	Category	Manufacturer	TotalSales	AvgPrice
101	Laptop	Electronics	ABC Electronics	$500,000	$800
102	Refrigerator	Appliances	XYZ Appliances	$300,000	$1,200
103	Chair	Furniture	PQR Furnishings	$100,000	$50

Figure 5.13 – Example of a denormalized products table with aggregated values

In this denormalized form, the `Products` table includes additional columns for total sales and average price. These values are pre-calculated and updated periodically. Now, when generating reports or dashboards that require information about total sales or average price, there's no need to join it with the `Sales` fact table, resulting in faster query performance.

Keep in mind the following considerations:

- Denormalization should be used judiciously based on the specific reporting and analytical requirements
- Regular updates to denormalized values are necessary to maintain accuracy
- Monitor the trade-off between improved query performance and increased storage space

Later, in *Chapter 12, Data Modeling and Managing Relationships*, we will be exploring the more advanced topic of modeling your data within Power BI for best practice approaches, particularly when working with different cardinalities.

Summary

In this chapter, we explored aspects of data quality assessment and preparation during the process of importing data into Power BI. The chapter began with an understanding of the significance of clean data and the need to address data quality concerns. It emphasized that the top three factors to consider are data completeness, accuracy, and consistency, as they lay the foundation for reliable analyses and visualizations.

You learned about using Power BI's data profiling capabilities to assess data completeness. By visualizing missing values and identifying columns that demand attention, you gained the skills to ensure a thorough and complete dataset.

Moving forward, your exploration of data accuracy unfolded with Power BI's versatile tools such as conditional formatting and data profiling. These tools empower you to validate accuracy, detect errors, and pinpoint outliers.

Delving into data consistency, Power BI's strong data modeling capabilities emerged as your guiding force. Building table relationships and following best practices gave you an overview of how to achieve accurate and consistent analyses.

Recognizing the importance of data relevance, you used Power BI's data transformation capabilities to filter and transform data, allowing you to focus on the correct data to begin your analysis.

You were introduced to formatting capabilities available in Power BI, enabling you to build a table with correct revenue formats that highlights outliers.

Finally, we gave a brief overview of the concept of data normalization in data preparation.

Now that we have brought this data into Power BI, we're ready to get started with some transformations. In the next chapter, we will explore the Query Editor in further detail to learn how to transform this data.

Questions

1. What is one of the concerns (described in this chapter) when importing data into Power BI?

    A. Location

    B. Size of data

    C. Data completeness

    D. Formatting

2. Which Power BI tool can be used to define rules and highlight data points that fall outside of the predefined accuracy ranges?

    A. Power Query

    B. Power Pivot

    C. Conditional formatting

    D. Data profiling

3. What does Power BI's DAX language allow users to create?

    A. Visualizations

    B. Semantic models

    C. Relationships between tables

    D. Calculated columns and measures

4. How can users filter out irrelevant data during the data import process in Power BI?

    A. Using DAX expressions

    B. Through conditional formatting

    C. By creating relationships

    D. Utilizing data transformation capabilities

5. What is the fundamental concept introduced in the last section?

    A. Data profiling

    B. Data transformation

    C. Data normalization

    D. Data completeness

6

Cleaning Data with Query Editor

Power BI's Query Editor is a powerful tool that allows you to connect, import, transform, and clean your data before visualizing it in Power BI reports and dashboards. With Query Editor, you can perform various data cleaning operations, such as removing duplicates, filtering rows, splitting columns, merging data, and more.

We will cover the following topics in this chapter:

- Exploring the Query Editor interface
- Data cleaning techniques and functions
- Using Query Editor versus DAX for transformation

By the end of this chapter, you will know about the essential techniques and functions for cleaning and transforming data using Query Editor.

Technical requirements

Using the following link, you will find the uncleaned dataset to be used during this chapter: `https://github.com/PacktPublishing/Data-Cleaning-with-Power-BI`.

Understanding the Query Editor interface

In this section, we will explore the essential components and functionalities of the Power Query interface in Power BI, along with some common techniques and functions to help you clean data.

To access Query Editor, open Power BI Desktop and navigate to the **Home** tab on the ribbon. Click on the **Transform data** button to launch Query Editor.

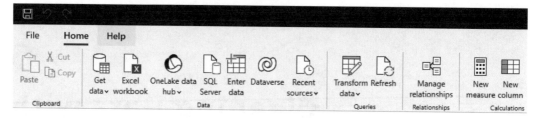

Figure 6.1 – Locating the Transform data button in the Home tab

Once inside Query Editor, you will notice the Power Query ribbon, which contains various groups of commands and tools to manage and transform your data, as shown in the following screenshot:

Figure 6.2 – Power Query ribbon with its important functions shown on the Home tab

The Query Editor navigation pane is on the left-hand side of the window. It lists all the queries in the current report and provides options to navigate between queries, as shown in the following screenshot:

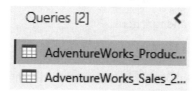

Figure 6.3 – Screenshot highlighting two queries within the Power Query window

In the center of the Query Editor window, you will see the **Query preview** pane, which displays a preview of the data after applying the transformation steps.

> **Important note**
>
> As you select different steps in the query settings, the preview will adjust to show what the data looked like in that transformation step.

The **Query Settings** pane is located on the right-hand side of the Query Editor window. It displays the applied steps of data transformations and provides options to manage query properties and connections (shown next). This is where we can often add further descriptions to help others understand the transformations we are adding, and other features such as **Query Folding** can be seen in this space.

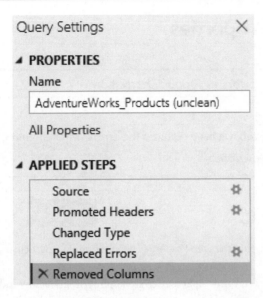

Figure 6.4 – Screenshot of some applied steps within Query Settings

For your reference, query folding is the process by which Power BI translates high-level data transformation requests into low-level SQL statements, which can be executed by the underlying data source. When query folding is used, the data source is responsible for performing the data transformation, rather than Power BI. This can result in faster query execution and reduced memory usage. The information on which steps are included in this fold will often show in the query settings, which helps users to understand where they might be "breaking the fold." We will cover this in further detail later in the book, in *Chapter 11, M Query Optimization*.

When naming the applied steps within **Query Settings** in Power Query (Query Editor), it's essential to follow some best practices to ensure the clarity, organization, and maintainability of your data transformation process. There are some additional best practices that are not just related to naming:

- **Use descriptive and meaningful names**: Choose names that clearly describe the purpose of each applied step. Avoid generic names such as `Step 1` or `Filter 2` and instead use descriptive names that convey the action taken, such as `Remove Duplicates`, `Convert to Date`, or `Filter Sales`.

- **Be consistent**: Maintain consistency in naming conventions throughout your applied steps. Use similar terminology for similar types of transformations. Consistency makes it easier for you and other users to understand the flow of the data transformation process.

- **Keep it concise**: While descriptive names are crucial, try to keep them concise and to the point. Long and wordy names can make the query steps pane cluttered and hard to read. You can right-click on a step and use **Step Properties** for longer text descriptions (as shown):

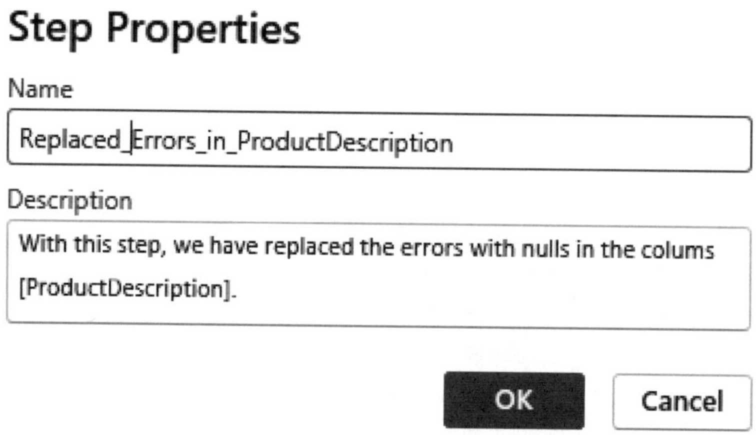

Step Properties

Name

Replaced_Errors_in_ProductDescription

Description

With this step, we have replaced the errors with nulls in the colums [ProductDescription].

OK   Cancel

Figure 6.5 – Screenshot of the Step Properties window within a particular step in Power Query

- **Avoid special characters and spaces**: Use alphanumeric characters and underscores in your step names. Avoid using special characters or spaces, as they might cause issues when referencing the steps in M code or when creating custom columns.

- **Use CamelCase or PascalCase**: For multi-word names, consider using CamelCase (for example, `splitColumns`) or PascalCase (for example, `CleanData`) to improve readability.

- **Include data source names**: If you have multiple data sources or connections, consider including the data source name as a prefix in your step names. This can be helpful when managing complex queries involving multiple sources.

- **Order sequentially**: This sounds obvious but can often be forgotten as you begin to make adjustments to a data model already built. Organize the applied steps in a logical and sequential order. Start with the initial data load and follow the sequence of transformations. This makes it easier to trace back and troubleshoot issues if necessary.

- **Simple and often**: It's often said that is it better to have multiple simple transformations that clearly convey what is being done rather than to have fewer but more complex transformations. This makes it simpler for people who are new to this particular data to understand what transformations have been applied.

- **Avoid ambiguous names**: Ensure that your step names are not ambiguous or open to interpretation. This will help prevent confusion and potential errors when working with the query. This is particularly relevant as you begin to repeat the cleaning steps listed later, in the *Data cleaning techniques and functions* section, with different mappings or tables in your dataset, where Power Query automatically labels them with `Removed Column`, `Lookup`, and so on.

- **Regularly review and clean up**: As your data model and transformation process evolves, regularly review and clean up the applied steps. Remove any unnecessary or redundant steps to keep the query efficient and organized.

As you have familiarized yourself with the Power Query interface and best practices for naming and organizing applied steps, you are well equipped to delve into the next section, where we will explore advanced techniques for efficient data transformation and delve into the nuances of query folding, optimizing your Power BI experience.

Data cleaning techniques and functions

In this section, you will deepen your understanding of Power Query's advanced features, unlocking a new realm of possibilities for efficient data transformation. We will delve into the intricacies of query folding, a process that translates high-level transformation requests into low-level SQL statements, optimizing query execution and minimizing memory usage. Additionally, we will explore techniques to further enhance the clarity and organization of your transformation process, ensuring your Power BI experience remains both streamlined and powerful.

Adding columns

Adding columns with calculated values enhances your dataset and enables you to derive new insights. This will be quite a common transformation, especially when looking to keep the original source column.

To note, this is a different way to add columns to your data from the method that was highlighted in *Chapter 4*, *The Most Common Data Cleaning Operations*, where we used DAX to add a column. As a reminder, although there are two ways to add an additional column, when possible, you should look to use this method as it's the preferred way to add columns in Power BI if they cannot be added directly to the source system.

Follow these steps to add columns (a screenshot of the **Add Column** tab is shown):

- **Using existing columns**: In Query Editor, you can add a new column based on existing column values or calculations. Select the **Add Column** tab on the ribbon.

Figure 6.6 – Various options under the Add Column tab

- **Column calculations**: Choose from various **Add Column** functions in the **Standard** dropdown, such as arithmetic operations, text concatenation, logical operations, and so on.

- **Custom calculations**: For more complex calculations, click on **Custom Column**. This will open the following window:

Custom Column

Add a column that is computed from the other columns.

Figure 6.7 – Screenshot of the Custom Column window in Power Query

This allows you to write M code using Power Query formula language to create the desired calculated column.

In later chapters, we will cover the M code language, but here is an example for us to create a new column that depicts whether the product has a color or not:

```
=if [ProductColor] = "NA" or [ProductColor] = null or [ProductColor] =
"" then false else true
```

This returns a new column that shows a value of True if the product has a color. The nice thing about this custom column function is that you have the ability to check available columns and also check whether there are any syntax errors with your code.

Data type conversions

Data type conversions are crucial for ensuring accurate calculations and visualizations. Power BI allows you to transform data types in Query Editor. Follow these steps to perform data type conversions:

1. **Selecting columns**: In Query Editor, select the column(s) you want to convert data types for.

2. **Data type conversion**: Go to the **Transform** tab on the ribbon. Click on the **Data Type** dropdown and choose the desired data type for the selected column(s).

3. **Custom code**: If Power BI doesn't automatically detect the correct data type, or you need a specific conversion, you can use custom code. Click on **Advanced Editor** in the **Home** tab to write M code or Power Query formula language code for complex conversions. We will cover this in later chapters.

Date/time

Date/time functions are essential for extracting specific components from date and time columns or performing date-related calculations. Here's how to use date/time functions:

1. **Selecting columns**: In Query Editor, select the date/time column you want to work with.

2. **Date/Time functions**: Go to the **Transform** tab on the ribbon. Click on the **Date** or **Time** dropdown to access various functions such as **Year**, **Month**, **Day**, **Quarter**, and so on.

Rounding

Rounding functions are useful for controlling precision and simplifying visualizations. Here's how to apply rounding in Query Editor:

1. **Selecting columns**: In Query Editor, select the numeric column(s) you want to round.

2. **Rounding functions**: Go to the **Transform** tab on the ribbon. Click on the **Standard** dropdown to access common rounding functions such as **Round**, **Round Down**, **Round Up**, and so on.

3. **Custom rounding**: To round to a specific number of decimal places, click on **Custom Column** in the **Add Column** tab. Use M code such as `Number.Round([ColumnName], numDecimalPlaces)` for custom rounding.

Pivot/unpivot columns

Pivoting and unpivoting are essential for transforming your data between wide and tall formats. Here's how to use these functions:

- **Pivot columns**:

    I.   Select the column you want to use as the pivot column.

    II.   Go to the **Transform** tab and click on **Pivot Column**.

    III. Choose the values column containing the data to be spread across new columns.

    IV.   Optionally, you can use an aggregation function to summarize values if duplicates are found during pivoting.

- **Unpivot columns**:

  I.   Select the columns you want to unpivot (convert into rows).

  II.   Go to the **Transform** tab and click on **Unpivot Columns**.

Power BI will create two new columns, **Attribute** and **Value**, containing the original column names and values, respectively.

Merge queries

Merging queries allows you to combine data from multiple sources into a single dataset. This is particularly useful as you begin to build out dataflows within the Power BI service, which has a similar look and feel to Query Editor. Here's how to perform query merging:

- **Creating queries**: Before merging, create two or more queries containing data to be combined.

- **Merge queries**: Select the first query from the **Queries** pane. Go to the **Home** tab and click on **Merge Queries**. Then choose the second query and specify the join conditions (columns) for merging.

- **Options for merging**: You can choose from different join types: inner, left outer, right outer, and full outer.

Additionally, you can choose which columns to include in the result.

Another option might be to append two queries together. This is particularly useful when combining two datasets to make a larger dataset. For example, if you have an Excel sheet with sales data for a particular month and would like to combine it with another Excel sheet for another month's data, you could use append queries to combine this data together.

As you conclude this exploration of advanced Power Query features, you are now equipped with the knowledge to tackle the intricacies of adding columns, mastering data type conversions, harnessing date/time functions, applying rounding techniques, and employing pivotal transformations. This deeper dive will empower you to wield the full potential of Power BI in transforming and enhancing your datasets for more robust analyses and impactful visualizations.

Using Query Editor versus DAX for transformation

In Power BI, Power Query and **DAX** (short for **Data Analysis Expressions**) are both powerful tools for data transformation, but they serve different purposes and are used at different stages of the data preparation process. There's a simple workflow we can reference when deciding on which tool to use for your transformations. Let's review them in detail.

Power Query Editor

Power Query Editor in Microsoft Power BI is a powerful data transformation tool designed for cleaning and refining data before analysis. It features an intuitive interface, allowing users to connect to various data sources, import raw data, and perform diverse transformation tasks such as filtering, sorting, and merging. The editor operates step by step, enhancing transparency and facilitating error identification. Noteworthy is its ability to record transformations as reproducible steps, and it supports a formula language called M for advanced scripting. Overall, it's a versatile tool for ensuring data accuracy and consistency, making it essential for effective data preparation in analytics projects.

- **Purpose**:

  - **Data loading and transformation**: Power Query is primarily used for loading and transforming data from various sources before it is imported into the Power BI data model.

  - **Extract, Transform, Load (ETL)**: It's great for tasks such as cleaning, filtering, shaping, and merging data from different sources.

- **Interface**:

  - **Graphical User Interface (GUI)**: Power Query uses a graphical user interface that allows users to apply a series of step-by-step transformations to the data using a point-and-click interface.

- **Language**:

  - **M Language**: Power Query uses the M language for expressing data transformation logic. While you can perform many tasks using the GUI, the underlying code is written in M.

- **Transformations**:

  - **Wide range of transformations**: Power Query offers a wide range of built-in transformations and functions that allow you to clean, reshape, and transform data easily.

- **Flexibility**:

  - **User-friendly**: It's user-friendly and suitable for users with a non-programming background. You can perform complex transformations without writing code.

Data Analysis Expressions (DAX)

As introduced in *Chapter 1, Introduction to Power BI Data Cleaning*, DAX is a formula language that plays a pivotal role in Power BI, helping users of Power BI to perform complex calculations and analysis on their data.

- **Purpose**:

  - **Data modeling and analysis**: DAX is primarily used within the Power BI data model for creating calculated columns, measures, and calculated tables. It's used for defining business logic and calculations.

- **Interface**:

  - **Formula language**: DAX is a formula language used for creating custom calculations. Formulas are written in the DAX language, and they define calculations based on the data model.

- **Language**:

  - **The DAX language**: DAX is its own formula language specifically designed for creating custom calculations in Power BI. It's similar to Excel formulas but extends to support more complex analysis in a BI context. However, it should be noted that DAX is also a query language that the tabular engine uses to grab and generate data.

- **Transformations**:

  - **Aggregations and calculations**: DAX is used for creating aggregations, calculated columns, and measures. It's not designed for the detailed data manipulation that Power Query excels at.

- **Flexibility**:

  - **Business logic**: DAX is essential for creating business logic within your reports. You can use it to define complex calculations, such as **Key Performance Indicators** (**KPIs**), time-based calculations, and other custom metrics.

Workflow

Now to help you decide when to use Power Query and when to use DAX, I've provided a short summary workflow to make this decision simpler:

- **Typical workflow**:

  - **Power Query first**: Generally, you use Power Query to load and transform data from source systems. This includes cleaning data, filtering, and shaping it to your needs. This also includes adding columns. There's an entire tab in Power Query editor devoted to adding columns.

  - **DAX later**: Once the data is loaded into the data model, you use DAX to create calculations and measures based on the transformed data.

- **Integration:**

  - **Seamless integration:** Power Query and DAX are seamlessly integrated within Power BI. Power Query handles the ETL process, and DAX is used for creating calculations and measures based on the transformed data.

To conclude, Power Query is used for the ETL process and data preparation, while DAX is used for creating calculations and measures within the Power BI data model. They work together to provide a comprehensive solution for data transformation and analysis in Power BI.

Summary

In this chapter on cleaning data with Power BI's Query Editor, you embarked on a journey of mastering essential techniques and functions for transforming and refining your datasets. You began by learning more about the Query Editor interface, understanding its crucial components such as the Power Query ribbon, navigation pane, preview pane, and settings pane. You explored the significance of maintaining clear and descriptive names for applied steps, ensuring consistency and conciseness, and avoiding ambiguous terms to enhance the organization and readability of your data transformation process.

Moving forward, you delved into advanced features such as query folding, where high-level transformation requests seamlessly translate into low-level SQL statements, optimizing query execution. Armed with best practices, you navigated through the Power Query interface, learning the art of naming, organizing, and cleaning up applied steps.

You then covered data cleaning techniques and functions, such as adding columns, performing data type conversions, utilizing date/time functions, applying rounding transformations, merging queries, and combining data from multiple sources.

You covered the strategic use of Power Query and DAX, recognizing their distinct roles in the data preparation process. Power Query, with its user-friendly graphical interface and M language, excels at data loading, cleaning, and shaping tasks, while DAX is there for defining business logic within the Power BI data model.

Questions

1. What are the crucial components of the Query Editor interface discussed in the chapter?

    A. Power Query help

    B. Navigation compass

    C. Power Query ribbon

    D. Settings

2. What is query folding, and how does it optimize query execution in Power BI?

    A. Folding multiple tables

    B. Duplicate queries in Power Query

    C. Translating high-level transformations into low-level SQL statements

    D. Executing queries slowly for precision

3. Which technique allows the creation of new data based on existing columns?

    A. Filtering

    B. Sorting

    C. Adding columns

    D. Removing duplicates

4. What determines how records are matched between tables in merging queries?

    A. Query folding

    B. Join types

    C. Preview settings

    D. Ribbon functions

5. What is Power Query used for in the data preparation process?

    A. Creating calculated columns

    B. Defining complex business logic

    C. Loading, cleaning, and shaping data

    D. Folding queries

Further reading

- Power Query documentation – Power Query | Microsoft Learn: `https://learn.microsoft.com/en-us/power-query/`

- What is Power Query? – Power Query | Microsoft Learn: `https://learn.microsoft.com/en-us/power-query/power-query-what-is-power-query`

7

Transforming Data with the M Language

As we have seen throughout this book so far, Power BI and Power Query are powerful tools designed to help transform, clean, and shape data for effective visualization and analysis. Central to their data transformation capabilities is a functional, case-sensitive language called **M**, which serves as the backbone for performing data transformations within these tools.

in this chapter, we will delve into the essence of M, exploring its significance, structure, and common use cases, and get hands-on with some examples, which will be covered in the following topics:

- Understanding the M language
- Filtering and sorting data with M
- Transforming data with M
- Working with data sources in M

By the end of this chapter, you will have built a basic foundation of knowledge and hands-on experience using M within the advanced editor – useful for creating complex data transformations that are not easily achievable through the **graphical user interface** (**GUI**). As an outcome of reading this chapter, you will feel more confident about reviewing and creating code for use in the advanced editor.

Technical requirements

Using the following link, you will find the uncleaned dataset to be used during this chapter: `https://github.com/PacktPublishing/Data-Cleaning-with-Power-BI`.

Understanding the M language

M, also known as the Power Query formula language, is an integral part of Power BI and Power Query. It facilitates the transformation of raw, unstructured, or messy data into organized, refined datasets that are ready for analysis and visualization. Unlike traditional formulas in Excel that operate on cell-level data, M operates on entire columns or tables, enabling complex data transformations across large datasets.

M and DAX are two coding languages within Power BI; however, M is also very different from DAX. It's a functional, case-sensitive language (similar to F# for those familiar) that employs a sequence of steps to transform data. In Power Query's M language, each step in the query editor represents a transformation or operation applied to the data. While not explicitly defined as functions, these steps function in a manner similar to functional programming. The steps operate sequentially, with the output of one step serving as the input for the next. This sequential arrangement allows for the creation of a transformation flow where each step builds upon the results of the preceding ones, enabling a structured and organized approach to data manipulation and shaping. Let's take a brief overview of the basic structure of M that you'll find in **Advanced Editor**.

Structure of M

The M language in Power Query follows a step-by-step structure, with each step representing a transformation applied to the data. It begins with the `let` keyword, followed by the definition of variables using the = operator. These variables hold the intermediate results of data transformations. The code is organized into a series of expressions, and the final result is typically specified in the last expression of the `in` clause. The language emphasizes a functional approach, with functions and operators used to manipulate and shape the data throughout the query.

The let keyword

In most cases, nearly every M query begins with `let` to open the code and begin reading the query steps. There are exceptions to this in the advanced editor where you can nest calls to Power Query functions but this isn't common and would be seen as bad practice. This part of the code is used to define variables and store immediate results. Variables are defined by using the following syntax:

```
let Variable = Expression
```

in this example, `Variable` is the name of the variable you're creating and `Expression` is the value or calculation you're assigning to it.

Identifiers

Depending on which area of Power Query you're looking at, you might refer to the following as a step or a variable, more commonly known as identifiers. Identifiers are names given to variables, functions, and other entities.

These are often recognizable in the **Advanced Editor** view of Power Query Editor because they are placed in double quotes and have a hashtag as a prefix.

For example, look at the following screenshot from the Power Query Editor UI:

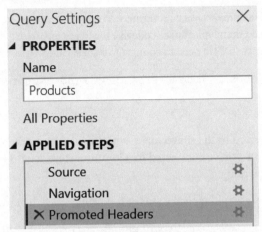

Figure 7.1 – Screenshot of the applied steps in Power Query Editor

This would be seen in the M query from the advanced editor as follows:

```
#"Promoted Headers"
```

Data source

M starts by first connecting to a data source such as a CSV file, database, web service, or one of many other options. This is often done using a variable often assigned the name Source, which begins by specifying the location of the data.

An example of this could look like the following:

```
let
    Source = Excel.Workbook(File.Contents("C:\Users\GusFrazer\Downloads\
    products.xlsx"), null, true),
```

In this example, we have opened the code with let and have then introduced our first step. Source is the name we have given to this step or variable, which, as the name suggests, is there to represent where the data has come from. Typically, this is already created for you when you connect to your data via the GUI. However, it's useful to understand what's happening here:

- Excel.Workbook() tells Power Query to connect to an Excel workbook and its contents
- File.Contents("C:\Users\GusFrazer\Downloads\products.xlsx") then tells Power Query where to locate the workbook and the Contents function reads the binary contents of the file

- **null** is there to specify that no specific sheet is being loaded from the workbook, meaning that the data from all the sheets will be loaded into the query

- The **true** parameter specifies that the first row of the data should then be used as column headers

When connecting to Excel documents, we typically need to specify where we are loading the data. From the previous examples, we would then typically see code like the following to load data from specific locations in a file. This will then specify that we need to connect to a sheet called Products from the workbook:

```
Products_Sheet = Source{[Item="Products",Kind="Sheet"]}[Data],
```

Query steps

Now that you have connected to the source data, you will want to begin to define a series of query steps to transform the data you've connected to. Common steps would include filtering, sorting, merging, grouping, and pivoting.

In the previous example, we would typically see the following code when we open **Advanced Editor**:

```
#"Promoted Headers" = Table.PromoteHeaders(Products_Sheet,
[PromoteAllScalars=true]),
```

The # symbol is used as a placeholder to refer to the current step or the result of the previous step in the query. This symbol is commonly employed within let statements to represent the data generated by the most recent transformation.

For example, if you have a variable with spaces or special characters in its name, like the previous example "Promoted Headers", you can use the # symbol at the beginning of its name within double quotes (#"Promoted Headers") to reference it in subsequent steps. This enables a structured approach to data manipulation, and variables can either be a single word like "Source" or include spaces and special characters, with the # symbol aiding in their identification and utilization within the query.

We will cover the other functions seen in the previous code, such as PromoteHeaders, in the next section.

Data types and functions

M operates on data types such as text, numbers, dates, and lists. These data types form the building blocks of M functions, which can be used to manipulate these data types, perform calculations, and create new columns or tables.

In the previous example, we can see the "Promoted Headers" variable contains a few other functions and data types. Here is a breakdown of what is happening in the previous function:

- #"Promoted Headers" is the name of the current step, which defines a new step called "Promoted Headers" while referencing the previous steps. The aim of this step is to result in a table where the first row becomes column headers.

- `Table.PromoteHeaders()` is the function used to actually action the promotion of the first row to column headers. It takes two arguments within the brackets.

  - The first argument in the function is `Products_Sheet`, which symbolizes the table we are performing the function on. This is typically the output name of the previous step.

  - `[PromoteAllScalars=True]` is an optional argument that is used to modify the behavior of the function. It's there to indicate that all scalar values (non-tabular values) in the first row should be promoted to headers.

in expressions

An `in` expression is used to specify the final result of the query. It helps in separating the variable definitions from the main computation. The `in` expression comes after all the `let` expressions and indicates what the final output of the script should be.

In our example, if we were happy with the data and just wanted to return this as is, we would use the following expression to end the code. This signifies that we want to return the output from the last step in the `let` series:

```
in
    #"Promoted Headers"
```

Literals

In Power Query, literals refer to constant values that are directly written within the M query and represent specific data types. These values are not variables or references to other data sources but are fixed, unchanging values embedded directly into the M language code.

Here are just a few of the common types of literals in Power Query:

Literal type	Example	Description
Text	`"Hello, Power Query!"`	Represents a sequence of characters enclosed in double quotes
Number	`42`	Represents numeric values, including integers and decimals
Logical	`true` or `false`	Represents Boolean values for logical conditions
DateTime	`#datetime(2022, 1, 1, 0, 0, 0)`	Represents a specific point in time
List	`{1, 2, 3}`	Represents a list of values enclosed in curly braces

Record	`[Field1=1, Field2="Value"]`	Represents a record with named fields and corresponding values
Table	`#table({"Column1", "Column2"}, {{1, "A"}, {2, "B"}})`	Represents a table with specified columns and rows
Duration	`#duration(0, 1, 0, 0)`	Represents a duration of time (days, hours, minutes, seconds)

Table 7.1 – Table referencing the literal types available in Power Query along with some examples

Literals are useful when you need to include specific constant values directly in your Power Query code. They provide a way to define fixed data points or structures without the need for external data sources or dynamic calculations.

Common use cases of M

As you can imagine from the name of this chapter and the book, the biggest use case for M is to help with cleaning and transforming data. In addition to this, though, it can be used to help with standardizing formats for data being loaded to ensure accuracy and integrity. Merging and appending data from different data sources becomes seamless with M, enabling you to consolidate data for your analysis.

In the next section of this chapter, we will look at some of the most common functions used within M. However, another great use for this language is when you need to do some custom complex calculations as it allows you to go beyond the built-in functions from the GUI.

> **Important note**
>
> Lastly, like other coding languages, you can add comments to different parts of your code. Adding comments to M is a great practice to enhance readability and understanding, especially when sharing your code with others. Comments provide explanations and context about what each step is doing. This is particularly important when you start building long complex queries into your code. Comments can be initiated by starting a new line with the // characters. When you do this within **Advanced Editor**, it will typically show the comments in green to highlight that these are not coded values.

Here's an example of how you can add comments to the previous M:

```
let
    //Load Excel workbook from specified file path
    Source = Excel.Workbook(File.Contents("C:\Users\GusFrazer\
Downloads\products.xlsx"), null, true),
    Products_Sheet = Source{[Item="Products",Kind="Sheet"]}[Data],
    //Promote headers from the first row of the Products_Sheet table
    #"Promoted Headers" = Table.PromoteHeaders(Products_Sheet,
```

```
[PromoteAllScalars=true]),
in
    #"Promoted Headers"
    //Final step where the transformed data is output
```

In this section, you learned more about the foundation and structure of the M language used within Power Query to transform data. As you progress to the next section, you will build on this knowledge with techniques to filter and sort your data with M.

Filtering and sorting data with M

Filtering and sorting are essential data transformation tasks that help you extract relevant information from large datasets and organize it in a meaningful way.

Power Query's M language offers a range of functions to efficiently filter rows based on conditions and sort data according to specific criteria. In this section, we'll explore how to filter and sort data using M, accompanied by step-by-step examples and explanations of key functions.

First of all, filtering data from your analysis typically involves selecting certain rows from a dataset based on certain conditions. M has a function named `Table.SelectRows` for this exact purpose. As it suggests, it allows you to specify a condition within the argument that determines which rows should be retained.

Following on from the `Products` table we connected our M to earlier, we can add an additional step to help us filter the data for analysis.

For example, suppose for our analysis we only need to pull data on products that have a cost greater than $10. We could adjust the preceding steps with the following code to make this filter:

```
    #"Filtered Products"= Table.SelectRows(#"Promoted Headers", each
[Product_Cost] >= 10)
in
    #"Filtered Products"
```

We could also add a sorting function to this so that we can sort the data in a particular manner. To do this, we would typically use the `Table.Sort` function, which then allows us to pass a similar argument as shown:

```
Table.Sort("Filtered Products",{{"Product_Cost", Order.Ascending}})
```

If you are trying this on the products data, you'll notice that the filter function will return an error. This is because when you load the data into Power Query from Excel, it doesn't recognize the [Product Costs] column as a number but instead as a text type due to the $ symbol in the data. The error is because we are trying to apply a number filter on a text column.

This leads us to the next section because in order to remove this error, we will need to carry out some transformations on the data first.

Transforming data with M

Now, there are a plethora of transformation functions that can be used within **Advanced Editor** to transform your data. With the issue/error we faced when trying to apply the filter, there are a certain number of functions we will need to use, such as `Table.TransformColumns` and `Table.RemoveLastN`.

As mentioned earlier, the first issue we can see in the data that might prevent us from filtering is that the values for cost and price contain a $ character. This is leading Power BI to read this as a text value. So our first port of call should be to remove this value from the column.

Now, of course, you could use the **Split column** function in the Power Query UI but it's important to understand what M code is created behind the scenes from using such buttons. Using M will also help reduce the steps you need to get to the desired goal. This will particularly help when you're looking to script more complex queries in M later in your data journey.

So, we will begin by using the `Table.TransformColumns` function to advise Power Query to remove the currency symbol and also return the value as a number. We will add the following M step to the previous code in order to first remove the currency symbol:

```
#"Remove Currency" = Table.TransformColumns(#"Promoted Headers",
    {
        {"Product_Cost", each Number.From(Text.AfterDelimiter(_,
"$")), type number},
        {"Product_Price", each Number.From(Text.AfterDelimiter(_,
"$")), type number}
    }
),
```

We have labeled this step pretty clearly to highlight what this variable is doing; however, we could also add some commentary to this to provide further context that this is not only removing the currency symbol but also transforming the value into a number type.

The `Table.TransformColumns` function is then used to apply a transformation to one or more columns of a table. It takes two main arguments: the source table, which in this example is `#"Promoted Headers"`, and a list of columns within this table that we'd like to transform.

As we need to transform more than one column, we will need to create two separate arguments within this `Table.TransformColumns` function. This is referred to as the list of transformations and can be seen enclosed in curly brackets { }.

Within the transformations and curly brackets, we have specified the column we want to transform, such as `Product_Cost`. We then use a function such as `each` to state that this will apply to each value in this column:

```
each Number.From(Text.AfterDelimiter(_, "$"))
```

To decipher what this code is doing, it's actually best to read it backward. The `Text.AfterDe-limiter(_, "$")` section of the code is a function that extracts the text portion after the dollar symbol for each value within the `Product_Cost` column. The `Number.From()` function is then used to convert the extracted text into a numeric value. Lastly, for assurance, we include the type specifier `number` to specify that the results of the transformation should have a data type number.

In order to transform multiple columns, we must bracket these arguments as such:

```
Table.TransformColumns (Previous step,
    {
        {"column 1", type DesiredType},
        {"column 2", type DesiredType},
        {"column 3", type DesiredType}
    }
)
```

Now that we have removed the currency symbol and converted the values/columns to a number type, we have one more error that might cause a problem, which is the bottom row, which has null values and errors.

In order to eliminate this problem, we can use the following code to remove the last row from the dataset, which happens to be our blank row:

```
#"Removed Bottom Rows" = Table.RemoveLastN(#"Remove Currency",1),
```

This function uses the `Table.RemoveLastN` function to then remove the number of rows specified in the argument from the table highlighted. In this scenario, we are only removing 1 row, which is identified after the comma.

Now that we have removed the bottom row, we can apply the filter code we used previously to create the following M code:

```
let
    Source = Excel.Workbook(File.Contents("C:\Users\GusFrazer\
Downloads\products.xlsx"), null, true),
    Products_Sheet = Source{[Item="Products",Kind="Sheet"]}[Data],
    #"Promoted Headers" = Table.PromoteHeaders(Products_Sheet,
[PromoteAllScalars=true]),
    //the following functions removes the $ sign and converts these
columns to numbers from text
    #"Remove Currency" = Table.TransformColumns(
        #"Promoted Headers",
        {
            {"Product_Cost",each Number.From(Text.
AfterDelimiter(_, "$")), type number},
            {"Product_Price", each Number.From(Text.
AfterDelimiter(_, "$")), type number}
```

```
            }
    ),
    //the next function removes the row at the bottom of the table
that contains nulls and errors
    #"Removed Bottom Rows" = Table.RemoveLastN(#"Remove Currency",1),
    // the following carries out the filter on the table to only show
products that cost more than $10
    #"Filtered Products" = Table.SelectRows(#"Removed Bottom Rows",
each [Product_Cost] >= 10)
in

    #"Filtered Products"
```

> **Important note**
>
> As you can see, it's important to add descriptions using comments here. This will also help if you need to share this with others so they can understand what has been built and why.

Now that you have a basic understanding of the M language, you will begin to look at how you can optimize your M with the use of parameters in the next section.

Working with data sources in M

To effectively work with different data sources, you need a good grasp of M's capabilities for more dynamic and flexible data transformations. It's essential to understand how M can be used to customize and parameterize data source connections. In short, this will help you to enhance reusability and facilitate easy adjustments to queries without manual code modification, thus saving you time later down the line.

In the following sections, you will learn about how to actually go about creating parameters with the help of examples for you to follow along and implement in your own environment.

Creating parameters and variables

Parameters and variables can be used for a number of different uses in M queries. One of which is to allow you to decouple your data source details from your M query, making it easy to switch between different sources. By defining parameters for key attributes such as file paths or server addresses, you can change data sources without modifying the code, enhancing maintainability and flexibility.

We'll start by creating parameters to store data source details. These parameters will make your data source connections dynamic and easy to switch. Parameters are all managed within a particular window on the Power Query UI, which is shown next, making it easier for you to manage multiple parameters in one location.

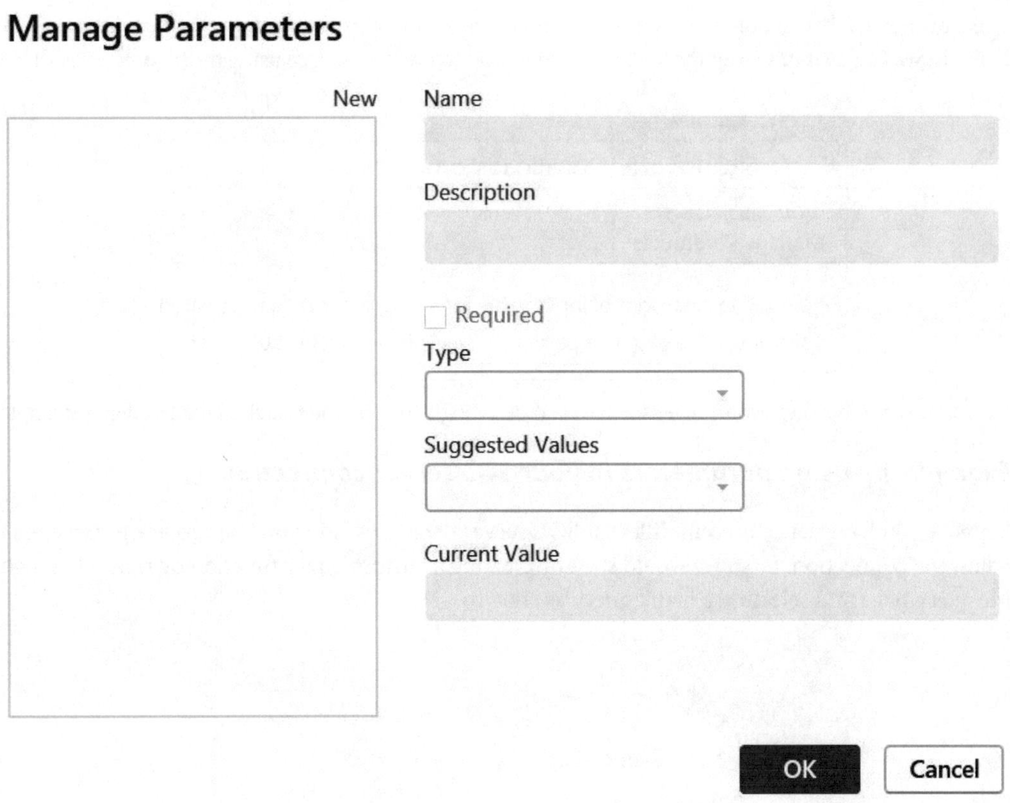

Manage Parameters

New   Name

Description

☐ Required

Type

Suggested Values

Current Value

OK   Cancel

Figure 7.2 – Screenshot of the Manage Parameters window within Power Query

Follow these steps to create a new parameter:

1. In Power Query, go to the **Home** tab and select **Manage Parameters**.

2. Define parameters for aspects such as file paths, server names, or API endpoints. For example, you can create a `DataSourcePath` parameter for file paths and a `ServerName` parameter for server connections.

Now that we have created that parameter, we can then add it to our M by referencing the parameter where the file path previously was. The following example shows just the beginning of an M query that we have adjusted to include the reference of the parameter we created:

```
let
Source = Excel.Workbook(File.Contents(DatasourcePath), null, true),
```

This now means that, should we need to change the data source to, say, a production environment, for example, we could simply swap the file path for the production data source using the parameter as shown:

Figure 7.3 – Screenshot of input value for a parameter we have created
showing a file path to a particular Excel file named Products.xlsx

Now, there are other steps you can perform to add more logic to your code, such as the following examples.

Example 1 – using parameters in your SQL server connection

Suppose you have data stored in different SQL server databases, and you want to use parameters to adjust the connection. First, we would start by creating a custom query function by right-clicking in the query pane and selecting a blank query as shown:

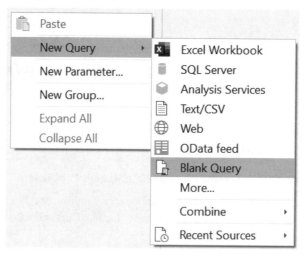

Figure 7.4 – Screenshot of the menu when right-clicking in the query pane within Power Query

Here's an example of an M function to achieve this parameterized connection:

```
(ServerName as text, DatabaseName as text) =>
    let
        Source = Sql.Database(ServerName, DatabaseName)
    in
        Source
```

Let's see a breakdown of this example and what is happening during the query:

- `(ServerName as text, DatabaseName as text) =>`: This part of the code defines the parameters that the function expects (`ServerName` and `DatabaseName`), along with their data types (`text`).

- `Source = Sql.Database(ServerName, DatabaseName)`: This line of code establishes a connection to a SQL Server database using the `ServerName` and `DatabaseName` parameters. It retrieves data from the specified database.

- `ConnectToSqlServer`: Finally, the function is closed and returns `ConnectToSqlServer`, making it available for use in your queries.

In this example, we have used the parameter we created within `sql.database`. This is handy particularly when you need to swap the connection that you are using within Power Query. For example, if you are developing in a test environment or SQL Server, you might use this parameter to point at your test server and tables. When you have completed your transformations though, you will be ready to publish this to the Power BI service. At this point, it's easier to adjust the parameter as opposed to the query code to define the production server.

If you are using deployment pipelines in the Power BI service, you can then set up rules that adjust the parameters when you deploy from test to production workspaces, for example, as shown in the following screenshot. There are deployment rules for data source rules when using this service, but this will only allow you to adjust the server name for the connection and only supports certain data sources.

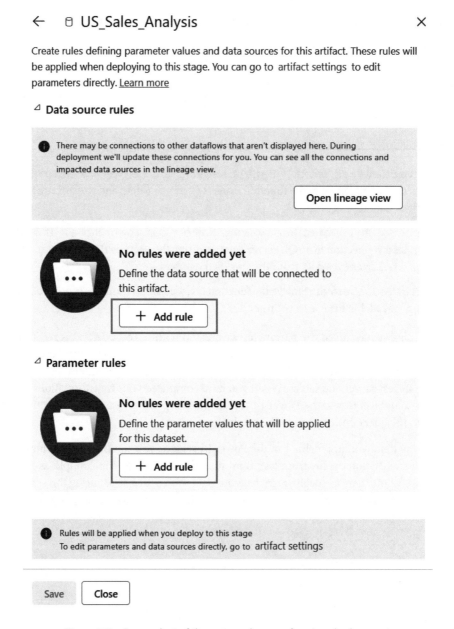

Figure 7.5 – Screenshot of the menu when configuring deployment
rules within a deployment pipeline in the Power BI service

If you didn't use parameters for this, you would need to manually go into your M query to adjust the server name and table name from within Sql.Database. You could also potentially do this in the Power Query GUI, but again, this would be manually done during deployment to production workspaces.

Example 2 – using parameters to filter data and conditional data source selection

There are often times when you will need to change the filter of a query to obtain different results. Now, it would be a lot simpler if you could do this without either editing the query or making slightly different copies of the same query. In this example, we will change the data source filter from CSV to Excel. You can then use a parameter and conditional logic to select the appropriate data source function.

Without a parameter, you would do this by creating another blank query as shown in the following screenshot:

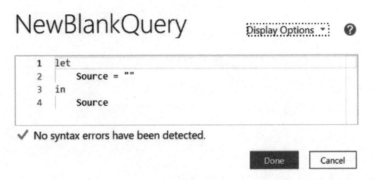

Figure 7.6 – Screenshot of Power Query Advanced Editor when creating a new query

Add the following code:

```
let
    DataSourceType = "CSV", // or "Excel"
    ConnectToDataSource =
        if DataSourceType = "CSV" then
        Csv.Document(File.Contents("C:\Local\File.csv"), [Delimiter =
",", Encoding = 1252])
        else
Excel.Workbook(File.Contents("https://example.com/RemoteFile.xlsx"),
null, true)
in
    ConnectToDataSource
```

This M query uses the if...then...else construct to connect to either a local CSV file or a remote Excel file based on the value of the DataSourceType variable.

The challenge here though is that to adjust the data source from CSV to Excel, you would need to open this query and manually adjust the variable.

If you create a parameter as seen in the earlier steps of this section, you would then be able to use the parameter in the `DataSourceType` variable. This could be set to a list of values that included CSV and Excel, as shown in the following configuration:

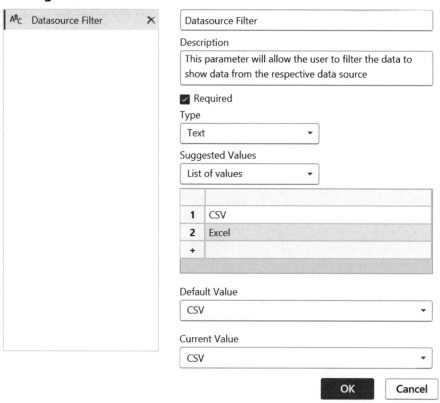

Figure 7.7 – Screenshot of the new parameter configuration named Datasource Filter

Now let's evolve the previous code and build upon it. To follow along, ensure you have downloaded the Excel file named `AdventureWorks_Sales_2017.xlsx` from GitHub. In this example, we are going to connect to a CSV file (labeled `AdventureWorks_Sales_2017.CSV`) in the GitHub repo if the parameter is set to `CSV`. Otherwise, our query will open the local Excel file:

1. Select **Transform data** from within Power BI.

2. From the **Home** tab, select **Manager parameters** and then select **New parameter** from the dropdown.

3. Enter the configuration shown in *Figure 7.7*.

4. Select **New source** from the **New query** group under the **Home** tab of the ribbon toolbar.

5. Select **Blank query**.

6. Select **Advanced Editor** and now enter the following code:

```
let
    DataSourceType = #"Datasource Filter",
    ConnectToDataSource =
    if DataSourceType = "CSV" then
        let
            csvurl = "https://raw.githubusercontent.com/
PacktPublishing/Data-Cleaning-with-Power-BI/main/AdventureWorks_
Sales_2017.csv",
            csvcontent = Text.FromBinary(Web.Contents(csvurl)),
            csvtable = Csv.Document(csvcontent, [Delimiter =
",", Encoding = 1252])
        in
            csvtable
    else
        let
            Excelworkbook = Excel.Workbook(File.Contents("C:\
Users\GusFrazer\Downloads\AdventureWorks_Sales_2017.xlsx"),
null, true){[Item="Sales",Kind="Sheet"]}[Data],
            #"Promoted Headers" = Table.
PromoteHeaders(Excelworkbook, [PromoteAllScalars=true]),
            #"Changed Type" = Table.
TransformColumnTypes(#"Promoted Headers",{{"OrderDate", type
any}, {"StockDate", type any}, {"OrderNumber", type text},
{"ProductKey", Int64.Type}, {"CustomerKey", Int64.Type},
{"TerritoryKey", Int64.Type}, {"OrderLineItem", Int64.Type},
{"OrderQuantity", Int64.Type}})
        in
            #"Changed Type"
in
    ConnectToDataSource
```

7. Select **Done**.

In this example, you can see we introduced nested `let` statements to load CSV data directly from a specified URL as well as to load and transform an Excel workbook.

The CSV nested `let` statements take the contents for the URL and retrieve the binary content to convert to text. The last variable parses this into a table using the `Csv.Document` function.

Now it isn't actually necessary to add the Excel Workbook nested `let` statement; however, if you simply used the following code, Power Query would not know that you would actually want to extract the data from the sheet within the file:

```
else
    Excel.Workbook(File.Contents("C:\Users\GusFrazer\Downloads\
AdventureWorks_Sales_2017.xlsx"), null, true)
```

So, you would see the following output when you switch the parameter to `Excel`:

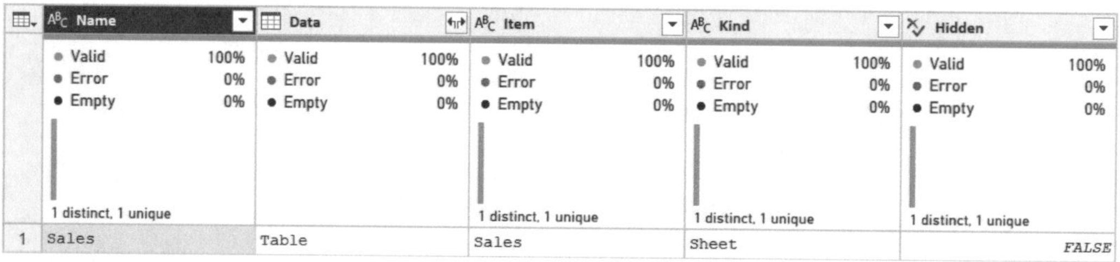

ABC Name		Data	ABC Item		ABC Kind		Hidden	
● Valid	100%	● Valid 100%	● Valid	100%	● Valid	100%	● Valid	100%
● Error	0%	● Error 0%	● Error	0%	● Error	0%	● Error	0%
● Empty	0%	● Empty 0%	● Empty	0%	● Empty	0%	● Empty	0%
1 distinct, 1 unique			1 distinct, 1 unique		1 distinct, 1 unique		1 distinct, 1 unique	
1 Sales		Table	Sales		Sheet			FALSE

Figure 7.8 – Screenshot of the output using the previous code when the parameter created is set to Excel

By using the nested `let` statement for Excel, we can then add additional logic to the query, which then opens the specific sheet we want to view, and carry out the transformations that are usually carried out by default when opening an Excel sheet using Power Query.

This result will show the same data but you will have the option to specify from the drop-down parameter whether you are using a local copy or the version hosted on GitHub.

Example 3 – combining multiple CSV files

The last example is one I see used often, particularly with companies looking to combine financial files or exported data files.

Suppose you have a folder containing several CSV files that you want to combine into a single table. You might want to create a parameter to filter the data for a specific date (another very common use case for a parameter). To do this, let's first walk through how you might do this in the Power Query UI and then inspect the query in **Advanced Editor** to add our parameters.

To follow along, ensure you have downloaded and extracted the folder named AdventureWorksSales from within the ZIP file named AdventureWorksSales.zip from GitHub:

1. Select **Transform data** from within Power BI.

2. Select **New source** and then select **More…** from the dropdown.

3. Select **Folder** and then select **Connect** as shown:

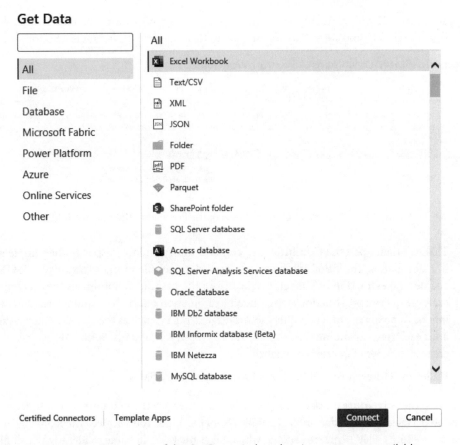

Figure 7.9 – Screenshot of the Get Data window showing connectors available

4. The next window will allow us to specify the path to the folder containing our CSVs. Here, we either type out the file path by selecting **Browse**, or we can create a new parameter using the dropdown under the folder path. Select **Browse…** and then navigate to the folder you have downloaded. Select **OK**.

Folder

Folder path

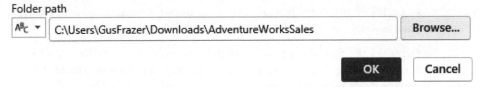

Figure 7.10 – Screenshot of the user entering the folder path into the connector

5. Selecting **OK** will open another window, which lists a preview of the files in the folder, as shown. Select **Combine & Transform Data** to then open the Power Query Editor interface.

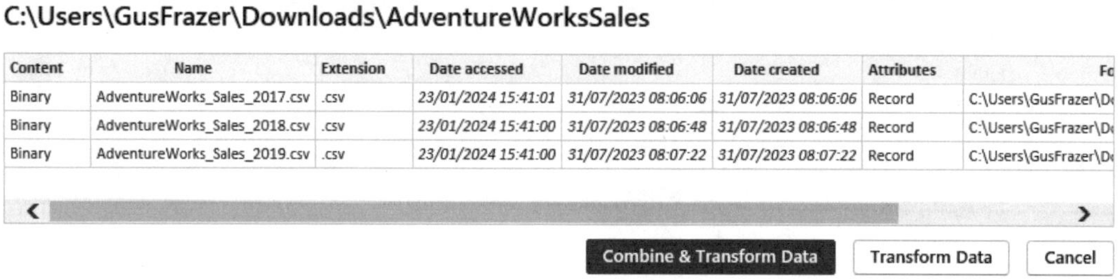

C:\Users\GusFrazer\Downloads\AdventureWorksSales

Content	Name	Extension	Date accessed	Date modified	Date created	Attributes	Fo
Binary	AdventureWorks_Sales_2017.csv	.csv	23/01/2024 15:41:01	31/07/2023 08:06:06	31/07/2023 08:06:06	Record	C:\Users\GusFrazer\D(
Binary	AdventureWorks_Sales_2018.csv	.csv	23/01/2024 15:41:00	31/07/2023 08:06:48	31/07/2023 08:06:48	Record	C:\Users\GusFrazer\D(
Binary	AdventureWorks_Sales_2019.csv	.csv	23/01/2024 15:41:00	31/07/2023 08:07:22	31/07/2023 08:07:22	Record	C:\Users\GusFrazer\D(

| Combine & Transform Data | Transform Data | Cancel |

Figure 7.11 – Screenshot of the preview of the files within the selected folder

6. This will then open the **Combine files** configuration window to specify the sample file for transformation. The **Combine files** transform identifies file formats (text, Excel, JSON) and enables the extraction of a specific object from the first file. It automates the creation of an example query for extraction steps, linked to a function query that parameterizes file/binary inputs. Applying the function query to the original query, such as the `Folder` query, executes it for each row, expanding the extracted data as top-level columns. Select **OK**, which will then create a number of queries automatically.

7. Under the **Other queries** folder, select **AdventureWorksSales**.

By selecting the **AdventureWorksSales** query, you can then see the output from the functions that have created a table from the data in the CSV files from the folder you selected. The following example includes a column called `Source.Name`, which takes the CSV filename to identify which file that row was extracted from.

As we can see from the **Query Settings** window, there are a number of steps that have been carried out on this table. However, before we dive into this, it's worth highlighting what Power Query has created in the background as we were loading this data, which can be seen on the left-hand side under the queries window. These are created in the folder named `Helper Queries`:

*   `Sample File`: This query selects the first file from within the folder that we specified.

*   `Parameter1`: Power Query created a binary parameter automatically with a current and default value of `Sample File`. It is used to select the file in the previous query.

*   `Transform File`: This is a custom function that is updated directly from the query called `Transform Sample File`. This function is then used in later queries to carry out the transformations performed on the sample file on all the files in the folder.

*   `Transform Sample File`: This is a query that uses the parameter to open `Source File`. There is, by default, one transformation applied (promoted headers). Here, you would be able to add further transformations that would then be applied to all the files in the folder.

Returning to the `AdventureWorksSales` query within the **Other Queries** folder, let's unpack the transformations that have been applied to transform and combine these CSV files, which can be seen in the following screenshot:

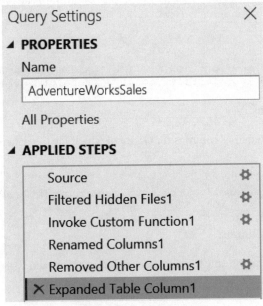

Figure 7.12 – Screenshot of the query setting and applied steps for the query named AdventureWorksSales

Here is a further description of what each of these steps is carrying out and the M query behind this to help you develop your knowledge of M:

- **Source:**

  - **Description:** Retrieves information about all files in the specified folder.

  - **M query:**

```
Source = Folder.Files("C:\Users\GusFrazer\Downloads\
AdventureWorksSales"),
```

- **Filtered hidden files:**

  - **Description:** Excludes hidden files from the retrieved file information/folder.

  - **M query:**

```
#"Filtered Hidden Files1" = Table.SelectRows(Source, each
[Attributes]?[Hidden]? <> true),
```

- **Invoke custom function**:

  - **Description**: Applies the custom function that was automatically created called `"Transform File"` to each file's content. This adds a new column to the table with links to the table from each file.

  - **M query**:

    ```
    #"Invoke Custom Function1" = Table.AddColumn(#"Filtered Hidden
    Files1", "Transform File", each #"Transform File"([Content])),
    ```

- **Renamed columns**:

  - **Description**: Renames columns for clarity of which file the data is coming from.

  - **M query**:

    ```
    #"Renamed Columns1" = Table.RenameColumns(#"Invoke Custom
    Function1", {"Name", "Source.Name"}),
    ```

- **Removed other columns**:

  - **Description**: Retains only the necessary columns to extract.

  - **M query**:

    ```
    #"Removed Other Columns1" = Table.SelectColumns(#"Renamed
    Columns1", {"Source.Name", "Transform File"}),
    ```

- **Filtered hidden files**:

  - **Description**: Expands the table column containing the transformed file data from each CSV.

  - **M query**:

    ```
    #"Expanded Table Column1" = Table.ExpandTableColumn(#"Removed
    Other Columns1", "Transform File", Table.ColumnNames(#"Transform
    File"(#"Sample File"))),
    ```

Now this was a great introduction to how Power Query intuitively creates the steps to carry out the transformations needed to combine these files into one table, creating parameters, functions, and other queries along the way to make the journey simple for users like yourself to get started.

With an understanding of what Power Query is doing, we can look to build on this knowledge with a refined blank query that does this all in one query using M. From within Power Query, perform the following steps:

1. Select the **Home** tab in the ribbon and select **New source**.

2. From the dropdown, select **Blank Query**.

3. Select **Advanced Editor** from within the **Query** group under the **Home** tab.

4. Input the following M query:

```
let
    FolderPathParameter = "C:\Users\GusFrazer\Downloads\
AdventureWorksSales",
    Source = Folder.Files(FolderPathParameter),
    CombineFiles = Table.Combine(
        List.Transform(Source[Content], each Csv.Document(_,
[Delimiter = ",", Encoding = 1252]))
    ),
    #"Promoted Headers" = Table.PromoteHeaders(CombineFiles,
[PromoteAllScalars = true]),
    #"Changed Type" = Table.TransformColumnTypes(
        #"Promoted Headers",
        {
            {"OrderDate", type text},
            {"StockDate", type text},
            {"OrderNumber", type text},
            {"ProductKey", Int64.Type},
            {"CustomerKey", Int64.Type},
            {"TerritoryKey", Int64.Type},
            {"OrderLineItem", Int64.Type},
            {"OrderQuantity", Int64.Type}
        }
    )
in
    #"Changed Type"
```

5. Select **Done**.

6. In short, this M query creates a folder query that loads all CSV files from the specified folder and combines them into a single table. The output will be identical to the other query you created earlier in this section named **AdventureWorksSales** (where we used the UI to select a folder path and combine the files); however, you have created this with a much smaller query.

Here is a further breakdown of what each section of the query is doing:

- `FolderPathParameter = "C:\Your\Folder\Path\"`: Here, you define the `FolderPathParameter` variable, which specifies the path to the folder containing the CSV files to be combined.

- `Source = Folder.Files(FolderPathParameter)`: This line uses the `Folder.Files` function to retrieve a list of files within the specified folder.

- `CombineFiles = ...`: This variable holds the result of combining multiple CSV files into a single table.

- `Table.Combine(...)`: This function combines multiple tables into one. in this case, it's used to combine tables representing the content of individual CSV files.

- `List.Transform(...)`: This function iterates over the list of file content tables, parsing each with `Csv.Document` to load and parse the CSV data.

- `each Csv.Document(_, [Delimiter = ",", Encoding = 1252])`: This is an anonymous function (`each`) applied to each item in the list. It uses `Csv.Document` to load and parse the CSV content with specified delimiter and encoding settings.

We have only touched the surface of parameters and variables, but as you can see, parameters are a key part of the M language. In this section, you saw a number of good examples of how parameters can help you switch between different data sources, but there are many applications where you can incorporate this into your own analysis.

Summary

In this chapter, you gained an understanding of how to work with data sources using the M language within Power Query in Power BI. You learned about topics such as M queries, M structure, variable declarations, data source connections, query steps, data type manipulation, and the importance of comments for code readability. You also discovered the versatility of M in handling different data sources, customizing connections, and using parameters, offering step-by-step instructions on creating and using parameters to enhance code maintainability and flexibility.

Additionally, the chapter presented practical examples of using parameters in M when connecting to SQL Server databases, conditionally selecting data sources using parameters, and combining multiple CSV files from a folder. These examples illustrated how M can be used to perform advanced data transformations, beyond what the UI offers.

Overall, you gained valuable insights into the power of M for working with diverse data sources, customizing connections, and efficiently transforming data in preparation for analysis and visualization in Power BI.

In the next chapter, we will begin to delve deeper into the functionalities within Power BI that can aid and assist you with carrying out **Exploratory Data Analysis (EDA)**.

Questions

1.   What is the purpose of M in Power BI and Power Query?

      A.   Formatting cell-level data

      B.   Transforming entire columns or tables

      C.   Creating calculated tables

      D.   Sorting individual cells

2. What keyword marks the beginning of a new M variable declaration block?

   A. `Start`

   B. `Let`

   C. `let`

   D. `Define`

3. How is a data source typically connected using M?

   A. Through the **Connection** tab

   B. Via the **Import** button

   C. Using a variable, often named `Source`

   D. By applying filters

4. What does the # symbol represent in M?

   A. The next step in the query

   B. A step/identifier that includes a space or special characters

   C. Previous steps in a query

   D. An intermediate step

5. Which function is used to convert extracted text into a numeric value in M?

   A. `Text.Extract`

   B. `Number.From`

   C. `Transform.Text`

   D. `Numeric.Convert`

Using Data Profiling for Exploratory Data Analysis (EDA)

In today's data-centric world, the ability to extract actionable insights from your data is not just a competitive advantage, it's a necessity. To help you harness the full potential of your data, we will delve deep into the world of Power BI, where data profiling takes center stage in the art of **Exploratory Data Analysis (EDA)**.

Imagine having a tool that not only helps you explore your data but also illuminates the path to better decision-making. Power BI's data profiling features do just that. In this chapter, we will guide you through the process of activating and using these features effectively.

We will go through the following topics:

- Understanding EDA
- Exploring the data profiling features in Power BI
- Reviewing column quality, distribution, and profile
- Turning data profiles into high-quality data

By the end of this chapter, you'll be armed with the skills and knowledge needed to elevate your data analysis game with Power BI's data profiling capabilities.

Understanding EDA

EDA plays a pivotal role in the data analysis workflow, serving as an essential phase where the dataset undergoes initial scrutiny and exploration. Its primary purpose is to summarize the main characteristics of the data, uncover patterns, identify potential outliers, and gain insights into the data's underlying structure.

Well-carried-out EDA when first connecting to data provides the following benefits:

- It helps analysts and data scientists familiarize themselves with the dataset they are working with. It provides an overview of the data's scope, size, and complexity, allowing them to assess its suitability for their analysis objectives.

- Data quality issues such as missing values, duplicates, and inconsistencies are often identified.

- It reveals patterns, trends, and relationships within the data. Analysts use various graphical and statistical techniques to visualize data distributions, correlations, and outliers.

- It also helps you select appropriate modeling techniques based on the characteristics of the data. For example, understanding the distribution of a target variable can inform the choice of regression or classification models.

With this basic understanding of EDA, let's see what features within Power BI will help you carry out EDA on your data.

Exploring data profiling features in Power BI

Power BI offers a range of data profiling capabilities that empower users to explore and understand their data effectively. These capabilities are as follows:

- **Column quality assessment**: Power BI allows you to assess the quality of each column in your dataset. This assessment includes identifying data types, data completeness, and the presence of null or missing values. You can quickly spot inconsistencies and issues that may impact your analysis.

- **Column distribution analysis**: Understanding the distribution of data within each column is crucial for making informed decisions. Power BI provides visualizations and statistics to help you analyze data distributions. This includes histograms and summary statistics such as mean, median, and standard deviation.

- **Column profile views**: Power BI offers column profile views that give you a comprehensive overview of each column's characteristics. These views display summary statistics, data quality indicators, and data distribution visualizations in a single interface, making it easy to assess column quality and patterns.

These data profile views can be accessed by opening Power Query and selecting the **View** tab.

As we can see in *Figure 8.1*, within the **Data Preview** section of the **View** tab, there are three column-specific previews, which are **Column quality**, **Column distribution**, and **Column profile**:

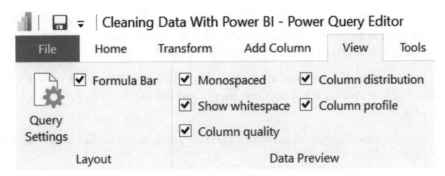

Figure 8.1 – The EDA functions within Power Query

In the next sections of this chapter, we will dive deeper into what each section can provide to help you profile your data.

Reviewing column quality, distribution, and profile

As mentioned earlier, **Column distribution**, **Column quality**, and **Column profile** views are the fundamental features of Power BI and Power Query, and they provide comprehensive insights into your dataset. These views are essential for EDA and help you understand the characteristics of individual columns in your data.

In the following sections, we will explore each view and how they report information.

Column distribution

The **Column distribution** view in Power BI and Power Query allows you to explore the distribution of values within a specific column. It provides visualization and statistics that help you understand how data is spread across different ranges or categories.

Let's see an example from the dataset provided in this book's GitHub repository. Here, we have only selected **Column distribution** and have then zoomed in on a particular value called **OrderQuantity**.

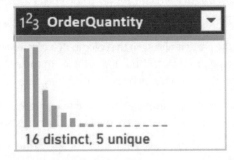

Figure 8.2 – Column distribution for the column named OrderQuantity

This example shows a histogram chart that displays the frequency or count of values within predefined intervals or bins. It visualizes the distribution of values, showing whether they are concentrated in specific ranges or evenly spread.

The example shows that there are 16 distinct values within the quantity data, with most of the records being within the first 2 bars. We will later dive deeper into the insights of this when we activate the column profile.

This view also lets us know about unique values. These are potential outliers or values that only appear once and might skew the readings.

Column quality

The **Column quality** view assesses the quality of data in a specific column. It helps you identify data issues, such as missing values, data type inconsistencies, and potential problems that may affect your analysis. If we activate **Column quality** in the previous view, we can see the following:

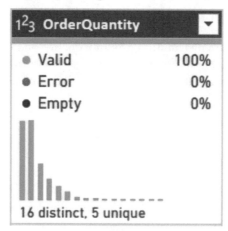

Figure 8.3 – Column quality and distribution for the column named OrderQuantity

In the context of the **Column quality** view in Power BI or Power Query, the percentage values for **Valid**, **Error**, and **Empty** represent the following:

- **Valid**: This represents the portion of data in the column that is considered valid or correct according to the specified data type or format. Valid data adheres to the expected data type, format, and constraints defined for the column. It does not contain any data quality issues or errors.

  For example, if you have a date column and the **Valid** percentage is 95%, it means that 95% of the rows in that column conforms to the expected date format and does not contain any data type errors.

  You might experience this if you have some text values within a column that has been set to contain a number values.

- **Error**: The **Error** percentage indicates the portion of data in the column that contains errors or does not meet the defined data quality standards.

  Data errors can include values that are of the wrong data type, do not follow the expected format, or violate any constraints defined for the column.

  For instance, if the **Error** percentage is 2%, it means that 2% of the values in the column contain data quality issues or errors that need attention and correction.

- **Empty**: The **Empty** percentage represents the proportion of missing or empty values within the column.

  Empty values are cells in your data column that have not been filled with any data, and they are often represented as null or blank cells in the dataset.

  For example, if the **Empty** percentage is 10%, it means that 10% of the cells in the column do not contain any data and are considered empty or missing values.

Column profile

Lastly, the **Column profile** view in Power BI and Power Query combines information from both the **Column distribution** and **Column Quality** views to provide a comprehensive profile of a specific column.

It offers an overview of the data's distribution, data quality, and other relevant insights in a single interface.

When switching on the data profile within Power Query, you can expect the **Column statistics** and **Value distribution** windows to open at the bottom of your screen:

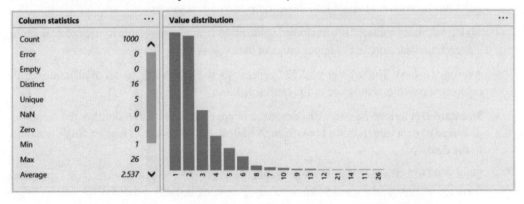

Figure 8.4 – View of the column profile for column named OrderQuantity

On the left, we can see a number of statistics that help us gain an insight into the profile of the data within this column. The availability of these statistics can vary depending on the nature of the data in that particular column.

Here is a breakdown of what we can see in the statistics in *Figure 8.4*:

- **Count** (total number of rows): This statistic shows that there are 1,000 rows in the column, which means your dataset contains 1,000 data points for this particular variable. It is worth noting here that when Power Query is loading a sample of data, it normally loads the first 1,000 rows, so the dataset could actually contain more rows.

- **Error**: The absence of any **Error** values (a count of **0**) suggests that there are no data quality issues or errors in this column. All the data appears to be correctly formatted.

- **Empty**: Similarly to **Error**, a count of **0** for **Empty** indicates that there are no missing or blank values in this column. Every row in the column contains data.

- **Distinct**: The **Distinct** count of **16** tells you that there are 16 unique values in this column. This is helpful for understanding the variety of data within the column.

- **Unique**: The **Unique** count of **5** indicates that there are 5 values that occur only once in the column. This provides insight into the diversity of values in the data.

- **NaN** (**Not a Number**): The count of **0** for **NaN** values suggests that there are no values in the column that are classified as Not a Number. This is typically relevant for numeric columns and indicates that all data points are numeric.

- **Zero**: The count of **0** for **Zero** values indicates that there are no data points with a value of 0 in this column.

- **Min** (minimum value): The minimum value of **1** is the smallest value present in the column. This statistic provides insight into the lower range of data values.

- **Max** (maximum value): The maximum value of **26** is the largest value in the column, giving you an understanding of the upper range of data values.

- **Average** (mean): The average of **2.537** represents the arithmetic mean of all values in the column. It provides a measure of the central tendency.

- **Standard Deviation**: The standard deviation of approximately **2.046** signifies the dispersion or spread of data values around the mean. A high standard deviation suggests high variability in the data.

- **Even** and **Odd**: These statistics categorize the data into even and odd values. You can see that there are 457 even values and 543 odd values, providing insights into the distribution of these two types of values in the column.

Now you have built a good foundation of knowledge of what the column quality, distribution, and profile views within Power Query are and how they can be used to gauge the cleanliness of your data. In the next section, you will dive deep into how they can be used to clean your data.

Turning data profiles into high-quality data

Along with the capability to provide insights on what this data represents, Power BI has now also made it easier to act on the insights provided. These features aim to help cleanse and transform the data faster so you can gain insights quicker. We'll review them in the next sections.

Recommended actions on column distribution

Figure 8.5 shows an example where Power BI has suggested one action we might take on this column is to remove duplicates. This can be seen by hovering over the distribution of the column.

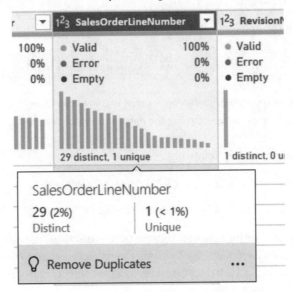

Figure 8.5 – Recommended action on the column named SalesOrderLineNumber

You can leverage the quick actions shown in the previous screenshot to clean and prepare the data you are analyzing more efficiently. Keep in mind that it might not always be the correct action to take; it depends on your analysis. For example, if you needed to see how many repeat orders there were within a sales order, it might not make sense to remove the duplicate line item numbers.

Value distribution

From within the **Column profile** view, we can see a large breakdown histogram of a column that we have selected. This view can be grouped on a number of different properties that are accessible in the top-right corner.

Similar to the previous section of this chapter, if you hover over a particular value, you will see the following information:

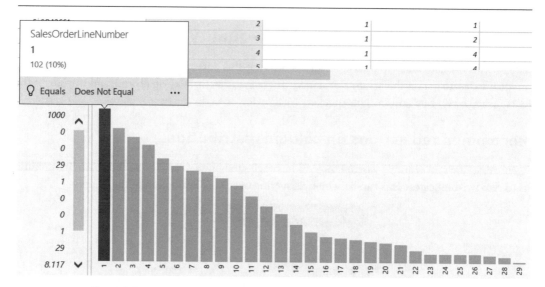

Figure 8.6 – The value distribution window within Power Query highlighting smart actions to filter the data to the value selected

We can see information such as the following:

- The value 1 appears 102 times in the **OrderQuantity** column
- The value 1 represents 10% of the data/number of rows

Should we wish to dive deeper into the data that makes up this value, or equally exclude it from our analysis, Power BI provides a recommended cleaning step to either filter to that value or exclude that value from the data. This is particularly great when you spot an outlier in the data and would like to investigate what that data point consists of.

By selecting the recommended cleaning action step, Power BI automates the creation of the cleaning steps within your Power Query interface. In the example shown in *Figure 8.6*, select the **Equals** button (with the lightbulb next to it highlighting that it's a smart recommendation) shown as follows:

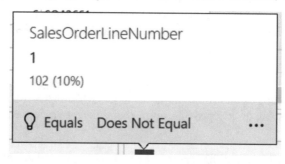

Figure 8.7 – Close-up of Figure 8.6

Power Query will then add a filter step within your query:

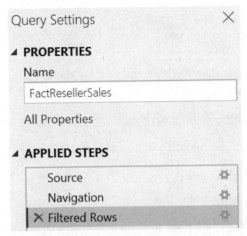

Figure 8.8 – The Applied Steps window within Power Query detailing the step added by selecting the equals action from Figure 8.7

This can be summarized by the following M code added to the advanced editor:

```
#"Filtered Rows" = Table.SelectRows(FactResellerSales1, each
[SalesOrderLineNumber] = 1)
```

Making use of the capabilities of the value distribution highlighted in this section can help you get started with the necessary transformations faster.

Summary

In this chapter, you were given an overview of Power BI's data profiling capabilities that can help with EDA. Beginning with an introduction to EDA's core concepts, you navigated the data profiling landscape within Power BI, mastering the interpretation and utilization of column quality, distribution, and profile views.

Throughout the chapter, the significance of EDA as a critical phase in data analysis was emphasized. EDA serves as a powerful tool for familiarizing yourself with datasets, identifying data quality issues, revealing patterns, and informing modeling choices.

You also learned how to use the **Column distribution** view to explore data distributions and identify unique values and potential outliers. The **Column quality** view allows you to assess data quality, including validity, errors, and empty values, ensuring data integrity. Furthermore, the **Column profile** view combines data distribution and quality insights into a comprehensive profile of each column, offering a holistic understanding of your data.

In the next chapter, you'll further enhance your data preparation skills, enabling you to tackle even more complex data challenges and optimize your datasets for robust analysis and visualization in Power BI.

Questions

1. What is the primary purpose of EDA?

    A. To finalize the dataset

    B. To summarize data characteristics and gain insights

    C. To create predictive models

    D. To validate machine learning algorithms

2. What are the benefits of conducting well-carried-out EDA when connecting to data?

    A. Identifying potential outliers

    B. Ignoring data quality issues

    C. Skipping data visualization

    D. Avoiding modeling choices

3. Which of the following is NOT a fundamental data profiling capability offered by Power BI?

    A. Column Quality Assessment

    B. Column Distribution Analysis

    C. Column Transformation

    D. Column Profile Views

4. How can you access the data profile views in Power BI?

    A. From the **Home** tab

    B. Within Power Query, open the **View** tab

    C. Using the **Visualization** pane

    D. Through Power BI Dashboard settings

5. What does the Column distribution view in Power BI provide?

    A. Assessment of data quality

    B. Histograms and statistics

    C. Data completeness percentage

    D. Visualization of column names

6. What does the Column quality view in Power BI assess, and how is it represented?

    A. Data distribution, shown in histograms

    B. Validity, Error, and Empty percentages

    C. Column names and types

    D. Visualization of data completeness

7. Which statistics are typically displayed in the Column profile view in Power BI?

    A. Count, Error, and Empty

    B. Min, Max, and Average

    C. Only Distinct count

    D. All of the above

8. Based on insights gained from data profiles, what action might Power BI recommend?

    A. Exporting the data

    B. Ignoring the insights

    C. Removing duplicates

    D. Changing the data source

9. How does Power BI automate the creation of cleaning steps based on recommended actions?

    A. By suggesting random actions

    B. Through the use of machine learning

    C. By providing recommended actions in the interface

    D. By requiring manual coding

Part 3 – Advanced Data Cleaning and Optimizations

This part navigates through advanced techniques for shaping and optimizing data within Power BI. You will dive into custom function creation in Power Query, mastering planning, parameters, and function creation. Later, you will explore M query optimization to gain insights into query optimization for peak performance, before concluding with an understanding of data modeling and relationship management to ensure that data models set the stage for success.

This part has the following chapters:

- *Chapter 9, Advanced Data Cleaning Techniques*
- *Chapter 10, Creating Custom Functions in Power Query*
- *Chapter 11, M Query Optimization*
- *Chapter 12, Data Modeling and Managing Relationships*

9

Advanced Data Cleaning Techniques

So far in this book, we have covered several techniques that range from basic to intermediary. Now, we are ready to progress to the next stage of this book, where we will explore more advanced techniques for cleaning, preparing, and enhancing data for analysis within Power BI and its toolkit.

In this chapter, you will learn about the following:

- Using Power Query Editor from within Dataflow Gen1 – fuzzy matching and fill down
- Using R and Python scripts
- Using ML to clean data

By the end of this chapter, you will have learned how to build complex functions within Power Query. In addition to this, you will also learn how to begin bringing other advanced languages such as R or Python into your data model.

The key aim of this chapter is to provide an introduction to techniques that you can leverage as you clean, prepare, and enhance your data for analysis, as well as to introduce you to working with dataflows from the Power BI service.

Technical requirements

To follow along with the AutoML example and walk-through, you will require access to Dataflow Gen1 and a Power BI premium workspace.

To utilize R scripts within Power BI Desktop, it's essential to have R installed on your local machine. Fortunately, you can easily download and install R for free. Visit the official R project website (https://www.r-project.org/) to access the latest version of R. Once on the website, navigate to the **CRAN** (**Comprehensive R Archive Network**) section, and choose a mirror location close to you. From there, select the appropriate version of R for your operating system (Windows, macOS, or Linux) and initiate the download.

After downloading the installer, follow the installation instructions provided to complete the setup process. Once R is successfully installed on your local machine, you'll be equipped to seamlessly run R scripts in conjunction with Power BI Desktop for enhanced data analysis and visualization capabilities. You can get further details on R scripts from the Microsoft website: `https://learn.microsoft.com/en-gb/power-bi/connect-data/desktop-r-scripts`.

Once installed, you will need to run the following code in your workspace to ensure the necessary packages are installed:

```
> install.packages("dplyr")
```

To run Python scripts in Power BI Desktop, you will need to install Python on your local machine. You can download Python from the Python website: `https://www.python.org/`. Further details on installing Python are also available at `https://learn.microsoft.com/en-us/power-bi/connect-data/desktop-python-scripts`.

To install the relevant packages (`pandas` and `matplotlib`), you need to open the command line on your local device and enter the following commands:

```
py -m pip install --user matplotlib
py -m pip install --user pandas
```

Data for the examples used in this chapter can be found in the following GitHub repo: `https://github.com/PacktPublishing/Data-Cleaning-with-Power-BI/blob/main/online_shoppers_intention.csv`.

Using Power Query Editor from within Dataflow Gen1 – fuzzy matching and fill down

Data is the lifeblood of any analytics project, and Power BI offers a powerful toolset to help users clean and prepare their data for analysis. The Power Query Editor from within Dataflow Gen1, an integral part of Power BI, provides a range of techniques to streamline data cleaning. In this section, we'll explore two essential techniques: **fuzzy matching** and **fill down**, and discover how they can elevate your data preparation game.

Fuzzy matching

Data from various sources can be notoriously inconsistent. Spelling mistakes, abbreviations, and different naming conventions can wreak havoc on your data analysis efforts. **Fuzzy matching** is a powerful technique that helps you match similar strings within your data, making it invaluable for consolidating information and reducing data inconsistencies.

Fuzzy matching uses a similarity score to determine how closely two strings match. It assigns a similarity score between 0 (no similarity) and 1 (perfect match) based on the comparison of two strings. The higher the similarity score, the more likely it is that the strings represent the same entity.

There are a number of use cases for how fuzzy matching can help when preparing data but here are just a few of them:

- **Merging duplicate records**: Fuzzy matching can help you identify and merge duplicate records, even when there are slight variations in the data

- **Standardizing text**: If your data includes variations of the same text (for example, "USA" and "United States of America"), fuzzy matching can standardize it

- **Handling misspelled names**: When dealing with names or product titles with spelling variations, fuzzy matching can identify and link similar entries

It's important to note that features of fuzzy matching can only be used from within the Power BI web service. Here is a walk-through of how this can be implemented in Power BI:

1. **Create a dataflow**: Log in to your Power BI service and workspace. Select **Create new dataflow**. Ensure you select **Create from within the Power BI workspace**; otherwise, you will potentially create a dataflow using the Dataflow Gen2, which is part of Fabric.

2. **Define your data**: Select **Define your data** to add new tables to the dataflow, opening up the next page, showing all the connectors.

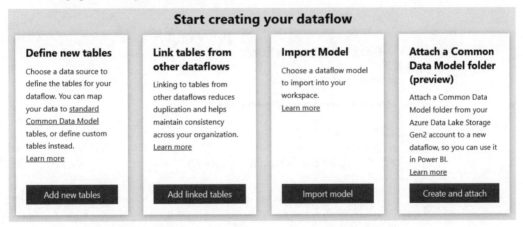

Figure 9.1 – Screenshot showing the options available when creating
a new dataflow within the Power BI workspace

3. **Select the connector**: Select **Text/CSV connector**, which will then prompt you to add the file path for the data you'd like to connect to. Add the following URL for the data in this example: `https://raw.githubusercontent.com/PacktPublishing/Data-Cleaning-with-Power-BI/main/mtcars.csv`.

4. **Transform data**: When the preview file window opens, select **Transform data** to then open Power Query within the service.

5. **Select your data column**: From the Power Query Editor within the Dataflow Power Query Editor from within Dataflow Gen1, select the relevant columns, and choose **Select the column** for the column we would like to apply the **Fuzzy Grouping** option to. In this example, we can see there is a column with lots of misspellings named `Car Brand`.

6. **Adding columns**: Navigate to the **Add Columns** tab. Then select the **Cluster** icon. This will open the following window:

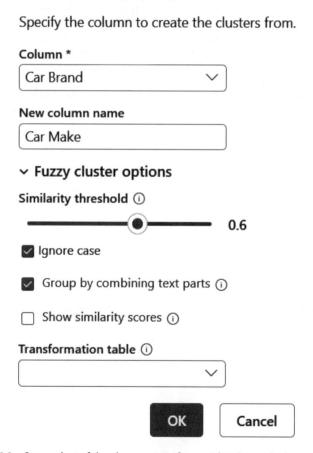

Figure 9.2 – Screenshot of the cluster menu from within Power BI/Power Query

7. **Configure settings for the cluster**: Adjust the name of the new column. Here, you can also configure the fuzzy cluster by adjusting the similarity threshold.

8. **Review the results**: In the following figure, you can review the results of the newly created column:

	A⒝C Car Brand	A⒝C Car Model	1.2 mpg	1²₃ cyl	1.2 disp	1²₃ hp	1.2 drat	1.2 wt	1.2 qsec	1²₃ vs	1²₃ am	1²₃ gear	A⒝C Car Make
1	Mazda	Mazda RX4	21	6	160	110	3.9	2.62	16.46	0	1	4	Mazda
2	Mazdaa	Mazda RX4 Wag	21	6	160	110	3.9	2.875	17.02	0	1	4	Mazda
3	Datsun	Datsun 710	22.8	4	108	93	3.85	2.32	18.61	1	1	4	Datsun
4	Hornet	Hornet 4 Drive	21.4	6	258	110	3.08	3.215	19.44	1	0	3	Hornet
5	H0rnet	Hornet Sportabout	18.7	8	360	175	3.15	3.44	17.02	0	0	3	Hornet
6	Valiant	Valiant	18.1	6	225	105	2.76	3.46	20.22	1	0	3	Valiant
7	Duster	Duster 360	14.3	8	360	245	3.21	3.57	15.84	0	0	3	Duster
8	Mercedes	Merc 240D	24.4	4	146.7	62	3.69	3.19	20	1	0	4	Mercedes
9	Mercedes	Merc 230	22.8	4	140.8	95	3.92	3.15	22.9	1	0	4	Mercedes
10	Mercede$	Merc 280	19.2	6	167.6	123	3.92	3.44	18.3	1	0	4	Mercedes
11	Mercede$	Merc 280C	17.8	6	167.6	123	3.92	3.44	18.9	1	0	4	Mercedes
12	Mercedez	Merc 450SE	16.4	8	275.8	180	3.07	4.07	17.4	0	0	3	Mercedes
13	Mercedes	Merc 450SL	17.3	8	275.8	180	3.07	3.73	17.6	0	0	3	Mercedes
14	Mercedes	Merc 450SLC	15.2	8	275.8	180	3.07	3.78	18	0	0	3	Mercedes
15	Cadillac	Cadillac Fleetwood	10.4	8	472	205	2.93	5.25	17.98	0	0	3	Cadillac
16	Lincoln	Lincoln Continental	10.4	8	460	215	3	5.424	17.82	0	0	3	Lincoln
17	Chrysler	Chrysler Imperial	14.7	8	440	230	3.23	5.345	17.42	0	0	3	Chrysler
18	Fiat	Fiat 128	32.4	4	78.7	66	4.08	2.2	19.47	1	1	4	Fiat
19	Honda	Honda Civic	30.4	4	75.7	52	4.93	1.615	18.52	1	1	4	Honda
20	Toyota	Toyota Corolla	33.9	4	71.1	65	4.22	1.835	19.9	1	1	4	Toyota
21	Toyota!	Toyota Corona	21.5	4	120.1	97	3.7	2.465	20.01	1	0	3	Toyota
22	Dodge	Dodge Challenger	15.5	8	318	150	2.76	3.52	16.87	0	0	3	Dodge
23	AMC	AMC Javelin	15.2	8	304	150	3.15	3.435	17.3	0	0	3	AMC
24	Camaro	Camaro Z28	13.3	8	350	245	3.73	3.84	15.41	0	0	3	Camaro
25	Pontiac	Pontiac Firebird	19.2	8	400	175	3.08	3.845	17.05	0	0	3	Pontiac
26	Fiat	Fiat X1-9	27.3	4	79	66	4.08	1.935	18.9	1	1	4	Fiat
27	Porsche	Porsche 914-2	26	4	120.3	91	4.43	2.14	16.7	0	1	5	Porsche
28	Lotus	Lotus Europa	30.4	4	95.1	113	3.77	1.513	16.9	1	1	5	Lotus
29	Ford	Ford Pantera L	15.8	8	351	264	4.22	3.17	14.5	0	1	5	Ford
30	Ferrari	Ferrari Dino	19.7	6	145	175	3.62	2.77	15.5	0	1	5	Ferrari
31	Maserati	Maserati Bora	15	8	301	335	3.54	3.57	14.6	0	1	5	Maserati
32	Volvo	Volvo 142E	21.4	4	121	109	4.11	2.78	18.6	1	1	4	Volvo

Figure 9.3 – Preview of the data after adding a new column and configuring the cluster option within Power BI/Power Query

In this example, we can see that by using fuzzy matching, we have been able to use smart technology within Power Query to automate the correction in the data.

Although we didn't use a transformation table in this example, it's important to understand what this feature does when clustering values. In *Figure 9.2*, at the bottom of the configuration window, we can see there is an option to reference a transformation table. This can be a table or query you have created in your dataflow, which becomes really useful if you want to include abbreviations or acronyms from your data in the mapping of the clusters. An example of this could be using a transformation table to help associate acronyms such as **BDCF** with **Bidirectional Cross Filtering**.

> **Important note**
>
> It is crucial that the transformation table you use includes the columns named `From` and `To`. Without these named columns, Power Query will not recognize the table as a transformation table, resulting in no transformation.

Fill down

Data gaps are common and can lead to inaccurate analyses. The **fill down** technique in Power BI's Power Query Editor from within Dataflow Gen1 can help fill in these gaps, creating a consistent and complete dataset.

Fill down is an operation that copies the value from the previous row to fill in missing values in the current row. This is particularly useful when you have a series of data points with occasional gaps.

Here are some use cases where fill down might be best applicable:

- **Time series data**: When working with time series data, fill down can populate missing values in a time sequence, ensuring the continuity of your data
- **Categorization**: If you have categorical data where values should remain consistent until changed, fill down can help maintain the continuity of categories
- **Calculations**: In situations where you need to perform calculations on missing values, fill down can prepare the data for mathematical operations

Here is a walk-through of how this can be implemented in Power BI:

1. **Select your data**: Open the Power Query Editor from within Dataflow Gen1, and select the column with missing values (in this example, we can see that the `Wheels` column has a number of rows with missing values). We know that the data is looking at cars, so we can assume that all the cars in this category of data have four wheels, making it an ideal example to use the *fill* feature. Navigate to the **Transform** ribbon on the toolbar and choose the **Fill Down** option. You can also choose to fill up from this button.

2. **Configure fill down**: Choose the desired options, such as the direction (down or up) and the handling of null values. In this example, we will select **Down** to fill down. Once selected, Power Query will apply the fill down operation to your data, and the gaps will be filled automatically.

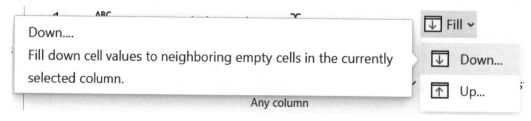

Figure 9.4 – Screenshot of the fill down function available within
the Power Query Editor view from the Dataflow

Compared to fill down, fill up works in a similar manner but in the opposite direction: populating rows with values from the row below.

Best practices for using fuzzy matching and fill down

Here are just some useful best practice tips when working with fuzzy matching and fill down within the Power Query Advanced Editor:

- **Data backup**: Always create a backup of your data before applying any changes, especially when using fuzzy matching, as it may result in data consolidation that cannot be undone.

  If you are in Power BI Desktop, you could simply save a local copy of your file or use integrations such as GitHub to help with rolling back to a previous version of your changes. From dataflows though, this is not as simple as, although you can export your query to JSON, you can't exactly save a local copy of the query. So, one method I have always found safest is to duplicate the query before making adjustments. That way, you always have a rollback copy of the query should you need it. To do this, follow these steps:

  I.   **Duplicate the query**: In the Power Query Editor, duplicate the query you are working on by right-clicking on the query you'd like to back up. From the menu that appears (shown in the following figure), select **Duplicate**. This creates a copy of your data transformation steps without affecting the original data.

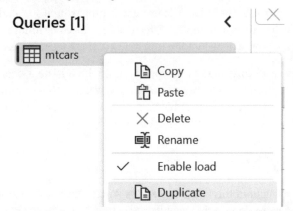

Figure 9.5 – Screenshot of the menu that appears from right-clicking a query within the Power Query Editor from within a dataflow

  II. **Rename the original query**: Right-click on the original query and use a clear and distinct name, indicating that it is a backup or a copy. This helps in easily identifying and distinguishing the backup from the main query. For example, a name such as `mtcars_ROLLBACK_GF_05022024` provides clear detail that this is a rollback version of the query and when it was created.

III.   **Disable the loading of the backup query**: To prevent the dataflow from duplicating efforts or impacting performances, it's best to disable the loading of the rollback copy of the query. The **Enable load** option allows users to control whether the results of a specific query should be loaded into the data model of Power BI or other destinations. By default, Power Query loads query results into the data model for analysis, but clicking on **Enable load** (as shown in *Figure 9.5*) enables the option to disable loading. This is also useful for performing intermediate data transformations or cleaning without adding unnecessary data to the final dataset. This feature helps manage the size and content of the Power BI data model.

- **Threshold sensitivity**: Adjust the similarity threshold in fuzzy matching to achieve the desired balance between strict and loose matching.

- **Data validation**: Regularly validate the results of your data cleaning efforts to ensure that the fuzzy matching and fill down operations yield the expected results.

- **Documentation**: Maintain documentation of the steps taken during data cleaning. This is crucial for reproducibility and troubleshooting.

- **Iterative process**: Understand that data cleaning is often an iterative process. You may need to revisit and refine your cleaning operations as you gain deeper insights into your data.

The Power Query Editor from within Dataflow Gen1 in Power BI empowers analysts and developers like yourself to take control of their data, cleaning and preparing it for analysis effectively. Fuzzy matching and fill down are just two examples of the many advanced techniques available to tackle data inconsistencies and gaps. You will be looking into many of these techniques in the coming chapters.

By leveraging the power of fuzzy matching, you can unify inconsistent data, while fill down helps maintain data continuity, even in the presence of missing values. These techniques, when used with best practices in mind, can significantly enhance the quality of your data and, in turn, improve the accuracy and reliability of your Power BI reports and visualizations.

Using R and Python scripts

As you have learned throughout this book, Power BI's Power Query Editor from within a dataflow or Power BI Desktop is a versatile tool that enables users to shape, transform, and cleanse data before it's used for analysis and visualization.

While the built-in capabilities that have been highlighted in the previous sections are robust, sometimes you may encounter data manipulation tasks that require more advanced processing. This is where the feature of using R or Python scripts in coding languages such as R and Python, for example, comes to the rescue.

Before jumping into how you might go about doing this, it's worth understanding why you might use these languages. Custom data scripts enable users to extend the capabilities of Power BI by leveraging the rich ecosystems of R and Python.

Although this chapter will not go into depth about how to code in these languages, here are some scenarios where you might consider using custom scripts:

- **Complex transformations**: When your data transformation needs to go beyond the standard capabilities of the Power Query M formula language, R or Python scripts provide a way to perform complex operations.

- **Statistical analysis**: If you need to run statistical analyses, predictive modeling, or machine learning algorithms on your data within Power BI, R or Python scripts are your allies.

- **Third-party libraries**: Access to the extensive libraries available in R and Python can be a game-changer. From natural language processing to image analysis, you can tap into a vast array of pre-built functions and packages.

- **Data integration**: When you want to integrate data from various sources, databases, or web services, using custom scripts allows you to fetch and process the data seamlessly.

Benefits of using R or Python scripts

There are many advantages of using R and Python scripts in Power BI, which I've summarized as follows:

- **Advanced data manipulation**: Both R and Python offer powerful data manipulation capabilities, making it easier to handle complex transformations, missing data imputation, and more

- **Statistical and machine learning capabilities**: Leverage the rich ecosystems of R and Python to run sophisticated statistical analyses or build machine learning models directly within Power BI

- **Integration with external data sources**: Access data from various sources, including APIs, databases, and web services, by using the extensive libraries available in R and Python

- **Reproducibility and documentation**: Scripts can be saved and documented within Power BI, ensuring transparency and reproducibility of data transformation processes

Getting started with using R or Python scripts in Power BI

Let's walk through a basic example of how to use R and Python scripts within Power BI's Power Query Editor. It's important to note that, in this section, we will need to jump back into Power BI Desktop as dataflows do not currently support the use of R or Python scripts. In this example, we'll use a simple dataset of sales transactions to carry out some simple transformations using R and Python. It's important to note that these are just to demonstrate how to leverage these languages in Power BI. The simple transformations in this example could also be done using Power Query. The code has also been added to the GitHub repo should you wish to copy the code from there (given that Python is line-sensitive, copying directly from the snippets may introduce errors otherwise).

The steps to using R in Power BI are as follows:

1. **Select your data**: Load your data into Power BI using the techniques we discussed earlier in this book, in *Chapter 5, Importing Data into Power BI*, by selecting **Get data** and then select **R script**, as shown:

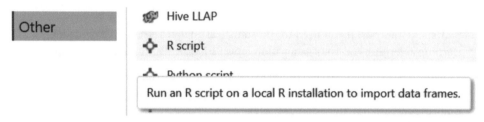

Figure 9.6 – Screenshot of the Get data menu from within Power BI Desktop

2. **Enter the following code**: This will open a dataset that is available by default within R, which we can use for an example:

    ```
    data(mtcars)
    ```

3. **Select Transform data**: You need to select the **Transform data** option, which will open the Power Query Editor, showing the following preview:

1.2 mpg	1.2 cyl	1.2 disp	1.2 hp	1.2 drat	1.2 gear
21	6	160	110	3.9	4
21	6	160	110	3.9	4
22.8	4	108	93	3.85	4
21.4	6	258	110	3.08	3
18.7	8	360	175	3.15	3
18.1	6	225	105	2.76	3

`= Table.ReorderColumns(mtcars1,{"mpg", "cyl", "disp", "hp", "drat", "gear", "wt", "qsec", "vs", "am", "carb"})`

Figure 9.7 – Screenshot of the data preview within Power Query

4. **Invoke R script**: Under the **Transform** tab, choose **Run R Script**.

5. **Write R Script**: Write your R script to perform the desired transformation. For instance, you could use R to group the cars by the number of gears they have and then the average **miles per gallon (mpg)** they have of sales for each category:

    ```
    # R Script Example
    library(dplyr)
    result <- dataset %>%
      group_by(gear) %>%
      summarize(AverageMPG = mean(mpg))
    ```

6. **Apply the script**: Click on the **OK** button to apply the R script, and the result will be added as a new column in your data.

7. **Select privacy**: For the R script to work properly in the Power BI service, all data sources need to be set to public.

The output of this script will transform the data showing the average mpg value per gear category, as shown:

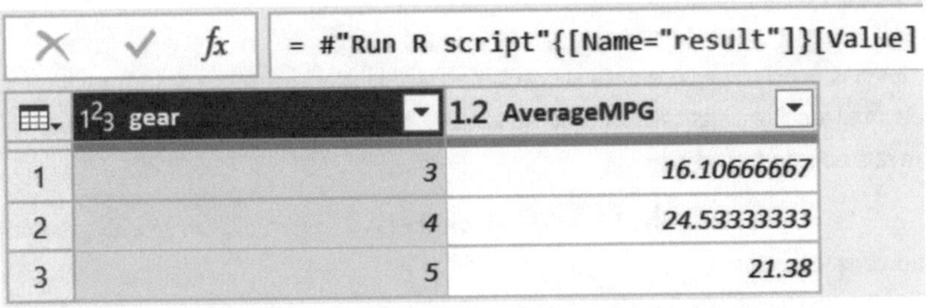

	1²3 gear	1.2 AverageMPG
1	3	16.10666667
2	4	24.53333333
3	5	21.38

`= #"Run R script"{[Name="result"]}[Value]`

Figure 9.8 – Screenshot of the results from the R script

As you can see from this example, this has returned a simplified view of the data calculating that those cars with four gears have the optimum mpg value. It's important to note that the simple grouping transformations we carried out in the previous example can also be done in Power Query using the grouping functions. The key aim is to give you an introduction to how to actually leverage your R scripts in Power BI.

The steps to use **Python** for the same transformations in Power BI are as follows:

1. **Repeat steps 1–3 from the previous example**: Connect to the same data as the previous example.

2. **Invoke Python script**: Under the **Transform** tab, choose **Run Python Script**.

> **Tip**
> Ensure you have installed `pandas` and `matplotlib`.

3. **Write Python script**: Write your Python script to perform the desired transformation. An example would look like the following; you could use Python to calculate the average sales price:

```python
# Python Script Example
import pandas as pd
dataset = pd.DataFrame(dataset)
# Group by 'gear' and calculate the average of 'mpg'
result = dataset.groupby('gear').agg({'mpg': 'mean'}).reset_index()
# Rename the column to match the R example
result = result.rename(columns={'mpg': 'AverageMPG'})
```

4. **Apply the script**: Click on the **OK** button to apply the Python script, and the result will be added as a new column in your data.

5. **Select privacy**: For the Python scripts to work properly in the Power BI service, all data sources need to be set to public (out of the **Public**, **Organizational**, or **Private** options).

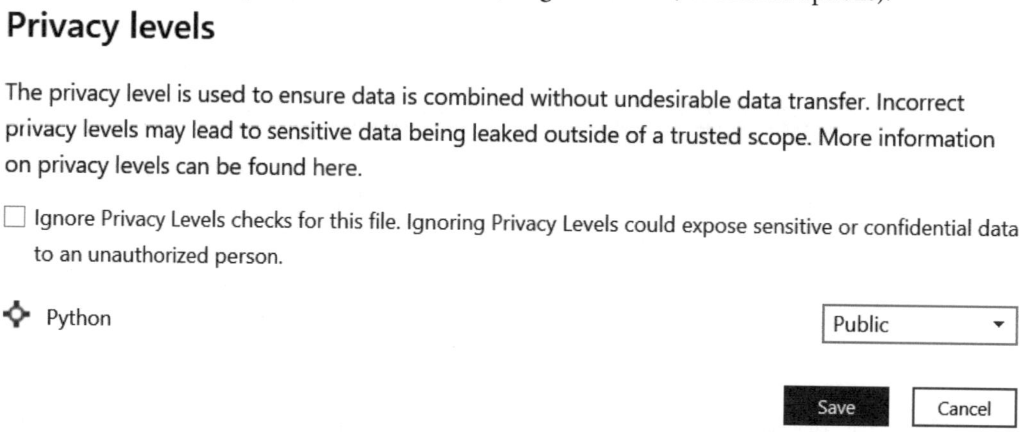

Privacy levels

The privacy level is used to ensure data is combined without undesirable data transfer. Incorrect privacy levels may lead to sensitive data being leaked outside of a trusted scope. More information on privacy levels can be found here.

☐ Ignore Privacy Levels checks for this file. Ignoring Privacy Levels could expose sensitive or confidential data to an unauthorized person.

◆ Python   Public   ▼

                                                    Save   Cancel

Figure 9.9 – Screenshot of the privacy levels from the Python script

> **Important note**
>
> Privacy levels in Power Query define the sensitivity of data sources and control their visibility and interaction with each other. When a data source is set to **Private**, it contains confidential information, and access is restricted to authorized users. **Organizational** privacy levels allow data sources to fold into private and other organizational sources, with visibility limited to a trusted group. **Public** privacy levels apply to files, internet sources, and workbooks, allowing data to fold into other sources while being visible to everyone in the business. Examples of the **Public** privacy level include freely available data from the Azure Marketplace or information from a public web page stored in a local file.
>
> To highlight, though, setting this to **Public** doesn't mean that your data will be made accessible to anyone and everyone outside your company. If you set a data source to the **Public** privacy level, it means that the data from that source can be shared and combined with other data sources, but it doesn't imply that the data itself is accessible externally. The privacy levels primarily control the interaction and integration of data within the Power BI environment. Regardless of the privacy level, the actual security and access control of the data are managed by the underlying data sources and the Power BI service.

6. **Open result table**: The script will return the view shown in the following figure. Select the **Table** link next to the result value to complete the script.

	AᴮC Name			Value	
1	dataset			Table	
2	result			Table	

Figure 9.10 – Screenshot of the results from the Python script

The results that match the results from the R script are shown here:

	1²₃ gear		1.2 AverageMPG	
1	3		16.10666667	
2	4		24.53333333	
3	5		21.38	

Figure 9.11 – Screenshot of the results from the Python script after
selecting Table from within the Value column

R and Python scripts provide Power BI users with an expanded toolkit for data transformation and preparation. This feature opens up opportunities for advanced data manipulation, statistical analysis, and machine learning within the familiar Power BI environment. As you become proficient in using scripts, you'll unlock the full potential of your data and create more insightful and sophisticated reports and visualizations.

To facilitate the scheduled refresh of datasets that use R or Python scripts in Power BI, it is essential to set up a personal gateway on the computer hosting the workbook and the Python installation. This process allows for the automated and regular updating of Python visuals or datasets, ensuring that the information remains current and relevant. The personal gateway serves as a crucial link between Power BI and the local environment, enabling seamless communication and data refreshes for datasets that leverage R or Python functionalities. If you would like more information about setting up a gateway, please refer to the links in the *Further reading* section of this chapter.

The preceding examples provide an introduction to the potential scripts you can run using R and Python within Power BI and Power Query. In the next section, you will learn how you can use machine learning to clean your data.

Using ML to clean data

In addition to being a market-leading visualization platform, Power BI offers a suite of built-in machine learning features that empower users to take their data analysis and preparation to the next level. In this section, we will explore those features within Power BI and understand how they can be harnessed to streamline data cleaning, preparation, and enhancement.

Data cleaning with anomaly detection

Data cleaning is often the first step in the data preparation process. Anomalies or outliers in the data can skew analysis results and compromise the quality of reports. Power BI's built-in anomaly detection feature can automatically identify and flag data points that deviate significantly from the norm. Power BI's anomaly detection leverages machine learning algorithms to detect data points that are statistically different from the rest. Users can set the sensitivity level to control the number of anomalies detected.

Here are some examples of how anomaly detection could be implemented:

- **Quality control**: Identify defective products or data entry errors in manufacturing and production data

- **Financial fraud detection**: Automatically flag suspicious transactions in financial datasets

- **Network security**: Detect abnormal network behavior and potential security breaches

Data preparation with AutoML

Data preparation often involves transforming and shaping data to make it suitable for analysis. Power BI's **automated machine learning (AutoML)** capabilities can simplify the process by providing data transformation suggestions and automating routine tasks.

AutoML in Power BI suggests and generates transformation steps based on the data's characteristics, such as missing values, data types, and patterns. It uses machine learning to understand the data's structure and provides actionable recommendations.

This feature has some powerful applications and uses, so here are some of the most common use cases for AutoML:

- **Feature engineering**: Automatically create new features from existing data, such as aggregations, one-hot encoding, and time-based calculations. For those not familiar with data science or machine learning practices, these can be summarized as follows:

  - **Feature engineering** is a crucial aspect of machine learning that involves transforming and creating new features (variables) from existing data to improve the performance of a predictive model. The goal is to provide the model with more relevant and informative input features, ultimately enhancing its ability to make accurate predictions.

  - **Aggregations** in feature engineering involve summarizing or combining multiple data points into a single value. For example, you might calculate the average, sum, or count of a specific attribute for a group of related data points.

- **One-hot encoding** is a technique used to represent categorical variables numerically. In many machine learning algorithms, including those based on mathematical equations, categorical data needs to be converted into a numerical format. One-hot encoding achieves this by creating binary columns for each category and assigning a 1 or 0 to indicate the presence or absence of that category for each data point. This ensures that the algorithm can effectively interpret and utilize categorical information.

- **Handling missing data**: Automatically impute missing values using appropriate methods

- **Data type conversion**: Suggest data type conversions based on the data's statistical properties

The steps to implement AutoML are as follows (you'll need to log in to your Power BI service and workspace, as AutoML is not available in Power BI Desktop):

1. Create a new dataflow: Within your Power BI online service workspace, create a new dataflow (Dataflow Gen1), named `Dataflows` in my example workspace, as shown:

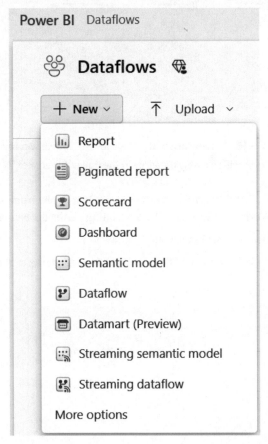

Figure 9.12 – Screenshot of the drop-down menu from selecting New within a Power BI workspace

2. Select **Define new table**: Out of the four presented options, select **Define new table**.

3. Select **Text/CSV**: You will be presented with many connector options to connect to your data or simply upload a file. Here, we can select **Text/CSV** and then use the following file path linked to the GitHub repo: `https://raw.githubusercontent.com/PacktPublishing/ Data-Cleaning-with-Power-BI/main/online_shoppers_intention.csv`.

    Select **Next** to continue.

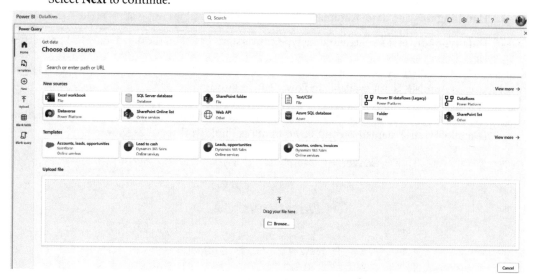

Figure 9.13 – Screenshot of the Choose data source window from
within a new dataflow in the Power BI service

4. Select **Transform Data**: This will open the Power Query view from within the dataflow. Here, you can choose to carry out further EDA or cleaning on the file before we add AutoML to this.

5. Select **Save & Close**: This will save your dataflow as is.

6. Name your dataflow: Here, we will be prompted to add a name to the dataflow, as shown:

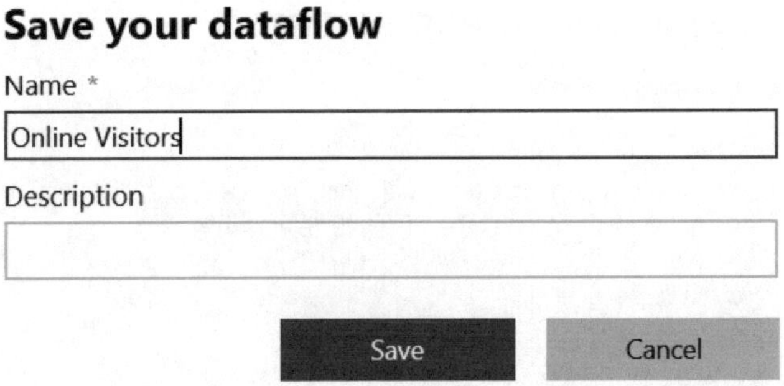

Save your dataflow

Name *

Online Visitors

Description

Save	Cancel

Figure 9.14 – Screenshot of the Save your dataflow window from within the Power BI service

7. Next, you will be presented with a view from within the dataflow, which shows the tables currently being returned/output from this dataflow. It's important to note that there may be more than the ones shown if some tables/queries have the **Enable load** option unselected. An example of the actions that will appear on the right-hand side of the dataflow is shown here:

ACTIONS

Figure 9.15 – Screenshot of the actions available to apply against
a particular table or query within a dataflow

Before continuing with the example steps, you might be interested in what each of these actions does. Here is a breakdown summary for you to better understand the outcome of each button:

- **Edit Table**: This will allow you to edit or transform the table, effectively reopening the Power Query window from within the dataflow.

- **Apply ML Model**: This will allow you to apply the ML model to the selected table, which you will be doing shortly.

- **Properties**: This will open the **Properties** window for this particular table, and more importantly, the description of this table. Here, you can add further detail on what information is held in this table.

- **Incremental Refresh**: This will open the window shown as follows, which will allow you to configure **Incremental refresh** on this particular table of the dataflow. This can be extremely useful when you have large data tables within your dataflow. Note that you will need a Date column in your table in order for this to work.

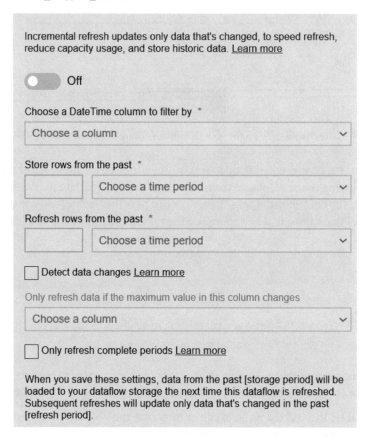

Figure 9.16 – Screenshot of the Incremental refresh window within a dataflow
where users can set up and manage their incremental refreshes

8. Select **Apply ML Model** and then select **Add a machine learning model**: In the dataflow editor,
    click on **Add a machine learning model** to begin our model.

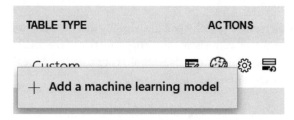

Figure 9.17 – Screenshot of the options menu when selecting Apply ML Model in the dataflow

9. Select tables and columns: Next, select the tables and columns we would like to use within our model predictions, as shown. In this example, let's try to predict whether someone will revisit at the weekend.

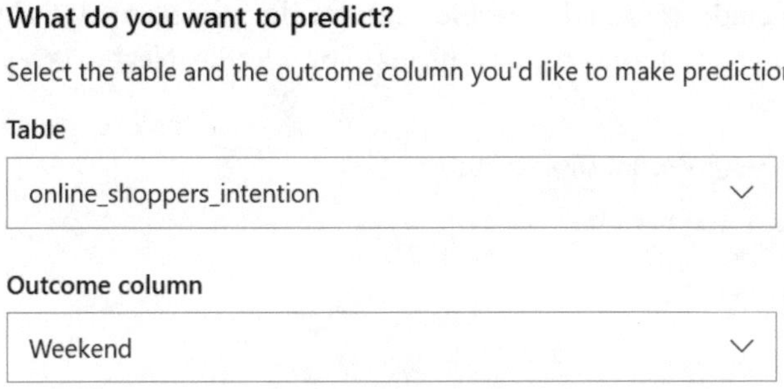

What do you want to predict?

Select the table and the outcome column you'd like to make predictions about so we can recommend the best model.

Table

online_shoppers_intention ⌄

Outcome column

Weekend ⌄

Figure 9.18 – Screenshot of the model creation window highlighting
which table and column we would like this model to apply to

10. Choose the model: The next window will present you with the option to select which classification model to use based on the column you selected in the previous step. Here, we only have the option to select the **Binary Prediction** classification because the field we selected, Weekend, is a **true/false** field. You can continue by selecting **true** in the **Choose a target outcome** field and selecting **Next**.

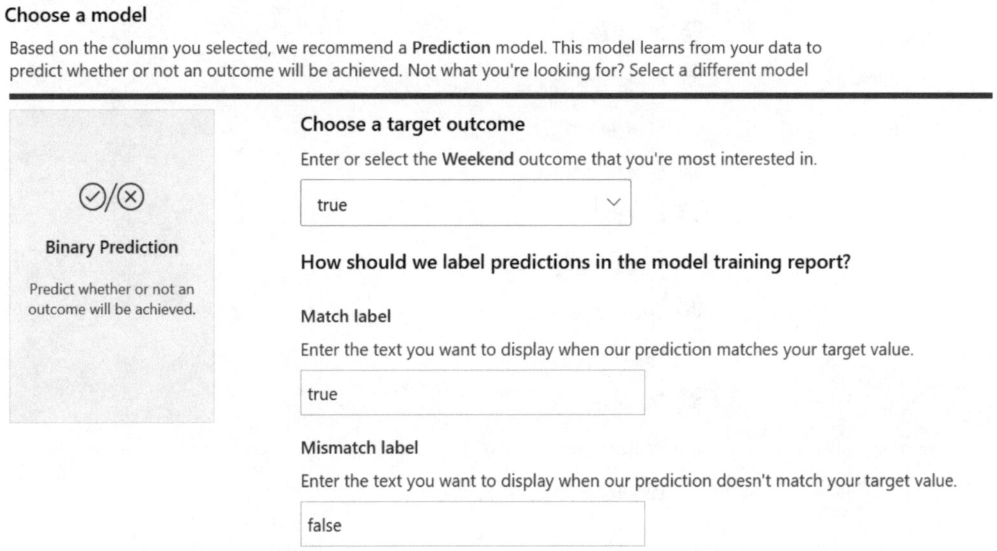

Choose a model

Based on the column you selected, we recommend a **Prediction** model. This model learns from your data to predict whether or not an outcome will be achieved. Not what you're looking for? Select a different model

⊘/⊗

Binary Prediction

Predict whether or not an outcome will be achieved.

Choose a target outcome

Enter or select the **Weekend** outcome that you're most interested in.

true ⌄

How should we label predictions in the model training report?

Match label

Enter the text you want to display when our prediction matches your target value.

true

Mismatch label

Enter the text you want to display when our prediction doesn't match your target value.

false

Figure 9.19 – Screenshot of Choose a model from with the model creation wizard

11. Select columns to be included in the model: Power BI conducts an initial examination of a data sample and proposes potential inputs to enhance prediction accuracy. If a specific column is not recommended, Power BI provides explanations alongside it. You have the flexibility to modify selections, choosing to include or exclude specific fields for the model's analysis by toggling checkboxes next to column names. The process is finalized by selecting **Next** to accept the chosen inputs, as shown:

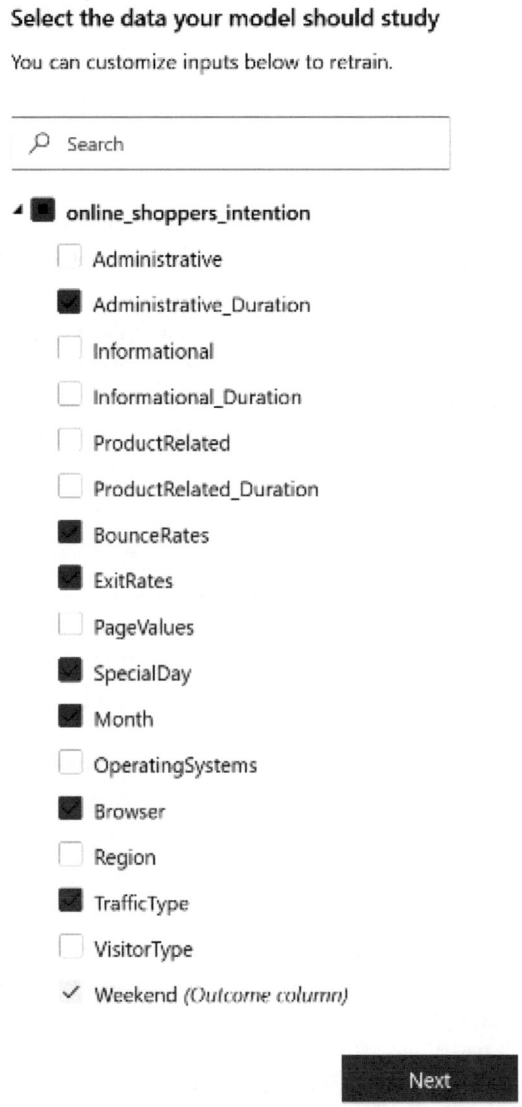

Select the data your model should study

You can customize inputs below to retrain.

🔍 Search

▲ ◼ online_shoppers_intention

   ☐ Administrative

   ☑ Administrative_Duration

   ☐ Informational

   ☐ Informational_Duration

   ☐ ProductRelated

   ☐ ProductRelated_Duration

   ☑ BounceRates

   ☑ ExitRates

   ☐ PageValues

   ☑ SpecialDay

   ☑ Month

   ☐ OperatingSystems

   ☑ Browser

   ☐ Region

   ☑ TrafficType

   ☐ VisitorType

   ✓ Weekend *(Outcome column)*

[Next]

Figure 9.20 – Screenshot showing the recommended columns Power BI has selected to be included within your model study

12. **Name and train your model:** In the final window, you will be presented with the option to name your model and, most importantly, set the time allotted to train your model. The longer you train your model, the more accurate the results.

Name and train your model

Model name

WeekendVisitors

Description

(Optional)

Training time

The longer you train your model, the more accurate the results. Train for a short time if you just want to make sure you've selected the right data. Keep in mind, this won't result in the best model.

5 minutes ——————————————— 360 minutes | 54 minutes

What happens next?

We'll take a statistically significant sample of your data and train the model using 80% of it. We'll then test the model on the remaining 20% and go over the Prediction accuracy in a report. You can find the training and test data we used in your workspace.

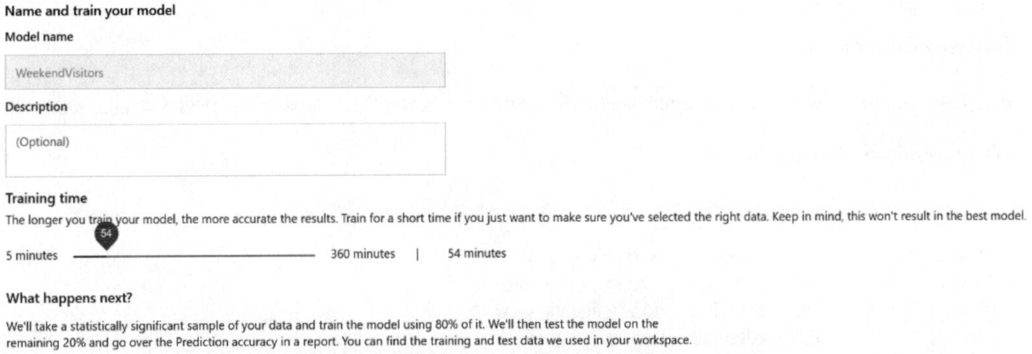

Figure 9.21 – Screenshot of the final window to name your model
and set the allotted training time for the model

13. **Review and apply:** Review the suggested settings, adjust if needed, and apply them to your model to complete the setup. It's important to note that the training of the model doesn't start until you click on the **Save and Train** button.

> **Connectivity issues**
>
> If you get errors from within your dataflow, this might be due to your connections. To adjust this, simply select **Edit the dataflow**. This will open warnings across the new ML tables that suggest you need to edit credentials to access the table. Alternatively, this can be done by selecting **Settings** in the header bar and then selecting owner BI Settings. This will open the following settings page, where you can then navigate to the **Dataflows** tab. Here, you will see the settings for your particular dataflow, including credentials. Then, simply edit the connections that have warning signs, as shown in the following figure.

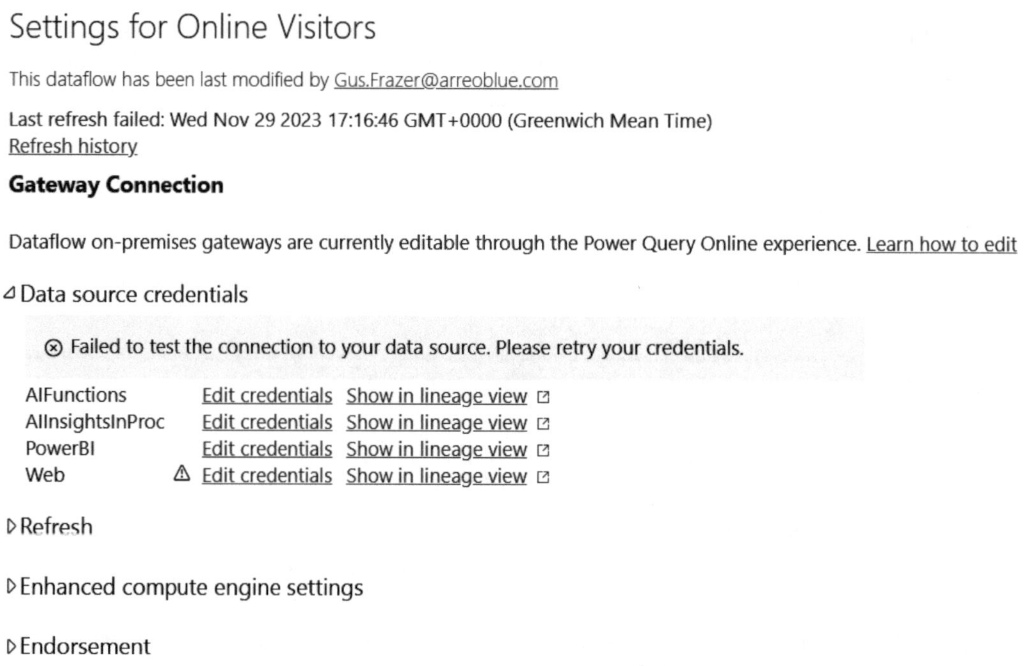

Settings for Online Visitors

This dataflow has been last modified by Gus.Frazer@arreoblue.com

Last refresh failed: Wed Nov 29 2023 17:16:46 GMT+0000 (Greenwich Mean Time)
Refresh history

Gateway Connection

Dataflow on-premises gateways are currently editable through the Power Query Online experience. Learn how to edit

◁ Data source credentials

⊗ Failed to test the connection to your data source. Please retry your credentials.

AIFunctions		Edit credentials	Show in lineage view ⌷
AIInsightsInProc		Edit credentials	Show in lineage view ⌷
PowerBI		Edit credentials	Show in lineage view ⌷
Web	⚠	Edit credentials	Show in lineage view ⌷

▷ Refresh

▷ Enhanced compute engine settings

▷ Endorsement

Figure 9.22 – Screenshot of the settings window for the dataflow we have
named Online Visitors detailing connection credential issues

14. **Return to the dataflow**: Now, return to the dataflow and select **Machine learning models**, as shown, to see the models we have created for this dataflow. Here, you will see that the model status has now been changed to **Trained**.

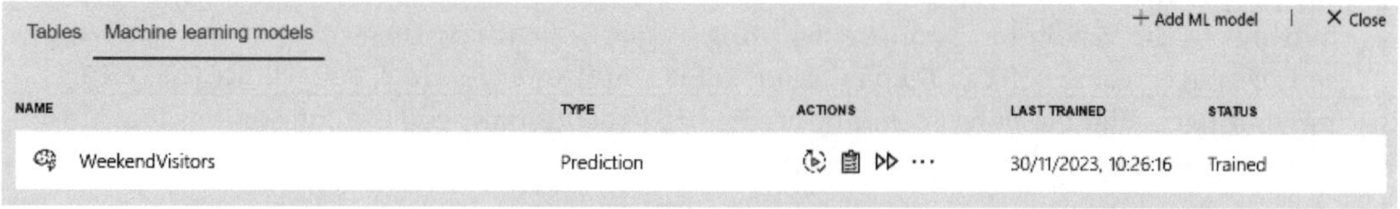

| | Tables   Machine learning models | | | | + Add ML model \| ✕ Close |
NAME		TYPE	ACTIONS	LAST TRAINED	STATUS
⏣ WeekendVisitors		Prediction	⏯ 🗎 ⏭ ⋯	30/11/2023, 10:26:16	Trained

Figure 9.23 – Screenshot showing the model created and the status, which is Trained

Once the machine model training has been completed and the time allotted for learning has passed, you will then be able to open the training report, which provides details on the results of the model training.

15. Select **View Training Report**: The second action button will allow you to view the training report of the model you just created. The following example shows the `WeekendVisitors` model.

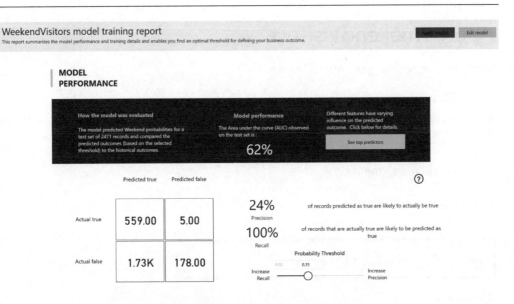

Figure 9.24 – Screenshot showing the model training report

This report allows you to review performance and statistics for the model created, with the ability to explore the top predictors as well as the options to adjust the probability thresholds of your model from recall to precision.

For those who are new to machine learning, you may not have heard terms previously such as *predictors* or *probability thresholds*. If you haven't seen these phrases before, then take note of the next paragraphs.

In the context of machine learning, **predictors** (which can also be known as features or independent variables) are the input elements that the model uses to make predictions. These can be various types of data, such as numerical values, categorical labels, or any other relevant information that helps the model understand patterns and relationships within the data. In the previous example, you selected predictors such as bounce rates and exit rates.

When working with machine learning models, we introduce classification and make decisions based on probabilities. The model assigns a probability to each prediction, indicating the likelihood of a certain class or outcome. The **probability threshold** is a value that determines how confident the model needs to be before making a prediction.

Training details provide a further breakdown of how the model was trained.

Having reviewed the model, we are now in a position to apply the model to our dataflow entity (the original table we loaded). You have to select **Apply model** to invoke the model. This will present the following screen and allow you to specify which dataflow entity to apply this model to:

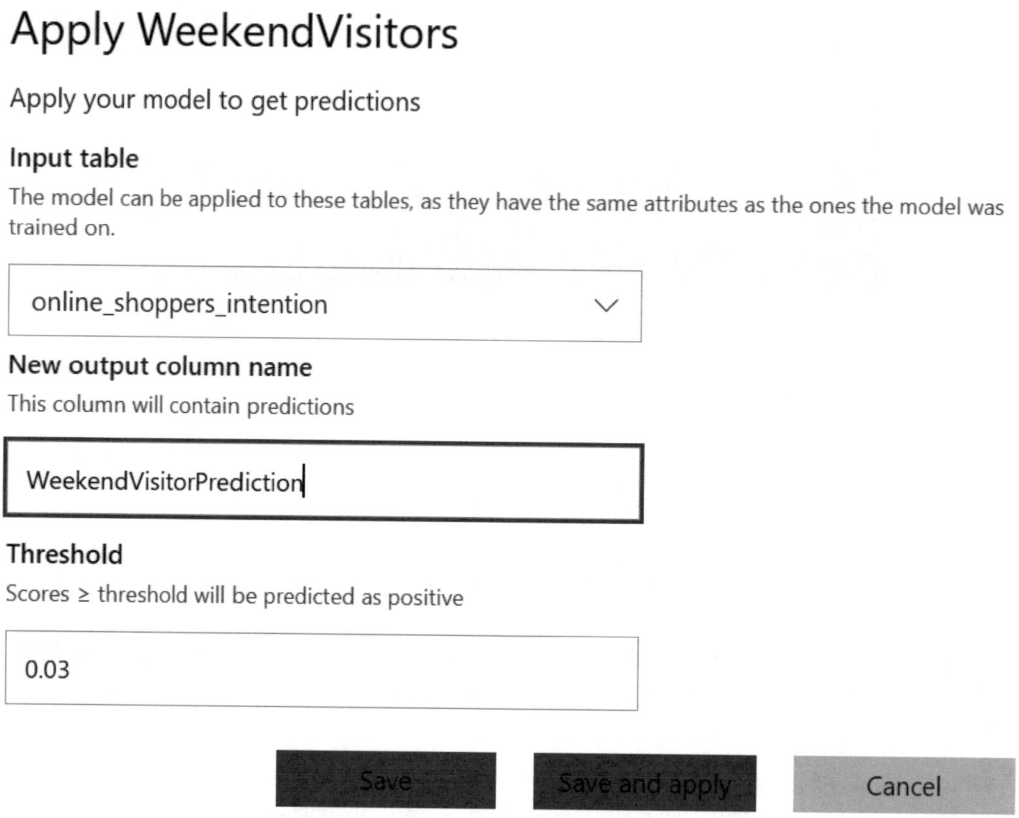

Apply WeekendVisitors

Apply your model to get predictions

Input table

The model can be applied to these tables, as they have the same attributes as the ones the model was trained on.

```
online_shoppers_intention                          ⌄
```

New output column name

This column will contain predictions

```
WeekendVisitorPrediction
```

Threshold

Scores ≥ threshold will be predicted as positive

```
0.03
```

Save | Save and apply | Cancel

Figure 9.25 – Screenshot of the confirmation window to apply the model to our original table

By selecting **Save and apply**, Power BI creates two new tables, with the suffix `enriched WeekendVisitors` (or whatever you have named your model). This is to differentiate between the original table and the enriched table of data we have just created.

In this case, applying the model to the `Online Visitors` table creates the following:

- `online_shoppers_intention enriched WeekendVisitors`, which includes the predicted output from the model. The following example shows the prediction of **TRUE** for a visit at the weekend as well as a scoring for this.

	VisitorType	Weekend	Revenue	1.2 WeekendVisitorPrediction.ExplanationIndex	WeekendVisitorPrediction.Outcome	WeekendVisitorPrediction.PredictionScore
1	Returning_Visitor	FALSE	null	1	TRUE	54
2	Returning_Visitor	TRUE	null	2	TRUE	55
3	Returning_Visitor	FALSE	null	3	TRUE	37
4	Returning_Visitor	TRUE	null	4	TRUE	56
5	Returning_Visitor	TRUE	null	5	TRUE	67
6	Returning_Visitor	FALSE	null	6	TRUE	63
7	New_Visitor	FALSE	null	7	TRUE	42
8	Returning_Visitor	TRUE	null	8	TRUE	49

Figure 9.26 – Screenshot shows the results from the predictions with an outcome and prediction score

- `online_shoppers_intention enriched WeekendVisitors explanations`, which contains top record-specific influencers for the prediction.

Applying the prediction model to our original table creates the preceding new tables and adds four columns to the original columns that were in the table: `Outcome`, `PredictionScore`, `PredictionExplanation`, and `ExplanationIndex`, each with a `WeekendVisitor` prediction prefix.

In this example, in the top row, you can see that although a visitor didn't visit at the weekend, the prediction model has predicted that they would visit at the weekend with a score of 54. This data can then be used within a visualization to tell a further story about the prediction data.

Although we won't deep dive into the queries within this section, it's important to note that newly created dataflow tables use M queries in the background to action the ML model. The following is an example screenshot of this from the table named `online_shoppers_intention enriched WeekendVisitors`:

Advanced editor   ×

```
1   let
2       Source = online_shoppers_intention,
3       AddExplanationsIndex = Table.AddIndexColumn(Source, Text.Combine({"WeekendVisitorPrediction", "ExplanationIndex"}, "."), 1, 1),
4       #"Invoked WeekendVisitors.Score" = WeekendVisitors.Score(AddExplanationsIndex, "WeekendVisitorPrediction", 0.03),
5       DataflowPrecalculatedSource = PowerBI.Dataflows(),
6       Workspace = DataflowPrecalculatedSource([workspaceId = "e8448fe8-69eb-454b-b15f-0a1156df3263"]){[Data],
7       Dataflow = Workspace{[dataflowId = "7d753Bcf-629f-4ddc-915a-cb3971597981"]}{[Data],
8       EnrichedPreview = Dataflow{[entity = "online_shoppers_intention enriched WeekendVisitors"]}{[Data],
9       #"Enriched results" = if (Table.First(#"Invoked WeekendVisitors.Score")[#"WeekendVisitorPrediction.PredictionExplanation"]="Unavailable"} = true then #"EnrichedPreview" else #"Invoked WeekendVisitors.Score"
10  in
11      #"Enriched results"
```

Figure 9.27 – Screenshot of the M query created for the online_
shoppers_intention enriched WeekendVisitors table

Here, we can see that the previous query then invokes a function that was created earlier in the background called `WeekendVisitors.Score`. This function consists of a more complex query to actually run the model and apply a score, as we can see in the following example:

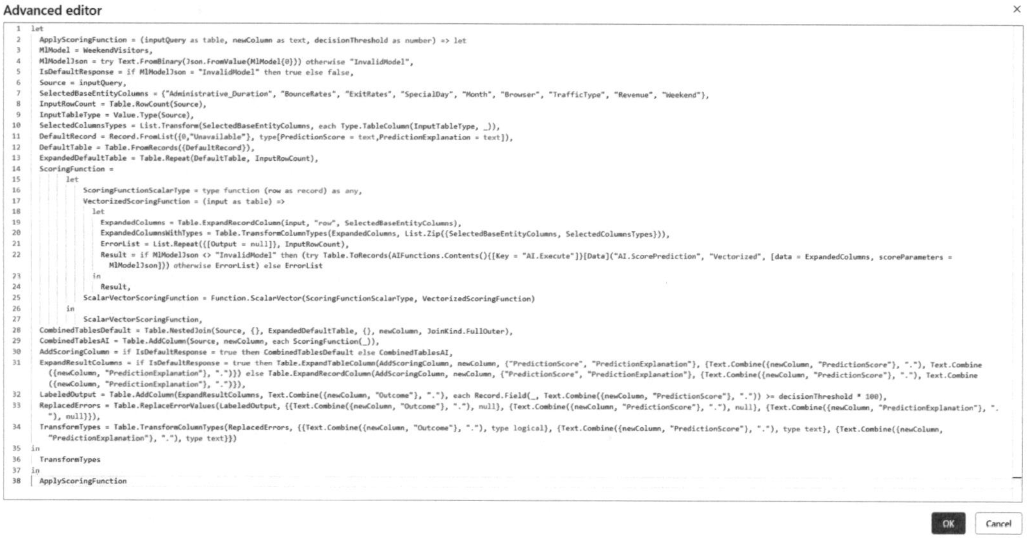

Advanced editor

```
let
  ApplyScoringFunction = (inputQuery as table, newColumn as text, decisionThreshold as number) => let
  MlModel = WeekendVisitors,
  MlModelJson = try Text.FromBinary(Json.FromValue(MlModel{0})) otherwise "InvalidModel",
  IsDefaultResponse = if MlModelJson = "InvalidModel" then true else false,
  Source = inputQuery,
  SelectedBaseEntityColumns = {"Administrative_Duration", "BounceRates", "ExitRates", "SpecialDay", "Month", "Browser", "TrafficType", "Revenue", "Weekend"},
  InputRowCount = Table.RowCount(Source),
  InputTableType = Value.Type(Source),
  SelectedColumnsTypes = List.Transform(SelectedBaseEntityColumns, each Type.TableColumn(InputTableType, _)),
  DefaultRecord = Record.FromList({0,"Unavailable"}, type[PredictionScore = text,PredictionExplanation = text]),
  DefaultTable = Table.FromRecords({DefaultRecord}),
  ExpandedDefaultTable = Table.Repeat(DefaultTable, InputRowCount),
  ScoringFunction =
        let
            ScoringFunctionScalarType = type function (row as record) as any,
            VectorizedScoringFunction = (input as table) =>
              let
                ExpandedColumns = Table.ExpandRecordColumn(input, "row", SelectedBaseEntityColumns),
                ExpandedColumnsWithTypes = Table.TransformColumnTypes(ExpandedColumns, List.Zip({SelectedBaseEntityColumns, SelectedColumnsTypes})),
                ErrorList = List.Repeat({[Output = null]}, InputRowCount),
                Result = if MlModelJson <> "InvalidModel" then (try Table.ToRecords(AIFunctions.Contents(){[Key = "AI.Execute"]}[Data]("AI.ScorePrediction", "Vectorized", [data = ExpandedColumns, scoreParameters =
                  MlModelJson])) otherwise ErrorList) else ErrorList
              in
                Result,
            ScalarVectorScoringFunction = Function.ScalarVector(ScoringFunctionScalarType, VectorizedScoringFunction)
        in
            ScalarVectorScoringFunction,
  CombinedTablesDefault = Table.NestedJoin(Source, {}, ExpandedDefaultTable, {}, newColumn, JoinKind.FullOuter),
  CombinedTablesAI = Table.AddColumn(Source, newColumn, each ScoringFunction(_)),
  AddScoringColumn = if IsDefaultResponse = true then CombinedTablesDefault else CombinedTablesAI,
  ExpandResultColumns = if IsDefaultResponse = true then Table.ExpandTableColumn(AddScoringColumn, newColumn, {"PredictionScore", "PredictionExplanation"}, {Text.Combine({newColumn, "PredictionScore"}, "."), Text.Combine
    ({newColumn, "PredictionExplanation"}, ".")}) else Table.ExpandRecordColumn(AddScoringColumn, newColumn, {"PredictionScore", "PredictionExplanation"}, {Text.Combine({newColumn, "PredictionScore"}, "."), Text.Combine
    ({newColumn, "PredictionExplanation"}, ".")}),
  LabeledOutput = Table.AddColumn(ExpandResultColumns, Text.Combine({newColumn, "Outcome"}, "."), each Record.Field(_, Text.Combine({newColumn, "PredictionScore"}, ".")) >= decisionThreshold * 100),
  ReplacedErrors = Table.ReplaceErrorValues(LabeledOutput, {{Text.Combine({newColumn, "Outcome"}, "."), null}, {Text.Combine({newColumn, "PredictionScore"}, "."), null}, {Text.Combine({newColumn, "PredictionExplanation"}, ".
    "), null}}),
  TransformTypes = Table.TransformColumnTypes(ReplacedErrors, {{Text.Combine({newColumn, "Outcome"}, "."), type logical}, {Text.Combine({newColumn, "PredictionScore"}, "."), type text}, {Text.Combine({newColumn,
    "PredictionExplanation"}, "."), type text}})
in
  TransformTypes
in
  ApplyScoringFunction
```

OK Cancel

Figure 9.28 – Screenshot of the M query created to output the WeekendVisitors.Score function

In this section, you took your first steps in creating machine learning models and applying them to your data. In the final section, you will learn more about using AI insights within your data analysis and preparation.

Data enhancement with AI Insights

Power BI also offers AI Insights, which allows users to integrate pre-built machine learning models into their reports. These models can generate additional insights and enhance the data with predictive analytics. This is a great feature to help automate the preparation of data if you need to add new data to your dataset quickly; however, this again depends on your data, as AI Insights has a limited number of models.

AI Insights provides pre-trained models that cover various use cases, such as sentiment analysis, image recognition, and text analytics. Users can easily integrate these models into their Power BI reports. In order to use this feature of Power BI, you will need a Premium license. Here are a few examples where this particular feature adds the most value:

- **Sentiment analysis**: Understand customer sentiment by analyzing textual feedback and reviews
- **Image recognition**: Automatically categorize and tag images in reports, such as identifying product categories
- **Text analytics**: Extract key phrases, entities, and sentiments from unstructured text data

Let's go through the steps to implement AI Insights. In this example, you will connect to Twitter/X data from celebrities and leverage AI Insights to help determine what language these social posts are in, thus allowing you to carry out analysis on social media posts in specific languages:

1. From Power BI Desktop, select **Get data** and then select **Text/CSV**.

2. Enter the following URL and select **Open**:

    ```
    https://raw.githubusercontent.com/PacktPublishing/Data-Cleaning-
    with-Power-BI/main/Twitter%20Tweets.csv
    ```

3. Select **Transform data** to open the Power Query Editor.

4. Select **Add Column** on the ribbon toolbar. You will see **AI Insights** on the far right-hand side of the ribbon, as shown:

Figure 9.29 – Screenshot of the Add Column ribbon in Power Query Editor

5. In the Power BI report, select the column you want to enhance with AI Insights, and then choose the relevant AI model. In this case, we would like to use **Text Analytics** as we want to analyze the language of the posts. This will open the AI Insights configuration window for **Text Analytics**.

6. Select **Detect language** from the configuration window for **Text Analytics**, as shown. Notice by default that it has already selected the column named content. In the lower-left corner, you can also adjust which Premium workspace you are using to run AI Insights.

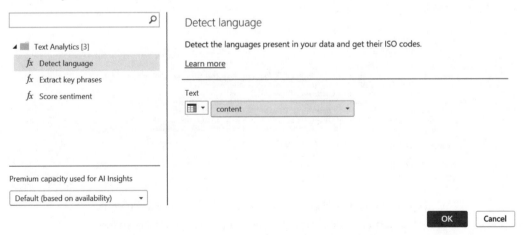

Figure 9.30 – Screenshot of the Text Analytics AI Insights configuration window in Power Query Editor

7. Data enhancement: The AI model will then process the data point and generate additional insights, which will be added to your data as shown in the following example:

ABC Detect language.Detected Language Name ▼	ABC Detect language.Detected Language ISO Code ▼
● Valid 100% ● Error 0% ● Empty 0%	● Valid 100% ● Error 0% ● Empty 0%
12 distinct, 3 unique	12 distinct, 3 unique
English	en
English	en
English	en
English	en
English	en
English	en
English	en

Figure 9.31 – Screenshot of the output from using AI Insights to detect the language of the social posts column ribbon in Power Query Editor

From these simple transformations, you could potentially now add a further layer to your social media analytics. Similar to the previous example in *Figure 9.27*, Power Query has used M to actually connect to cognitive services to carry out the AI Insights analysis. The following figure shows the M query generated by Power Query to do this:

Figure 9.32 – Screenshot of the M query created in the background to leverage AI Insights and cognitive services in Power Query Editor

As you explore these capabilities within Power BI, you'll be better equipped to work with data of varying complexities, leading to more accurate and insightful reports and visualizations. AI Insights is a great time-saver when it comes to automating the preparation of your data but it really does depend on the use case you have and the main point: whether you have a Premium license in order to be able to use it in the first place. By harnessing the power of machine learning in Power BI, you'll not only save time but also discover hidden patterns and gain deeper insights from your data.

Summary

In this chapter, you explored a range of advanced data cleaning and preparation techniques within Power BI's Query Editor.

The chapter began by introducing the power of this tool and highlighted two critical techniques: fuzzy matching, which identifies and consolidates similar strings within your data, and fill down, which fills gaps in your dataset with values from the previous row. We also outlined some best practices for using these tools, emphasizing data backup, sensitivity adjustment, regular validation, documentation, and the iterative nature of data cleaning.

The chapter also introduced the concept of using custom data scripts in languages such as R and Python, illustrating their benefits for complex transformations, statistical analysis, third-party libraries, and data integration.

The machine learning capabilities within Power BI were explored, including fuzzy matching, AutoML, and AI Insights, which enable anomaly identification, automated data preparation, and data enhancement with pre-trained models, respectively. These features empower users to streamline data cleaning, preparation, and enhancement, ultimately improving the quality of reports and visualizations.

The outcome of learning about the advanced data cleaning and preparation techniques presented in this chapter is that you have significantly enhanced your skill set for working with data in Power BI. You will have acquired proficiency in employing advanced tools and methodologies to address common challenges in data quality and consistency. The specific outcomes include the following:

- **Mastery of Query Editor techniques**: You have a deep understanding of advanced features within Power BI from within Dataflow Gen1, such as fuzzy matching and fill down. These techniques empower users to efficiently handle inconsistent data, merge duplicate records, standardize text, and fill gaps, ensuring a more accurate and reliable dataset.

- **Custom data scripting with R and Python**: You are equipped with the knowledge of integrating custom data scripts in the R and Python languages. This capability allows for more complex transformations, statistical analyses, and leveraging third-party libraries, expanding the scope of data manipulation beyond the capabilities of the standard Power Query M formula language.

- **Utilizing machine learning for data cleaning and preparation**: You have gained insights into leveraging machine learning capabilities within Power BI for data cleaning and preparation tasks. This includes fuzzy matching to build a more complete dataset, AutoML for insights into your website predictions, and AI Insights for integrating pre-built machine learning models into reports for predictive analytics.

- **Time savings and efficiency**: The adoption of these advanced tools and methodologies is designed to streamline the data cleaning and preparation processes. You will experience time savings and increased efficiency in handling diverse and complex datasets, allowing for a more agile and responsive approach to data analysis.

- **Foundation for further exploration**: The chapter served as a foundation for further exploration, encouraging you to delve into the creation of custom functions in the next chapter.

In the next chapter, you will delve into the creation of custom functions to automate complex data manipulations and further enhance data preparation capabilities.

Questions

1. What are the two essential techniques discussed in the chapter for cleaning and preparing data using the Query Editor in Power BI?

    A. Fuzzy matching and fill up

    B. Data profiling and sorting

    C. Fuzzy matching and fill down

    D. Data imputation and statistical analysis

2. In the context of fuzzy matching, what is the similarity score range, and what does it indicate?

    A. Range from 1 to 10, indicating similarity strength

    B. Range from 0 to 100, indicating confidence level

    C. Range from 0 to 1, indicating no to perfect similarity

    D. Range from -1 to 1, indicating negative to positive correlation

3. When is the fill down technique in Power BI's Query Editor particularly useful?

    A. When you want to skip data gaps

    B. When dealing with categorical data

    C. When you need to perform calculations on filled values

    D. When working with time series data and maintaining data continuity

4. What is a crucial best practice emphasized when working with fuzzy matching and fill down in Power BI?

    A. Occasionally document the steps taken during data cleaning

    B. Create and load multiple versions of the data

    C. Regularly refresh your data

    D. Regularly validate the results of data cleaning efforts and maintain documentation

5. What is the primary purpose of using scripts in languages such as R and Python in Power BI?

    A. To replace Power Query

    B. To add complexity to data models

    C. To extend the capabilities of Power BI by leveraging external ecosystems

    D. To simplify the data cleaning process

6. In the steps for using R in Power BI, what is the purpose of the **Run R Script** option in the Power Query Editor from within Dataflow Gen1?

    A. To download R packages

    B. To write R scripts

    C. To visualize R outputs

    D. To run machine learning models

7. What are the benefits of using R and Python scripts in Power BI for data preparation?

    A. Limited data manipulation capabilities

    B. Integration with external data sources

    C. Only suitable for simple transformations

    D. Exclusively designed for statistical analysis

8. Which built-in machine learning feature in Power BI is used for identifying and addressing outliers in data?

    A. AutoML

    B. AI Insights

    C. Anomaly Detection

    D. Predictive Modeling

9. What is the purpose of AutoML in Power BI?

    A. Manual data transformation

    B. Automated data preparation with machine learning suggestions

    C. Exclusive focus on statistical analysis

    D. Integration of pre-built machine learning models

10. What are some common use cases for AI Insights in Power BI?

    A. Fuzzy matching and fill down

    B. Feature engineering and data type conversion

    C. Sentiment analysis, image recognition, and text analytics

    D. Anomaly detection and statistical analysis

10

Creating Custom Functions in Power Query

In this chapter, we will learn how to create custom **Power Query** functions in Power BI, covering the planning process, **parameters**, and the actual creation of the functions. We will start by understanding data requirements and defining the function's purpose and expected output, then we will learn about the different types of parameters and how to use them to make functions more flexible and reusable, and finally, we will see step by step how to write M code functions, and test and debug them.

Specifically, the following topics will be covered in this chapter:

- Planning for your custom function
- Using parameters
- Creating custom functions

Overall, this chapter will provide a comprehensive guide to creating custom functions in Power BI. From reading this chapter, you can expect to feel more confident in approaching situations where you would need to create a custom function in Power Query. You will have gained hands-on experience on the steps needed to actually build this into your own work.

Planning for your custom function

Creating custom functions in Power Query can be a powerful tool for automating and streamlining your data transformation processes. However, before you dive into the world of custom functions, it's essential to plan your approach carefully. In this section, we'll explore the key aspects of planning for your custom function, including defining the problem, identifying parameters, and setting clear objectives. Proper planning will ensure that your custom functions are efficient, effective, and aligned with your data preparation needs.

Defining the problem

The first step in planning for a custom function is to clearly define the problem you want to solve. What specific data transformation or manipulation task do you need to perform regularly?

For example, you might need to calculate the rolling average of sales data or create a custom date hierarchy. Identifying the problem is essential as it serves as the foundation for building your custom function.

Identifying parameters

Parameters are the variables or values that your custom function will take as input. They allow you to make your custom function versatile and applicable to a range of scenarios.

When identifying parameters, consider the following:

- **Data inputs**: What data or columns will your function operate on?
- **Thresholds and criteria**: Are there specific thresholds or criteria that users should be able to customize?
- **Data types**: Will your function handle different data types, and how should it behave with each type?

Setting clear objectives

Once you have defined the problem and parameters, having clear objectives for your custom function is crucial. What do you aim to achieve with this function, and what are the expected outcomes? Defining objectives helps you stay focused and ensures that your custom function meets your data transformation goals.

Using parameters

Parameters are a vital component of custom functions in Power Query. They allow you to create dynamic and flexible functions that can be adapted to different datasets and scenarios. In this section, we will introduce parameters, exploring the types of parameters available, how to define them, and best practices for their use.

Types of parameters

Power Query offers several types of parameters that you can use in your custom functions:

- **Text parameters**: These parameters accept text input, such as column names or descriptions
- **Number parameters**: Number parameters accept numeric values

- **List parameters**: You can create lists of values that users can select from

- **Table parameters**: Table parameters accept tables as input, allowing for more complex data structures

- **Function parameters**: You can even pass functions as parameters to create dynamic behavior

Defining parameters

To define parameters in Power Query, you need to access the **Manage Parameters** dialog, which can be accessed in the main toolbar as shown in the following screenshot. Here, you can specify the name, data type, and description of your parameters. You can also provide a default value, making your function more user friendly. Defining parameters is an essential step in creating functions that are adaptable to different use cases.

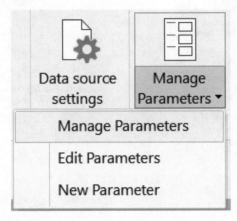

Figure 10.1 – Screenshot of the Manage Parameters menu in the Power Query toolbar

Example – Formula 1 wins

Let's put the skills we've taken from the previous two sections in planning and using parameters into practice as we begin by looking at a set of data. In this scenario, we will be looking at scraping some data from a website and then applying some transformations. This data will show us the top racing drivers of all time as well as their first or last wins (most recent wins). The problem here is that I only want to pull in one year and location column. To get around this, it would be ideal if we could create a parameter that can be used to select whether we want to pull in first or last win data.

The objective will be to then create custom columns that are dynamic and change depending on which parameter is selected. Let's get started by opening Power BI and executing the following steps:

1. **Selecting the connector**: Select **Get data** and then select the **Web** connector as shown:

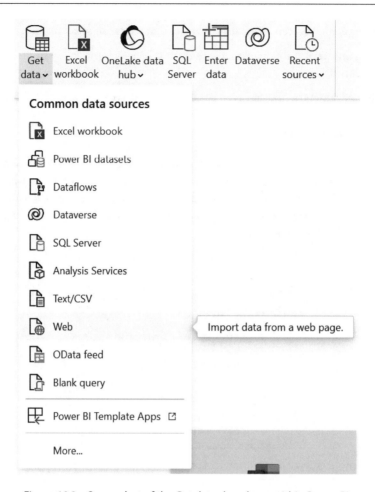

Figure 10.2 – Screenshot of the Get data dropdown within Power BI

2. **Input the URL**: In the prompt shown next, enter the following URL and then select **OK**: `https://en.wikipedia.org/wiki/List_of_Formula_One_Grand_Prix_winners`

From Web

◉ Basic   ◯ Advanced

URL

`https://en.wikipedia.org/wiki/List_of_Formula_One_Grand_Prix_winners`

OK   Cancel

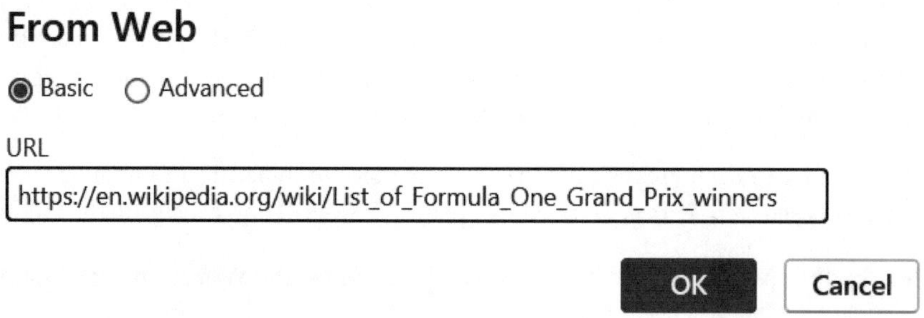

Figure 10.3 – Screenshot of the URL inputted into the web connecter window

3. This will bring up the **Access Web Content** window, where you can configure authentication to connect to the web content. For this example, we will use an anonymous authentication. Click on **Connect** to proceed.

4. **Select the tables and transform the data**: Once selected, the web connector will scrape the website URL for possible data entries and tables. The **Navigator** window (shown in the next image) will then appear with possible table options from scanning the web URL. On the left, you can see all the possible and suggested tables found within the web page. On the right, you can see a preview of this as well as the ability to switch the web page view, so you can also review this. In this example, you are going to select **Formula One Grand Prix Winners** and then select **Transform Data**.

Figure 10.4 – Screenshot of the Navigator window showing tables available from scanning the web page

5. **Split columns**: Before we begin creating a parameter and creating custom functions, we must first prepare the data. Currently, we have a column for the drivers' first win and a column for the drivers' last win, which includes a year and the Grand Prix location. Select the **First Win** column and select **Split Column** from the **Transform** tab. In the drop-down menu, select **By Delimiter**:

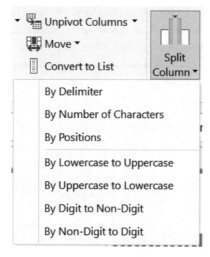

Figure 10.5 – Screenshot showing which of the Split Column functions to use

6. **Use space as delimiter**: Given the data, you want to extract two columns from the one, so in the example, we will select **Left-most delimiter** to avoid creating multiple columns, as you can see:

Split Column by Delimiter

Specify the delimiter used to split the text column.

Select or enter delimiter

    Space

Split at

⦿ Left-most delimiter

◯ Right-most delimiter

◯ Each occurrence of the delimiter

▷ Advanced options

Quote Character

    "

☐ Split using special characters

    Insert special character ▾

                        OK   Cancel

Figure 10.6 – Screenshot of the Split Column by Delimiter window

7. **Adjust the step properties**: Right-click on the step and select **Properties**. This will open the following window, allowing us to create a description and use a better naming convention for the step taken:

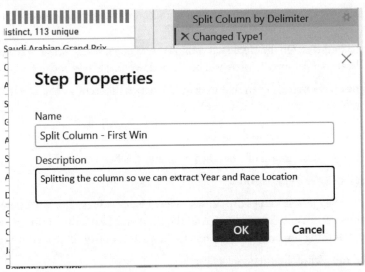

Figure 10.7 – Screenshot of the step being renamed and provided with a description of what the step is doing

8. **Repeat the steps for the Last Win column**: Now, repeat the previous steps for the final columns. You'll notice that when you use the split columns feature, it automatically adds a step to change the type of columns created by the split. This is to prevent an error from occurring by leaving un-typed columns in Power Query.

9. **Select Advanced Editor**: We now want to rename the four columns we have created. There are a number of ways we can do this; for example, we could adjust the previous M code used to split the columns, add four individual rename steps, or we could code in one rename step that adjusts all the columns. In this example, you will do the last option: creating a rename function in **Advanced Editor**.

10. **Add the M code**: The following M code should be added to the last line before the `in` function. Make a note to add a comma (,) at the end of the preceding line and also adjust the value after the `in` function:

```
    #"Renamed Columns" = Table.RenameColumns(#"Changed Type - Last
Wins",{{"First win.1", "First Win Year"},{"First win.2", "First
Win Location"},{"Last win.1", "Last Win Year"},{"Last win.2",
"Last Win Location"}})
in
    #"Renamed Columns"
```

The result should look like the following:

```
    #"Changed Type - Last Wins" = Table.TransformColumnTypes(#"Split Column - Last Wins",{{"Last win.1", Int64.Type}, {"Last win.2", type
text}}),
    #"Renamed Columns" = Table.RenameColumns(#"Changed Type - Last Wins",{{"First win.1", "First Win Year"},{"First win.2", "First Win
Location"},{"Last win.1", "Last Win Year"},{"Last win.2", "Last Win Location"}})
in
    #"Renamed Columns"
```

Figure 10.8 – Screenshot of the preceding code inputted within Advanced Editor

11. **Selecting parameter**: On the **Home** tab within Power Query, we can select **Manage Parameters** in order to create our parameter. There will be a dropdown that allows you to select **New Parameter**.

12. **Create your parameter**: Given that we would like two different values to select from, you will need to add these within the parameter settings:

    I.   Name the parameter as `First/Last Selector`.

    II.   Provide a description of what the parameter has been created for.

    III.   We can leave **Type** as **Any**.

    IV.   In the **Suggested Values** dropdown, select **List of values**. This will allow you to add the values you wish to use for this. Add the **First** and **Last** values into the list, as shown in the following screenshot, to be able to then select one of these values as a default value.

    V.   **Default Value** should be set as **First**.

    VI.   **Current Value** should be set as **First**.

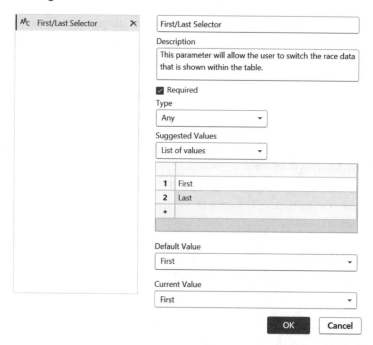

Figure 10.9 – Screenshot of the Manage Parameters window with inputs selected

13. **Add custom columns for first and last wins**: Now that we have added the parameter to achieve the output we would like, we can begin by creating a custom column that will return the year:

   I.   **Select Advanced Editor**: Instead of using the function custom column, we are going to script this into the code in **Advanced Editor**. This is because we also want to add a dynamic column title so that this changes depending on what we have selected in their parameter.

   II.   Add the following code to the bottom line of the code in **Advanced Editor**. Make sure to add a comma on the previous line to ensure there are no errors (taking care to ensure you are using the correct casing as M code is case sensitive):

```
#"Custom Column Year" = Table.AddColumn(#"Renamed Columns",
if #"First/Last Selector"= "First" then     "First Win -
Year" else "Last Win - Year", each if #"First/Last Selector"=
"First" then [First Win Year] else [Last Win Year]),

#"Customer Column Location" = Table.AddColumn(#"Custom Column
Year", if #"First/Last Selector"= "First" then "First Win -
Location" else "Last Win - Location", each if #"First/Last
Selector" = "First" then [First Win Location] else [Last Win
Location])

in

#"Customer Column Location"
```

These functions add an additional column to the table using the `Table.AddColumn` function. The syntax of these functions is as described here:

- `Table.AddColumn` (previous step/function name, new column name, the `IF` statement that will be applied for each row)

   - Note that you can use this function without the `IF` statement/argument

- This part of the code is used to create a dynamic column name:

```
if #"First/Last Selector"= "First" then "First Win Year" else
"Last Win Year"
```

- This part of the code is then used to dynamically change the contents of the column depending on which value of the parameter has been selected:

```
each if #"First/Last Selector"= "First" then [First Win Year]
else [Last Win Year]),
```

14. **Remove unwanted columns**: Now that we have created the dynamic columns, as a last step, you will need to remove the previous columns. As this step is happening last, it will not affect how the dynamic columns work. To do this, select the columns as shown, right-click, and select **Remove Columns**:

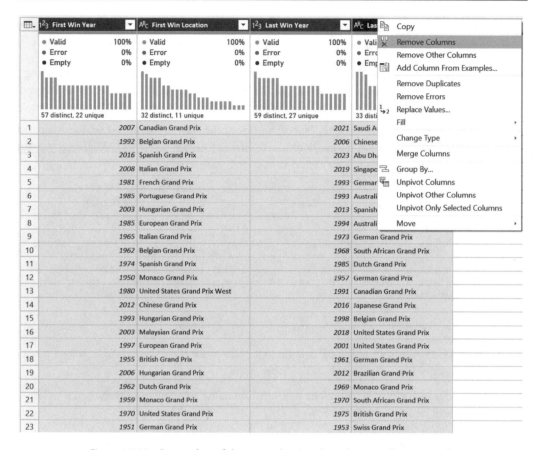

Figure 10.10 – Screenshot of the user selecting the columns to be removed

15. **Switch parameter**: Select **First/Last Selector** from the query list to open the parameter as shown:

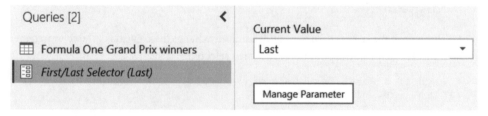

Figure 10.11 – Screenshot of the selected parameter query for First/Last Selector

16. **Select First from the dropdown**: This will adjust the parameter value.

17. **Select Formula One Grand Prix winners Query**: This will present the output of changing the parameter. As you'll see, this will change the columns in the data to show **First Win Year** and **First Win Location**.

The data is now prepared and ready for analysis. You have created a dynamic table/query that can now be quickly transitioned to show a different set of data at the switch of a parameter. In the next section, you can review some of the best practices for using parameters in the future.

Best practices for using parameters

When working with parameters, it's important to follow best practices:

- **Provide descriptive names**: Use clear and descriptive names for your parameters to make it easier for users to understand their purpose

- **Use default values**: Providing default values for parameters can make your function more user friendly and help users get started quickly

- **Test extensively**: Test your custom function with various parameter values to ensure it behaves as expected in different scenarios

- **Document parameters**: Document the purpose and usage of each parameter to help users understand how to use your custom function effectively

By adhering to these best practices, you can enhance the clarity, usability, and reliability of your custom functions within Power BI, ultimately improving the overall user experience.

Creating custom functions

With proper planning and an understanding of parameters, you're now ready to dive into creating custom functions in Power Query. This section will guide you through the process of building your custom function, including defining its structure, working with M code, and testing your function.

Defining the function structure

The structure of your custom function is crucial for its functionality and usability. Define the following aspects of your function:

- **Name**: Choose a descriptive name for your function

- **Parameters**: Specify the parameters your function will accept and their data types

- **Description**: Provide a clear and concise description of what your function does

- **Result**: Determine the expected result or output of your function

Writing M code

Power Query functions are created using the **M language**, which we touched upon earlier in this book. You'll need to write M code to define your function's behavior. It's essential to have a good grasp of M code to build effective custom functions as it allows you to perform data transformations, filter data, and create custom logic.

Testing and debugging

After writing the M code for your custom function, it's vital to thoroughly test and debug it. Test your function with different datasets and parameter values to ensure it works as expected. Debugging tools in Power Query, such as the formula bar and error messages, can help identify and fix issues in your code. One of the most common bugs found is when adding new code to the code in **Advanced Editor** and forgetting to add a comma after the last entry.

Documentation

This has also been mentioned a couple of times but is a key pivotal concept across all tools to help you prepare data: proper documentation is key to ensuring that users can understand and use your custom function effectively. Provide clear instructions on how to use the function, including explanations of parameters and expected outcomes. Good documentation promotes the adoption of your custom function among users.

Let's build upon the example in the previous section to create custom functions. There are two methods that stand out when creating a custom function, which could be to use the parameterized query you have created as a function. Or, alternatively, start a function from a blank query. In the following example, we will cover both scenarios.

Let's assume that I need to create multiple copies of the table with the different parameters selected. I could do this by using the entire query we created previously as a function. To do this, follow these steps:

1. Right-click on the query named `Formula One Grand Prix winners`.
2. Select **Create function…**.
3. Name the function `First/LastWinsToTable`. This will prompt Power Query to copy the query we created into a function while also grouping the queries together as shown:

First/LastWinsToTable [2]
Formula One Grand Prix winners
First/LastWinsToTable
Other Queries [1]
First/Last Selector (Last)

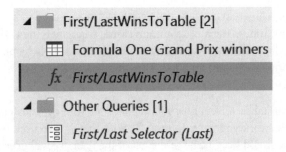

Figure 10.12 – Screenshot of the function created using the original query

As we can see in the query, our parameter is currently set to **Last**. If you wanted to invoke our function to create a new table with last wins highlighted, you could select **Invoke** from the function.

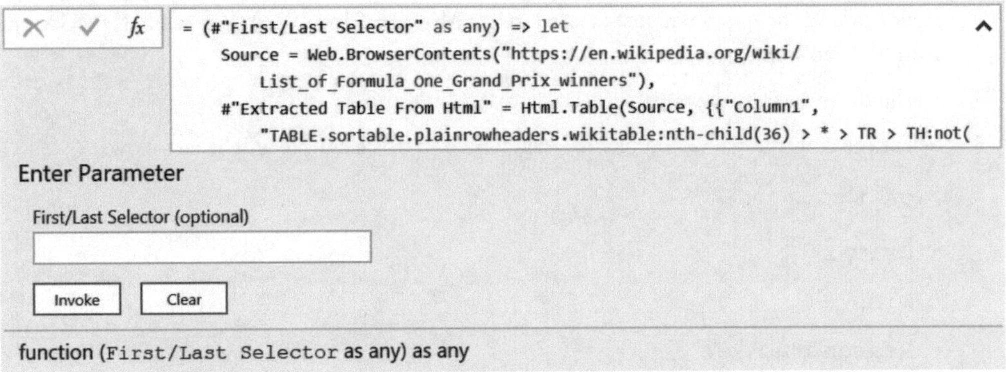

= (#"First/Last Selector" as any) => let
Source = Web.BrowserContents("https://en.wikipedia.org/wiki/List_of_Formula_One_Grand_Prix_winners"),
#"Extracted Table From Html" = Html.Table(Source, {{"Column1", "TABLE.sortable.plainrowheaders.wikitable:nth-child(36) > * > TR > TH:not(
Enter Parameter
First/Last Selector (optional)
Invoke
Clear
function (First/Last Selector as any) as any

Figure 10.13 – Screenshot of the function created named First/LastWinsToTable

4. Pressing **Invoke** will run the function query with the parameter selected and output a new table/query that can then be renamed `Last Wins` by right-clicking on the query name and selecting **Rename**.

First/LastWinsToTable [2]
Formula One Grand Prix winners
First/LastWinsToTable
Other Queries [2]
First/Last Selector (Last)
Invoked Function

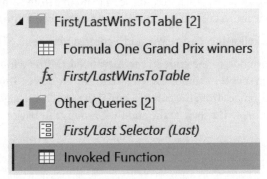

Figure 10.14 – Screenshot of the table created by invoking that function with the parameter set to Last

This example of creating a function could be really useful when you need to use parameters to apply the transformations multiple times. The most common case is when merging CSVs where the parameter could be the file path, thus, allowing you to clean multiple files simply by pointing the parameter at the new file and invoking the custom function. This, of course, happens provided that the CSVs have a similar structure in columns, and so on.

This is great, but let's now take a look at how you might create your own custom function from a blank query. Let's build on the work you have done so far with this data to now assess what each driver's wins per seasons active would be. Given the format of the data, we will need to start by doing some cleaning of the data using the following steps:

1. Duplicate the query you have built named `Formula One Grand Prix winners`.

2. Rename it `Driver Wins`.

3. Create a new group within the query page to separate this from the previous example. Simply right-click on the query you just created, select **Move to Group**, and then select **New Group…** from the sub-menu.

4. Name the group `CustomFunctionFromBlank` and select **OK**.

5. Select the columns we would like to keep, which in this example will be as follows:

    *   `Rank`

    *   `Driver`

    *   `Wins`

    *   `Seasons active`

6. From the **Home** ribbon, select **Remove columns** and then select **Remove other columns** from the submenu.

7. Before we start creating a function, let's first ensure the `Seasons active` columns are showing the correct values. We can see that some are missing the year values (likely because they are still active drivers). To correct this, we will use M to do this from within **Advanced Editor** (this could also be made into a custom function). Select **Advanced Editor** from the **Home** ribbon.

8. Before adding the following, ensure you add a comma to the end of the previous step.

9. Add the following code to the code in the **Advanced Editor** window. This will use nested expressions to then split the column named `Seasons active`. This then uses `if` statements to extract the year ranges from the column, and if the end-year range is blank, it will populate this with the year 2024. The logic at the end then groups this back together:

```
    AdjustedTable = Table.TransformColumns(#"Removed Other
Columns" , {"Seasons active", each
        let
            // Split the text by commas
```

```
                    YearsList = Text.Split(_, ", "),

                    // Process each item in the list
                    AdjustedYearsList = List.Transform(YearsList, each
                        if Text.Contains(_, "-") then
                            let
                                StartYear = Text.BeforeDelimiter(_, "-"),
                                EndYearText = Text.AfterDelimiter(_, "-"),
                                EndYear = if EndYearText <> "" then
EndYearText else Text.From("2024"),
                                AdjustedValue = StartYear & "-" & EndYear
                            in
                            AdjustedValue
                        else _),

                    // Combine the adjusted list back into a single text
                    AdjustedValue = Text.Combine(AdjustedYearsList, ", ")
            in
            AdjustedValue
        })
```

10. Then, adjust the variable after the final in from (#"Removed Other Columns" to AdjustedTable. This should look like the following screenshot:

```
17    AdjustedTable = Table.TransformColumns(#"Removed Other Columns" , {"Seasons active", each
18        let
19            // Split the text by commas
20            YearsList = Text.Split(_, ", "),
21
22            // Process each item in the list
23            AdjustedYearsList = List.Transform(YearsList, each
24                if Text.Contains(_, "-") then
25                    let
26                        StartYear = Text.BeforeDelimiter(_, "-"),
27                        EndYearText = Text.AfterDelimiter(_, "-"),
28                        EndYear = if EndYearText <> "" then EndYearText else Text.From("2024"),
29                        AdjustedValue = StartYear & "-" & EndYear
30                    in
31                    AdjustedValue
32                else _),
33
34            // Combine the adjusted list back into a single text
35            AdjustedValue = Text.Combine(AdjustedYearsList, ", ")
36        in
37        AdjustedValue
38        })
39    in
40        AdjustedTable
```

Figure 10.15 – An example of the query used in Advanced Editor to correct the missing years

11. The resulting output should have shaped the final column to ensure that any drivers that are still active have the year 2024 shown. In the following screenshot, we can see that Lewis Hamilton now shows **2007-2024** instead of **2007-**.

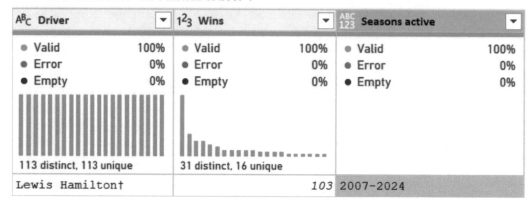

Figure 10.16 – Screenshot of the Seasons active column without the missing years in the ranges

12. Next, in order to figure out the average wins by active seasons, we need to cleanse the data to extract the number of years active. To do this, let's create a custom function from scratch so that we can then extract the number of years a driver has been active.

13. From the **Home** ribbon, select **New query** and then select **Blank query**. This will open a new query in the query window.

14. Rename this query YearsActiveFunction.

15. Select **Advanced Editor** so you can begin to build the function. As this is a blank query, you will see the following prepopulated by default:

```
let
    Source = ""
in
    Source
```

16. Remove these lines to start from a complete blank query and then type the following to define the function:

```
let
// Define the custom function to calculate years
    GetTotalYears = (textValue as text) as number =>
```

17. Now that we have defined the function, we will begin the transformations within a nested `let`. The first transformation we will need to do is to split out the year ranges as we did previously. Enter the following code:

```
let
    // Split the text by comma and trim each part
    yearsList = List.Transform(Text.Split(textValue, ","),
Text.Trim),
```

18. Next, add the following lines so you can define a function to calculate the number of years for each entry:

```
// Define a function to calculate years for a single entry
    GetYears = (entry as text) as number =>
        let
    // Split the entry by dash to get start and end years
            yearRange = Text.Split(entry, "-"),
            startYear = Number.From(List.First(yearRange)),
            endYear = if List.Count(yearRange) > 1 then
Number.From(List.Last(yearRange)) else startYear,

    // Calculate the number of years
            numYears = endYear - startYear + 1
        in
        numYears,
```

19. Now that our function is calculating the number of years for each entry, we need to add logic to pull this back together for each driver. Add the following lines:

```
// Calculate total years for each entry and sum them
    totalYears = List.Sum(List.Transform(yearsList,
GetYears))
```

20. All that's left to do is to close the `let` expression. Enter the following:

```
    in
        totalYears
in
    GetTotalYears
```

21. Now that you have completed your code, select **Done**. This should now show the following within the query for the function:

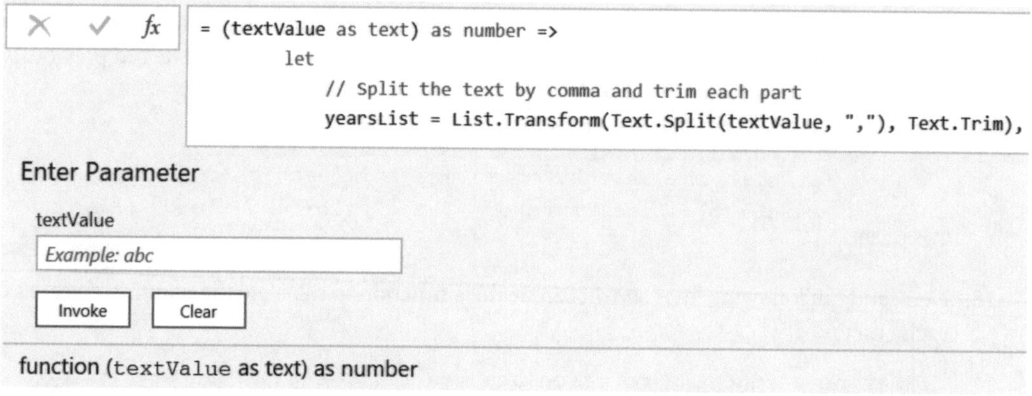

```
fx    = (textValue as text) as number =>
            let
                // Split the text by comma and trim each part
                yearsList = List.Transform(Text.Split(textValue, ","), Text.Trim),
```

Enter Parameter

textValue

Example: abc

| Invoke | Clear |

function (textValue as text) as number

Figure 10.17 – Screenshot of the function created named YearsActiveFunction

22. Now that you have created your custom function, return to the query you named `Driver Win`. Once you have navigated to the query, select the `Seasons active` column.

23. Select **Add column** from the ribbon and then select **Invoke custom function**.

24. Next, you will need to name the column you are creating, so, in this example, let's call it `Years Active`. Then, select the function you would like to use. Select the function we just created called `YearsActiveFunction`.

This will cause another configuration item to appear, which specifies the input for the function. In this example, as you already selected the `Seasons active` column, this should already appear as shown in the following. Select **OK** to invoke the function.

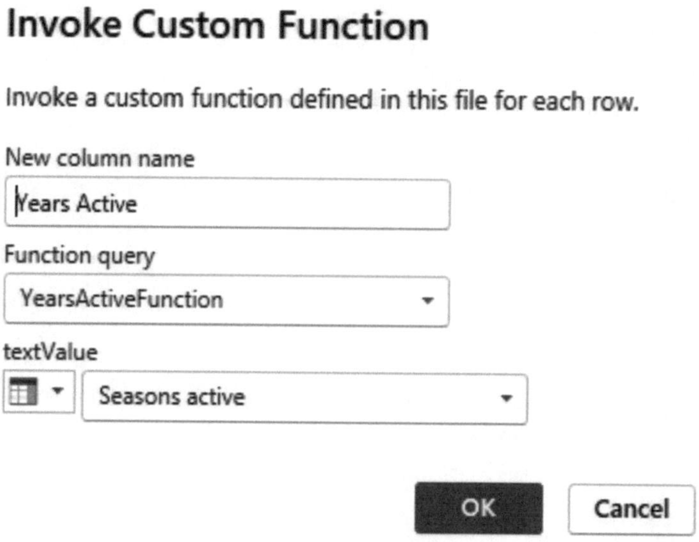

Invoke Custom Function

Invoke a custom function defined in this file for each row.

New column name

Years Active

Function query

YearsActiveFunction ▾

textValue

Seasons active ▾

| OK | Cancel |

Figure 10.18 – Screenshot of the Invoke Custom Function configuration

This will now create a new column that shows the number of years that the driver has been an active racer, which could later be used in a measure to calculate the average wins per active season. Thus, you can figure out which driver has the best all-round stats.

Summary

In this chapter, we explored the process of creating custom functions in Power Query. Effective use of custom functions in Power Query begins with proper planning, forming the cornerstone for building efficient and adaptable functions. This involves defining the problem, identifying parameters, and setting clear objectives to align with your data preparation needs. Parameters, as you learned, play a crucial role in enhancing the flexibility of your functions for various scenarios. The process of creating custom functions encompasses defining the function's structure, writing M code, thorough testing and debugging, and comprehensive documentation. Armed with these insights, you are well-prepared to leverage the full potential of custom functions in Power Query, with capabilities for seamless data transformation and preparation.

In the next chapter, you will learn more about the techniques and tips on how you can optimize your M code.

Questions

1. What is the first step in planning for a custom function in Power Query?

   A. Writing M code

   B. Testing and debugging

   C. Defining the problem

   D. Creating parameters

2. What role do parameters play in custom functions?

   A. Identifying issues in the code

   B. Enhancing documentation

   C. Making functions flexible and adaptable

   D. Debugging the function

3. Why is it important to provide default values for parameters in custom functions?

   A. To increase the complexity of the function

   B. To make the function less user-friendly

   C. To improve the overall user experience

   D. To avoid testing and debugging

4. What is crucial for defining the structure of a custom function?

    A. Complex M code

    B. Writing extensive documentation

    C. Choosing a descriptive name

    D. Setting default parameter values

11

M Query Optimization

In the previous chapter, you were introduced to custom functions, appropriate planning for functions, and also using the power of parameters within your functions. Across Power Query, there are a number of opportunities for you to express and code solutions with your knowledge of M code.

Like with any coding language, there are different ways in which you can write out your code, meaning there are often strategies and techniques that can help you achieve the optimum performance of your query. In this chapter, you will dive deep into four key tips for optimizing your M queries:

- Filtering and reducing the data you're working on to improve performance, such as removing unnecessary data early in the query

- Recognizing when to use functions optimized for specific tasks, reducing the need for custom code

- Employing lazy evaluation techniques and functions such as `Table.Buffer` and `Table.Distinct` to optimize memory usage and processing

- Using parallel query execution techniques, including functions such as `Table.Split`, to divide and conquer data transformation tasks and enhance query performance

We will cover these tips in the following sections:

- Filtering and reducing data

- Using native M functions

- Creating custom functions

- Optimizing memory usage

- Parallel query execution

With these techniques at your disposal, you'll be better equipped to tackle complex data transformation tasks in Power BI while maintaining optimal query execution speed.

Technical requirements

To follow the instructions in this chapter, you will need to connect to the data using the following URL: `https://raw.githubusercontent.com/PacktPublishing/Data-Cleaning-with-Power-BI/main/Retail%20Store%20Sales%20Data.csv`.

Creating custom functions

As we learned in the previous chapter, while native functions are powerful, there are scenarios where custom functions are necessary. In some scenarios, it might not even make sense to add the custom function through the **Queries** tab as it might only be used once. With that in mind, it sometimes makes more sense to build that custom function into the existing code within the advanced editor. We'll delve deeper into the process of creating efficient custom functions in M during this section.

As an example, start by building a table from a blank query. Follow these steps to do this:

1. Open Power BI Desktop.

2. Select **Transform data** from the Report, Table, or Model View to open the Power Query editor.

3. Select **New source** and then select **Blank query** from the dropdown. Select **Advanced editor** from the **Home** ribbon to open the Advanced editor.

4. Enter the following code into the Advanced editor:

```
let
Scorecard = Table.FromList(
    {"1,Test 1,98,0.2", "1,Test 2,78,0.1","1,Test
3,94,0.1","1,Test 4,88,0.2","1,Test 5,80,0.2","1,Test
6,43,0.2"},
    null,
    {"Participant","Test", "Score" ,"Weight"}
),
#"Changed Type" = Table.TransformColumnTypes(Scorecard
,{{"Score", type number}, {"Weight", type number}}), let
Scorecard = Table.FromList(
    {"1,Test 1,98,0.2", "1,Test 2,78,0.1","1,Test
3,94,0.1","1,Test 4,88,0.2","1,Test 5,80,0.2","1,Test
6,43,0.2"},
    null,
    {"Participant","Test", "Score" ,"Weight"}
),
#"Changed Type" = Table.TransformColumnTypes(Scorecard
,{{"Score", type number}, {"Weight", type number}}),
```

5. Click on **Done**.

   As you can see, this will have loaded some test results and their respective weightings. Suppose you need to calculate the weighted average of test scores based on specific criteria that native functions such as `List.Average` don't cover. Let's go through a custom function that optimizes the calculation, ensuring both accuracy and query performance.

6. Select **Advanced editor** from the **Home** ribbon.

7. Add a comma to the end of the preview step.

8. Then add the following:

```
CalculateWeightedAverage = (table, weights, values) =>
    let
        WeightedValues = Table.AddColumn(table, "Weighted Score",
each) Value.Multiply([Weight],[Score])),
        NormalAverage = Table.AddColumn(WeightedValues, "Normal
Average",each List.Average(WeightedValues[Score])),
        Result =  Table.AddColumn(NormalAverage,
"ResultWeightedAverage",each Value.Divide(List.
Sum(WeightedValues[Weighted Score]),List.
Sum(WeightedValues[Weight])))
    in
        Result
```

9. Now you'll notice that nothing happened. This is because we haven't invoked the function in the final `in` statement. You can do this by adjusting this as follows and clicking on **Done**:

```
in
    CalculateWeightedAverage(#"Changed Type")
```

This will add two columns to our table of test scores, which include the average and the weighted average score:

	Participant	Test	1.2 Score	1.2 Weight	Weighted Score	Normal Average	ResultWeightedAverage
	● Valid 100% ● Error 0% ● Empty 0%	● Valid 100% ● Error 0% ● Empty 0%	● Valid 100% ● Error 0% ● Empty 0%	● Valid 100% ● Error 0% ● Empty 0%	● Valid 100% ● Error 0% ● Empty 0%	● Valid 100% ● Error 0% ● Empty 0%	● Valid 100% ● Error 0% ● Empty 0%
			6 distinct, 6 unique	2 distinct, 0 unique			
1	1	Test 1	98	0.2	19.6	80.16666667	79
2	1	Test 2	78	0.1	7.8	80.16666667	79
3	1	Test 3	94	0.1	9.4	80.16666667	79
4	1	Test 4	88	0.2	17.6	80.16666667	79
5	1	Test 5	80	0.2	16	80.16666667	79
6	1	Test 6	43	0.2	8.6	80.16666667	79

Figure 11.1 – The query output, including the additional columns

In the code you created, you defined a custom function called `CalculateWeightedAverage`. This function optimizes the calculation of a weighted average, ensuring both accuracy and query performance for scenarios not covered by native functions. This function took one parameter: `table`.

Here's a breakdown of what this M query does:

- `WeightedValues`: Within the function, a new column named `Weighted Score` is added to the input table. This column is calculated by multiplying the corresponding row's `Score` with the row's `Weight`.

- `NormalAverage`: Within the function, a new column named `Normal Average` was added to the input table, `WeightedValues`. This used the `List.Average` function to return the average of the `Score` column.

- `Result`: The function returns a new column named `ResultWeightedAverage`, which carries out the weighted average calculation, obtained by dividing `List.Sum(Weighted Score)` by `List.Sum(WeightedValues[Weight])`.

In summary, this M query defines a custom function that calculates the weighted average of a given table of values. It does so by multiplying each value in the table by a corresponding weight, summing these weighted values, and then dividing the sum by the total weight. This can be useful when you want to calculate a weighted average for specific data in Power BI, where different values have different weights in the final average.

In the next section, you will build upon this knowledge as you learn more about how to optimize your M code when filtering and reducing data.

Filtering and reducing data

Efficiently handling large datasets is a common challenge in data transformation. Filtering and reducing data early in your query can significantly boost performance.

Let's walk through an example where we filter out unnecessary data. Consider a dataset with sales information for the past five years. If your analysis only requires data from the last year, filtering out the older records early in the query can save processing time and memory usage:

1. Open Power BI Desktop. We're going to be connecting to a new dataset.

2. Click on **Get Data | Text CSV**. You will then enter the following URL to access the file for our example: `https://raw.githubusercontent.com/PacktPublishing/Data-Cleaning-with-Power-BI/main/Retail%20Store%20Sales%20Data.csv`

3. Select **Transform Data** instead of **Load Now** so that you can explore the data before loading it all into memory.

4. Rename the query `Retail Store Sales Data - Problem Statement 1` using the **Properties** tab:

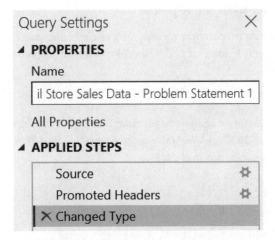

Figure 11.2 – The query settings renamed

5. Now, duplicate the queries by right-clicking on the query shown in the **Query** pane and selecting **Duplicate**. Create two duplicates of the query and follow the steps in *step 4* to rename these queries as follows:

- `Retail Store Sales Data - Problem Statement 2`
- `Retail Store Sales Data - Problem Statement 3`

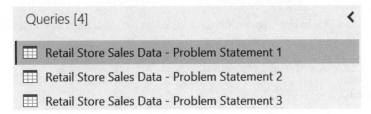

Figure 11.3 – The duplicate queries within Power Query

When we look at filtering data within our Power Query editor, we could of course begin manually using the UI to filter and reduce this data in multiple steps as we saw in *Chapter 4, The Most Common Data Cleaning Operations*. This is great; however, it will create many different steps within the applied window, which can of course make the window seem cluttered and complex.

Similarly, we could use techniques learned in *Chapter 7, Transforming Data with the M Language*, to code this in the advanced editor using M code, but again we are now looking at how we can optimize this code so that we can carry out the multiple filters within one step.

To do this, we are going to build upon what you learned in *Chapter 4* and *Chapter 7* to create more complex and logical functions within your M code. In the following steps, you will learn three different styles of filter logic to apply and optimize your M code.

In order to simulate the data preparation we are going to carry out, you will be presented with three different problem statements from your colleague. Your job is to prepare the data for your colleague to carry out their analysis.

Problem statement 1

Colleague: *We would like to run an analysis on the data, but the scope of this analysis should only include sales orders within the year 2023 and that have received more than a 20% discount. Please clean and prepare the data so I can analyze just that data.*

Here are the steps:

1. Select the query named `Retail Store Sales Data - Problem Statement 1`.
2. Select **Advanced editor** to open the M code for this query.
3. Add the following code within the Advanced editor. Remember to add a comma at the end of the previous line of code:

   ```
       #"ProblemStatement1" = Table.SelectRows(#"Changed Type",
   each [Discount]>=0.2 and Date.Year([Order Date])=2023)
   in
       #"ProblemStatement1"
   ```

4. Review and click on **Done** after checking for any errors.

The previous code will add one step within the applied steps rather than two individual filter steps. This can make the overall query more efficient.

We will now take a look at the next problem statement from our colleague.

Problem statement 2

Colleague: *I would like to take a look at a particular subset of the data regarding products that are in danger of being recalled. Could you prepare the data so that it also only returns the data on the following product lines?*

"OFF-BI-10001120","OFF-BI-10003527", "OFF-BI-10003527", "OFF-BI-10000545", "OFF-AP-10002534", "OFF-BI-10004632", "OFF-BI-10004584", "OFF-BI-10004632", "OFF-BI-10004632", "OFF-AP-10002684", "OFF-AP-10001205"

Here are the steps:

1. Select query named `Retail Store Sales Data - Problem Statement 2`.

2. Select **Advanced editor** to open the M code for this query.

3. Open **Advanced editor** and add the following code to the bottom of your existing query:

```
    #"ProblemStatement1" = Table.SelectRows(#"Changed Type",
each [Discount]>=0.2 and Date.Year([Order Date])=2023)
ProductIDFilterList = {"OFF-BI-10001120","OFF-BI-10003527",
"OFF-BI-10003527", "OFF-BI-10000545", "OFF-AP-10002534", "OFF-
BI-10004632", "OFF-BI-10004584", "OFF-BI-10004632", "OFF-BI-
10004632", "OFF-AP-10002684", "OFF-AP-10001205" },
    #"ProblemStatement2" = Table.
SelectRows(#"ProblemStatement1",each List.
Contains(ProductIDFilterList, [Product ID]))
in
    #"ProblemStatement2"
```

4. Click on **Done** after checking for any errors.

In this example, you learned to use lists to create a specific list of values that we will then use in the filter. This is great, but we can probably build upon this with the knowledge of parameters that we gained in the previous chapter. This will help with the scenario should the colleague need to adjust the given list of products. The steps are as follows:

1. Select **Manage Parameters | New Parameter**.

2. Configure the parameter as follows:

   - **Name**: `SelectedProducts`

   - **Description**: This parameter allows you to populate order IDs that you would like the datasource filtered by

   - **Required**: Checked

   - **Type**: **Text**

   - **Suggested Values: Any values**

   - **Current Value**: The list of products without the quotation marks

Manage Parameters

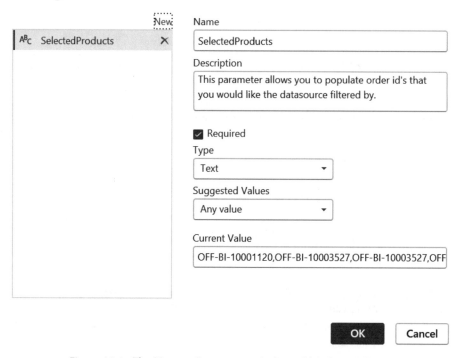

Figure 11.4 – The Manage Parameters window within Power Query

3. Now that you have created the parameter, you can adjust the following code in the Advanced editor:

```
ProductIDFilterList = {"OFF-BI-10001120","OFF-BI-10003527",
"OFF-BI-10003527", "OFF-BI-10000545", "OFF-AP-10002534", "OFF-
BI-10004632", "OFF-BI-10004584", "OFF-BI-10004632", "OFF-BI-
10004632", "OFF-AP-10002684", "OFF-AP-10001205" },
    #"ProblemStatement2" = Table.
SelectRows(#"ProblemStatement1",each List.
Contains(ProductIDFilterList, [Product ID]))
in
    #"ProblemStatement2"
```

Change that code to this:

```
    ProductIDFilterList = SelectedProducts,
    ProductIDFilterListTable = Text.
Split(ProductIDFilterList,","),
    #"ProblemStatement2" = Table.
SelectRows(#"ProblemStatement1",each List.
Contains(ProductIDFilterListTable, [Product ID]))
in
    #"ProblemStatement2"
```

This code will now reference the parameter we created called `SelectedProducts`. It will then convert that singular parameter to a list of values using the `Text.Split` function. That list is then used within the `List.Contains` function.

The output shown next returns a table of data with only the specified products, selected for the particular year of 2023 and with a discount greater than 20% applied:

Figure 11.5 – The result of adding the code to the advanced editor, with the table filtered to specific year, discount, and products

Having completed this, you can look at the final request from your colleague in the next example.

Problem statement 3

Colleague: *I would like to take a look at a particular subset of the data on products that have been sold for a higher profit than the average profit amount. Could you prepare the data so that it also only returns the data on those more profitable items?*

In this example, you are going to build upon the knowledge from the previous chapter to build a custom function within your M code that will do this logic for us filtering.

Let's go through the steps:

1. Select the query named `Retail Store Sales Data - Problem Statement 3`. Select **Advanced editor** to open the M code for this query.

2. Add the following code to the bottom of your existing query:

```
GetAverageProfitAmount = (ProductID) =>
        let
            AvgProfit = List.Average(Table.SelectRows(#"Changed
Type", each [Product ID] = ProductID)[Profit])
        in
```

```
            AvgProfit,
      #"FilteredTable" = Table.SelectRows(
          #"Changed Type",
          each [Profit] > GetAverageProfitAmount([Product ID])
      )
   in
      #"FilteredTable"
```

3. Select **Done** after checking for any errors.

This query will return a table of data for all the products with an above-average profit amount. Let's go through the breakdown of the code step by step.

The following defines a custom function named `GetAverageProfitAmount` that takes the `ProductID` parameter:

```
GetAverageProfitAmount = (ProductID) =>
      let
          AvgProfit = List.Average(Table.SelectRows(#"Changed Type",
  each [Product ID] = ProductID)[Profit])
      in
          AvgProfit,
```

Inside the function, a local `AvgProfit` variable is created. This variable represents the average profit amount for the specified `ProductID` parameter. The `Table.SelectRows` function is used to filter rows from the source table where the `ProductID` matches the provided `ProductID` parameter. The `List.Average` function is then applied to calculate the average of the `Profit` column for the filtered rows. The result is then stored in the `AvgProfit` variable, which is then used in the table filtering part of the M code.

The previous example would achieve the desired result; however, there is another way to achieve this, which would generally perform better and thus be more optimized. Using the previous custom function means that it must iterate this function on every row within the data. An alternative to this would be to use the `Group By` function instead of filtering rows based on a custom function. The `Group By` operation can calculate the average profit amount for each product ID in a single step.

To do this, remove the query you added in *step 2* and replace it with the following snippet:

```
    // Calculate average profit amount per product ID using the group
by function
    AvgProfitPerProductID = Table.Group(#"Changed Type", {"Product
ID"}, {{"AvgProfit", each List.Average([Profit]), type number}}),
    // Join the average profit amount back to the original table
    MergedTable = Table.Join(#"Changed Type", "Product ID",
AvgProfitPerProductID, "Product ID", JoinKind.Inner),
    // Filter rows where profit is greater than average profit amount
```

```
    FilteredTable = Table.SelectRows(MergedTable, each [Profit] >
[AvgProfit])
in
    FilteredTable
```

This optimized version reduces unnecessary iterations over the data and improves performance by calculating the average profit amount per product ID using the Group By operation instead of the custom function.

In this section, you have learned and explored how you can go about optimizing the M code queries you create by filtering the data to a smaller size, thus achieving better performance when it comes to analyzing the data.

In the next section, you will build upon this with other native functions that will help you optimize your M code.

Using native M functions

As highlighted earlier in this book, M, the language behind Power Query, offers a rich library of native functions designed for data transformation. Leveraging these functions can often be more efficient than custom code.

For instance, let's say you need to standardize product names by converting them to title case. Instead of writing custom code, you can utilize the Text.ToTitleCase function, making your query more concise and performant.

Here is an example of doing just this:

```
let
    Source = ... // Your data source
    StandardizedData = Table.TransformColumns(Source, {"ProductName",
Text.ToTitleCase})
in
    StandardizedData
```

In this code, we use the Table.TransformColumns function along with the Text.ToTitleCase function to standardize product names. Native functions are highly optimized for their specific tasks, resulting in more efficient and faster queries.

The Table.TransformColumns function is used to transform the data loaded in the source. Specifically, it's transforming a column named ProductName to title case. Title case means that the first letter of each word in the text is capitalized, and the rest of the letters are in lowercase. Here is a summary of the two values within the Table.TransformColumns function:

- ProductName: This is the name of the column in your data that you want to transform

- Text.ToTitleCase: This is a built-in function in Power Query that converts the text in the specified column to title case

After this transformation, the result is stored in the `StandardizedData` variable. The transformed data will have `ProductName` values, where each word starts with a capital letter, followed by lowercase letters. The rest of the data in the table will remain the same.

The final `StandardizedData` value is the result of this transformation and can be used for further data analysis, visualization, or other operations in your Power BI report.

In this section, you learned about how you can begin to use the `Table.TransformColumns` and `Text.ToTitleCase` functions to transform your data. Next, you will learn more about how you can use functions such as `Table.Buffer` to improve the efficiency and performance of your code.

Optimizing memory usage

Managing memory usage is vital for query optimization. Let's consider an example where you're dealing with a large dataset with repeated data. Instead of creating multiple copies of the same data, we can explore the `Table.Buffer` function.

This function loads a table into memory once, reducing memory duplication, which can lead to improved query speed, especially for large datasets with repeated data. This optimization can result in more efficient use of system resources and better overall performance during data transformation and analysis tasks.

On the other hand, though, there are some potential drawbacks to be aware of. One significant downside is that using `Table.Buffer` can actually slow down performance in certain scenarios.

One reason for this is that it loads the entire table into memory at once. For very large datasets, this can consume a significant amount of memory resources, potentially leading to memory pressure and slower overall performance, especially if your system doesn't have enough available memory to handle the entire dataset efficiently.

Additionally, using `Table.Buffer` may not always be necessary or beneficial. If you're working with relatively small datasets or if the dataset is already efficiently managed by Power Query's internal optimization mechanisms, using `Table.Buffer` might not provide any noticeable performance improvement but can still consume additional memory resources.

The following example shows how you could use this function in practice:

```
let
    Source = ... // Your data source
    TransformationSteps = ... // Your Transformation Steps
    BufferedTable = Table.Buffer(TransformationSteps) in
    BufferedTable
```

In this code, we use the `Table.Buffer` function to load the dataset into memory only once, reducing memory duplication. This optimization minimizes memory usage, resulting in faster query execution.

Here are a few additional details and memory-efficient coding practices to consider:

- The `Table.Buffer` function placement: If you are going to use this function, make sure to plan out where you will use this function. If you have or are working on a large dataset, or equally if you're performing computationally intensive operations early in your query, using `Table.Buffer` early on in your query can help by loading the data into memory early. This can be particularly useful when the subsequent steps involve filtering, sorting, or joining large tables. On the other hand, though, if you only need to buffer a subset of the data or if you're working with smaller data, then placing the `Table.Buffer` function later in your query can be more beneficial, helping to conserve your memory and buffering only the necessary data.

- **Minimizing variable use**: While variables can make your code more readable, excessive use of variables can also increase memory consumption. Consider using variables judiciously and avoid storing intermediate results in variables unless they are necessary for multiple steps in your transformation.

- **Recycling existing tables**: Instead of creating new tables for intermediate steps in your data transformation, try to reuse existing tables when possible. This can be achieved by referencing the previous step in the transformation process rather than creating a new table. For example, if you need to filter or transform data further, use the output of the previous step directly, which reduces the creation of unnecessary intermediate tables.

- **Using the Query Dependencies View**: Power Query's Query Dependencies View can help you understand how your queries are related and where memory may be consumed. It can assist in optimizing query execution and memory usage.

By applying these memory-efficient coding practices and using functions such as `Table.Buffer` wisely, you can create more efficient and performant Power Query transformations, especially when dealing with large datasets or complex data transformations. In the next section, we will walk through an example of using `Table.Buffer` with the `Table.Split` function.

Parallel query execution

Parallel query execution is a game-changer for performance. Suppose you have a massive dataset, and you want to process it more quickly. By splitting the table into smaller parts using `Table.Split`, you can enable parallel processing, drastically reducing query execution times.

This can be done using code such as the following in your M query:

```
let
    Source = ... // Your data source
    SplitTable = Table.Split(Source, 4) // Split the table into 4
partitions
in
    SplitTable
```

In this code, we use the `Table.Split` function to divide a large table into smaller partitions, enabling parallel processing. Each partition is processed simultaneously, which can often result in significantly reducing query execution times. It must be said, though, that using `Table.Split` in this code on its own won't inherently reduce query execution times, but it's a step towards enabling parallel processing, which can improve performance in certain scenarios. The effectiveness of parallel processing depends on various factors such as the nature of the data, the operations or transformations being performed, and the capabilities of the underlying hardware.

Here are a few additional details on what the previous code is doing and best practices when executing parallel queries:

- **The Table.Split function**: The `Table.Split` function is used to divide a table into multiple partitions or segments.

- **Partition count**: In the previous example, we have split the table into four partitions by specifying the number 4 as the second argument to `Table.Split`. You can adjust this number based on the available system resources, such as the number of CPU cores or the memory capacity. Experimenting with different partition counts may be necessary to find the optimal balance between parallel processing and resource consumption.

- **Parallel processing**: The key advantage of splitting a table into partitions is that each partition can be processed in parallel. This means that multiple CPU cores can work on different partitions simultaneously, which can lead to a substantial performance improvement. However, parallel processing is most effective when the underlying data source and the hardware support it.

- **Data source considerations**: It's important to note that not all data sources and data transformations can be parallelized effectively. Some data sources may not support parallel execution, and certain transformations may have dependencies that limit parallelism. You should test and profile your specific scenario to see how much performance gain you can achieve through parallel processing.

- **Query complexity**: The complexity of your data transformation steps also plays a role in the effectiveness of parallel processing. Simple, isolated transformations are more likely to benefit from parallelism than complex, interdependent transformations.

- **Combine data**: After processing each partition in parallel, you may need to combine the results back into a single table. Depending on your use case, you can use functions such as `Table.Combine` to merge the partitions into a unified dataset.

- **Resource management**: Keep in mind that parallel processing may require more system resources, so ensure that your hardware and Power Query configuration can support it effectively. Monitor memory and CPU usage during query execution to avoid resource exhaustion.

To conclude, using the `Table.Split` function to enable parallel processing is indeed a game-changer for performance when dealing with large datasets. It's a powerful technique, but it requires careful consideration of data source capabilities, hardware resources, and query complexity to achieve the best results. Experimentation and profiling are often necessary to fine-tune parallel processing for your specific use case.

Using Table.Buffer and Table.Split

Now that you have an understanding of these two functions, let's work on using them within an example dataset. In this example, we will also introduce you to the session diagnostic tool within the Power Query editor and how it can be used to measure the impact of your query and query optimization. This will provide a high-level introduction to the diagnostic tool, but if you would like to learn more about the tool and its outputs, then you can find a link in the *Further reading* section.

Let's connect to the data and build some scenarios:

1. Open Power BI Desktop.

2. Click on **Get Data | Text CSV**. Then enter the following URL to access the file for our example: `https://raw.githubusercontent.com/PacktPublishing/Data-Cleaning-with-Power-BI/main/Retail%20Store%20Sales%20Data.csv`

3. Select **Transform data**.

4. Rename this query in **Query settings** on the far right side of the Power Query editor to `StandardQuery`.

5. Duplicate the query by right-clicking on the query on the far left side of the Power Query editor and selecting **Duplicate**, renaming the duplicate `OptimizedQuery` as you go.

6. Return to **StandardQuery** and select the Advanced editor. Add the following code, making sure to add a **comma** to the previous step to prevent errors:

```
    #"Added Custom" = Table.AddColumn(#"Changed Type", "Cost",
each [Sales] - [Profit], type number),
    #"Added Custom1" = Table.AddColumn(#"Added Custom",
"TotalSales", each [Sales]*[Quantity],type number),
    #"Split Column by Delimiter" = Table.SplitColumn(#"Added
Custom1", "Country", Splitter.SplitTextByDelimiter(" ",
QuoteStyle.Csv), {"Country.1", "Country.2"}),
    #"Changed Type1" = Table.TransformColumnTypes(#"Split Column
by Delimiter",{{"Country.1", type text}, {"Country.2", type
text}}),
    #"Split Column by Delimiter1" = Table.SplitColumn(#"Changed
Type1", "Customer ID", Splitter.SplitTextByEachDelimiter({"-"},
QuoteStyle.Csv, false), {"Customer ID.1", "Customer ID.2"}),
    #"Changed Type2" = Table.TransformColumnTypes(#"Split Column
by Delimiter1",{{"Customer ID.1", type text}, {"Customer ID.2",
Int64.Type}}),
    #"Removed Columns" = Table.RemoveColumns(#"Changed
Type2",{"Customer ID.2"}),
    #"Renamed Columns" = Table.RenameColumns(#"Removed
Columns",{{"Customer ID.1", "Initials"}}),
    #"Replaced Value" = Table.ReplaceValue(#"Renamed
Columns",0,null,Replacer.ReplaceValue,{"Discount"}),
```

```
    #"Filtered Rows" = Table.SelectRows(#"Replaced Value", each
([Discount] <> null))

    in
    #"Filtered Rows"
```

7. Remove the following `in` statement:

```
    in
        #"Changed Type"
```

8. Click on **Done** to return to the Power Query editor. You should see that a number of steps have been added within the applied steps:

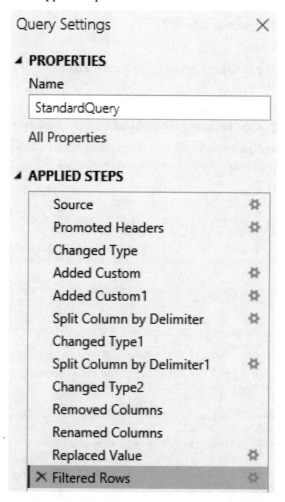

Figure 11.6 – The query settings showing the additional transformation steps added to this query

9. Select **Tools** from the ribbon. This will show us the available **diagnostic tools**.

10. Select **Diagnostic Options**. This will open the option settings for the diagnostic query. By default, this will have all options checked for **Diagnostic Level** and **Additional Diagnostics**. We don't need all of this for this simple test, so uncheck all but the **Aggregated** option:

Diagnostics Level

☑ Aggregated ⓘ

☐ Detailed ⓘ

Additional Diagnostics

☐ Performance counters ⓘ

☐ Data privacy partitions ⓘ

Figure 11.7 – The configuration for the diagnostic options settings

11. Click on **OK** to close the settings window.

12. Start diagnostics by selecting **Start diagnostics** in the **Session Diagnostics** group from the **Tools** ribbon. This will begin the recording. Ensure that you have the query **StandardQuery** selected.

13. Navigate to the **Home** ribbon and select **Refresh preview**.

14. Once this is done, navigate back to the **Tools** ribbon and select **Stop diagnostics**. This should automatically generate a query with a name formatted as **Diagnostics_Aggregated_Date_Time**.

15. Select this query and rename it `StandardQuery Diagnostic`.

16. This query still shows a lot of information on each of the applied steps. If you wish to understand more about each row and column from the results, then check the resources listed in the *Further reading* section for more details. We are going to aggregate this information using the **Group By** function. Select the column labeled `Query`.

17. Then, from the **Home** ribbon, select **Group By** function to open the configuration window. By default, this will open with the basic configuration. Adjust this by selecting the **Advanced** radial.

18. As you selected the column in step *15* before selecting **Group By**, the `Query` column should appear in the grouping. Add the aggregations as shown in the following screenshot:

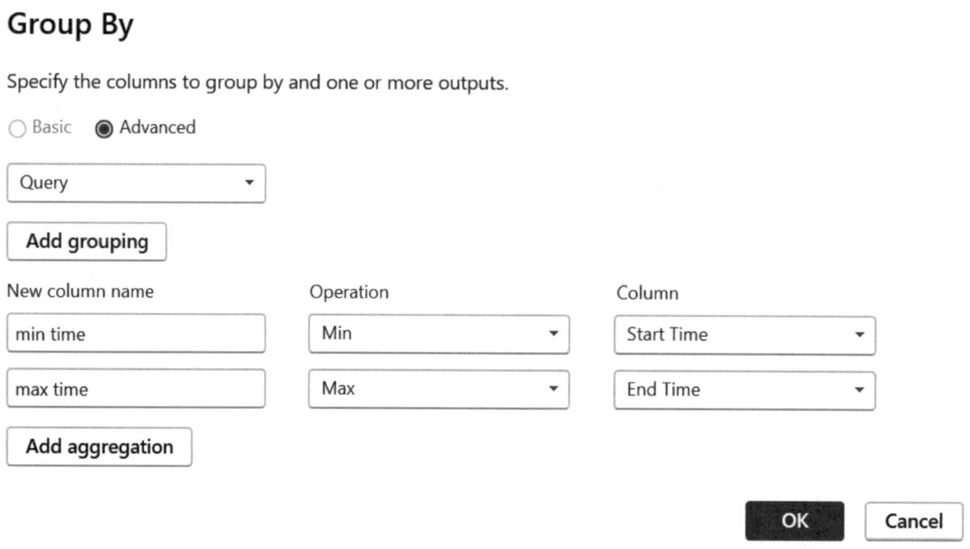

Group By

Specify the columns to group by and one or more outputs.

○ Basic ● Advanced

| Query ▾ |

| **Add grouping** |

New column name	Operation	Column
min time	Min ▾	Start Time ▾
max time	Max ▾	End Time ▾

| **Add aggregation** |

OK   Cancel

Figure 11.8 – The configuration for the Group By function

19. This will return a single row for the query we refreshed with the min (start time) and the max (end time) of the refresh preview. For ease, let's adjust the column types from **Date/Time** to **Time** by selecting both columns and right-clicking. Then, hover over **Change type** and select **Time**.

20. Let's add a new column to show the total time. To do this, navigate to **Add column** in the ribbon and select **Custom column**.

21. Give the new column a name such as Total Time (S) and enter the following formula:

```
Duration.Seconds([max time]-[min time])
```

22. Click on **OK**. This will now show the time taken in seconds to refresh the query. In my case, it took 1.08407 seconds, as shown in the following screenshot, but this might be different for you. Keep in mind that this data is pretty small and only has a handful of optimization steps, so naturally it is pretty quick already. However, if you were working with larger amounts of data, this could take minutes or even hours.

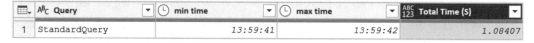

	ABC Query ▾	⏱ min time ▾	⏱ max time ▾	ABC 123 Total Time (S) ▾
1	StandardQuery	13:59:41	13:59:42	1.08407

Figure 11.9 – The results from the diagnostic on the query named StandardQuery

23. Before we progress to optimizing the query, it'd be worthwhile to create a custom function that we can use for future diagnostic results to quickly get to the total time. To do this, let's create a new blank query either by right-clicking in the **Queries** pane or by selecting a new source from the **Home** ribbon.

24. Rename the query Diagnostic Transformations.

25. Then paste the following code into the Advanced editor and click on **Done**:

```
= (x) as table =>
let
    #"Grouped Rows" = Table.Group(x, {"Query"}, {{"min time",
each List.Min([Start Time]), type nullable datetime}, {"max
time", each List.Max([End Time]), type nullable datetime}}),
    #"Changed Type1" = Table.TransformColumnTypes(#"Grouped
Rows",{{"min time", type time}, {"max time", type time}}),
    #"Added Custom" = Table.AddColumn(#"Changed Type1", "Total
Time (S)", each Duration.Seconds([max time]-[min time]))
in
    #"Added Custom"
```

26. Now, let's attempt to optimize this query using Table.Split. Select the query you created called **OptimizedQuery**.

27. In this example, we are going to need a function so we can perform the transformations to our split tables before we recombine them. To do this, repeat *step 23* to create a new blank query called SplitTableTransformations. This function will look to carry out the same transformations we did on **StandardQuery**.

28. Open the Advanced editor and paste the following code:

```
(X) as table =>
let
    #"Added Custom" = Table.AddColumn(X, "Cost", each [Sales] -
[Profit], type number),
    #"Added Custom1" = Table.AddColumn(#"Added Custom",
"TotalSales", each [Sales]*[Quantity],type number),
    #"Split Column by Delimiter" = Table.SplitColumn(#"Added
Custom1", "Country", Splitter.SplitTextByDelimiter(" ",
QuoteStyle.Csv), {"Country.1", "Country.2"}),
    #"Changed Type1" = Table.TransformColumnTypes(#"Split Column
by Delimiter",{{"Country.1", type text}, {"Country.2", type
text}}),
    #"Split Column by Delimiter1" = Table.SplitColumn(#"Changed
Type1", "Customer ID", Splitter.SplitTextByEachDelimiter({"-"},
QuoteStyle.Csv, false), {"Customer ID.1", "Customer ID.2"}),
    #"Changed Type2" = Table.TransformColumnTypes(#"Split Column
by Delimiter1",{{"Customer ID.1", type text}, {"Customer ID.2",
Int64.Type}}),
    #"Removed Columns" = Table.RemoveColumns(#"Changed
Type2",{"Customer ID.2"}),
    #"Renamed Columns" = Table.RenameColumns(#"Removed
Columns",{{"Customer ID.1", "Initials"}}),
    #"Replaced Value" = Table.ReplaceValue(#"Renamed
Columns",0,null,Replacer.ReplaceValue,{"Discount"}),
```

```
    #"Filtered Rows" = Table.SelectRows(#"Replaced Value", each
([Discount] <> null))

in
#"Filtered Rows"
```

29. Click on **Done**.

30. Select the query named OptimizedQuery and then duplicate this query. Rename the duplicate OptimizedQuery (NoTB).

31. Select Advanced editor and add the following to the editor – make sure to add a comma to the previous step and remove the in statement at the end:

```
    splittable = Table.Split(#"Changed Type",1000),
    ApplyTransformations = List.Transform(splittable,
SplitTableTransformations),
    CombineTables = Table.Combine(ApplyTransformations)
    buffertables = Table.Buffer(CombineTables),

in
buffertables
```

32. Click on **Done**.

Now, in the previous query, we used Table.Buffer and then Table.Split to partition the tables by 1,000 rows. Our function called SplitTableTransformations then applied the transformations to the list of tables, and lastly the Table.Combine function pulled them all together again to output the same results as **StandardQuery**. Let's see how this has affected the performance.

33. Select **Tools** in the ribbon and then select **Start diagnostics**.

34. Navigate back to **Home** in the ribbon and select **Refresh preview**. Make sure you have **OptimizedQuery** selected.

35. Return to **Tools** in the ribbon and select **Stop diagnostics**. Like before, this will create a new query in the Diagnostics query folder. Select the new query and rename it OptimizedQuery Diagnostic.

36. Select the **Home** ribbon and open the Advanced editor so you can apply the function you created to the final table. Adjust the in statement to show the following:

```
in
    #"Diagnostic Transformations"( #"Changed Type")
```

37. Click on **Done**.

Again, you may see a different result, but in my example this returned a total time of 1.0118774 seconds, as shown in the following screenshot, resulting in the query refreshing only marginally faster than the original **StandardQuery**. One of the reasons for this could be because of the use of `Table.Buffer` and, given the size of the data, this is actually not helping in the optimization.

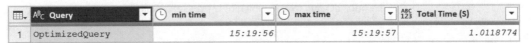

Figure 11.10 – The results from the diagnostic on the query named
OptimizedQuery that uses Table.Buffer and Table.Split

Notice that you added `Table.Buffer` at the end of the previous query. If you were to put it earlier in the query (for example, before the `Table.Split` function), you could expect to have seen very different results. The following screenshot shows the result if you were to implement this function earlier when working with this smaller data. As you can see, it resulted in the query running 12% slower than the original query.

Figure 11.11 – The results from the diagnostic on the query named OptimizedQuery
that uses Table.Buffer earlier in the query before the variable named splittable

Now, let's revisit this example and try to optimize this query by using just the `Table.Split` function.

38. Select the query named **OptimizedQuery (NoTB)** and open the Advanced editor.

39. This time, we will not use the `Table.Buffer` function to load our table into memory. Paste the following into the query with a comma after the previous step:

```
splittable = Table.Split(#"Changed Type", 1000),
ApplyTransformations = List.
Transform(splittable,SplitTableTransformations),
CombineTables = Table.Combine(ApplyTransformations)

in
CombineTables
```

40. Click on **Done**. This will not return the same results as before.

41. Repeat steps *33-37* with the query named **OptimizedQuery (NoTB)** selected. Rename the new query created from the diagnostic to `OptimizedQuery (NoTB) Diagnostic`.

After applying your diagnostic transformation function, you should see the results shown next. Here, we can see that by splitting the tables and applying our function to the partitions, we have been able to reduce the refresh to 0.6569053 seconds. Now, of course, this is looking at a small dataset, but that has allowed us to refresh nearly 40% faster than our standard query.

Figure 11.12 – The results from the diagnostic on the query named
OptimizedQuery (NoTB) which only uses Table.Split

On the flip side to this, we saw that by using the `Table.Buffer` function to load that table into memory actually caused a slower refresh in this instance, highlighting that you should always be careful when choosing when to use `Table.Buffer`.

Summary

In this chapter, we've covered several crucial techniques to enhance the performance of your Power Query workflows.

We began by emphasizing the importance of efficient data filtering and reduction, encouraging you to remove unnecessary data early in your query. We explored the use of native M functions, highlighting their efficiency compared to custom code for specific tasks. Optimizing custom functions was the next focus; we learned to optimize calculations not covered by native functions. The chapter also touched on the significance of optimizing memory usage, introducing `Table.Buffer` and other memory-efficient coding practices.

We then delved into the game-changing concept of parallel query execution, showcasing how functions such as `Table.Split` can drastically reduce query execution times by dividing large tables into smaller partitions and enabling parallel processing. These techniques will empower you to tackle complex data transformation tasks in Power BI while maintaining optimal query execution speed.

In the next chapter, we will dive into the critical topic of managing data relationships in Power BI and using them to clean data effectively.

Questions

1. What were the four key tips for optimizing M queries discussed this chapter?

    A. Sorting, filtering, grouping, summarizing

    B. Filtering and reducing data, using native M functions, creating custom functions, optimizing memory usage

    C. Conditional formatting, joins, aggregations, pivoting

    D. Concatenation, union, splitting, transforming

2. In the custom function for calculating the weighted average, what are the parameters of the function, and how is the weighted average calculated?

    A. Parameters: table, weights, values; the weighted average is calculated by summing the weighted values and dividing by the total weight

    B. Parameters: table, columns; the weighted average is calculated by multiplying values by weights

    C. Parameters: values, weights, total; the weighted average is calculated by summing the values and dividing by the weights

    D. Parameters: rows, weights, values; the weighted average is calculated by summing the values and multiplying by the weights

3. How can `Table.Buffer` optimize the performance of your query?

    A. It reduces the number of columns in a table

    B. It increases memory duplication for faster processing

    C. It loads a table into memory once, reducing memory duplication in subsequent steps

    D. It removes unnecessary rows from a table

4. What does the `Table.Split` function do in the context of parallel query execution?

    A. Combines multiple tables into one

    B. Splits a table into smaller partitions for parallel processing

    C. Removes duplicate rows from a table

    D. Filters rows based on a specified condition

Further reading

- `Table.Buffer`: https://learn.microsoft.com/en-us/powerquery-m/table-buffer

- `Table.Split`: https://learn.microsoft.com/en-us/powerquery-m/table-split

- **Diagnostic Tool Power Query**:

    - https://learn.microsoft.com/en-us/power-query/query-diagnostics

    - https://learn.microsoft.com/en-us/power-query/record-query-diagnostics

    - https://learn.microsoft.com/en-us/power-query/read-query-diagnostics

12

Data Modeling and Managing Relationships

After learning about how to write efficient and performant code, we must now take the next step in preparing and cleaning data for our analytics. This chapter is dedicated to comprehensively understanding and managing data relationships within Power BI to ensure clean and reliable data for effective decision-making. It addresses the often-overlooked issue of dirty data arising from poorly designed data models.

For those confused about why data modeling is part of this book, it's crucial to understand that without proper structuring and optimization of data, analysis and visualization in Power BI would be inefficient and unreliable. The desired Power BI semantic model often necessitates transformations to ensure data accuracy, consistency, and performance, thus emphasizing the indispensable role of data modeling in the process of data cleaning.

The chapter consists of the following topics:

- Understanding the basics of data modeling
- Using bidirectional cross-filtering
- Understanding what's the right cardinality
- Handling large and complex datasets
- Avoiding circular references

To be clear, this chapter will provide a lot of high-level information and techniques to adopt best practices when modeling data in Power BI. This particular topic is very deep, so the aim of this chapter is for you to gain knowledge on the topics included. If you would like to understand more about these topics, you can refer to the resources listed in the *Further reading* section at the chapter's end.

By the end of this chapter, you will have gained high-level insights into data modeling and relationship management, all while learning practical skills that guarantee the highest standards of data cleanliness within Power BI projects.

Understanding the basics of data modeling

In *Chapter 5, Importing Data into Power BI*, you were introduced to some key topics when it comes to importing data, such as dimension modeling, star schemas, and normalization/denormalization. This chapter will build upon this with further knowledge of the basics, introducing concepts such as bidirectional cross-filtering, cardinality, and other best practices.

Here is a summary of some of the basics to consider in this space. To highlight them, this section provides high-level descriptions along with some high-level examples.

Importing versus DirectQuery

In Power BI, we have two main methods of bringing data into our model: importing data and using DirectQuery. Let's have a brief overview of each to help get you up to speed on the difference between them.

Importing

Importing refers to the method of loading and storing data within a Power BI file itself. When you import data, Power BI brings a copy of the data into its internal storage engine, the VertiPaq engine. This engine compresses and optimizes the data, enabling fast query performance for analytical workloads. Importing is suitable for scenarios where data volumes are manageable within the Power BI file, and users can benefit from the performance gains provided by the in-memory storage and compression.

Naturally, this option comes with its pros and cons, which I've summarized for you here.

Here are the pros of importing:

- Fast query performance due to in-memory storage and compression
- Offline access to data since the data is stored within the Power BI file
- Easier to manage and suitable for smaller datasets

And here are the cons of importing:

- Data can become stale between refreshes
- Limited scalability for very large datasets
- Requires storage space within the Power BI file

Example scenario

Consider a scenario where you have a sales dataset in an Excel or a CSV file. Importing the data into Power BI would involve copying the dataset into the Power BI file, allowing users to create reports and dashboards based on this locally stored data. The refresh process is required to keep the imported data up to date with changes in the source.

DirectQuery

DirectQuery is an alternative mode in Power BI that allows the tool to send queries directly to the underlying data source in real time, without importing the data into the Power BI file. With DirectQuery, users can create reports and visualizations based on the live data stored in the source database. This mode is particularly useful when dealing with large datasets or when real-time access to the latest data is crucial.

This method of connecting to data comes with its benefits and challenges also, which I've summarized next.

Here are the pros of DirectQuery:

- Real-time access to the latest data in the source
- Scalability for large datasets since data is not stored in the Power BI file
- No need for scheduled data refreshes

And here are the cons of DirectQuery:

- Potentially slower query performance compared to importing, as queries are executed against the source database.
- DirectQuery defines a 1-million-row limit for data returned from cloud systems. This doesn't apply to aggregations or calculations but to the rows returned. It's important to know, though, when preparing your data, as if you go over that amount (except in Power BI Premium, which has different limits), you'll be presented with an error.
- Limited offline access since reports depend on a live connection to the source.
- Some features and transformations available in import mode may not be supported in DirectQuery mode. For example, you can parse JSON documents, or pivot data from a column to a row form with import mode, but these transformations are more limited in DirectQuery.

Example scenario

Imagine a scenario where your organization's data is stored in a SQL Server database. By using DirectQuery, you can create reports in Power BI that pull data directly from the SQL Server database in real time, eliminating the need to import and refresh the data periodically. This is configured when you first connect to the data source, as shown in the following screenshot:

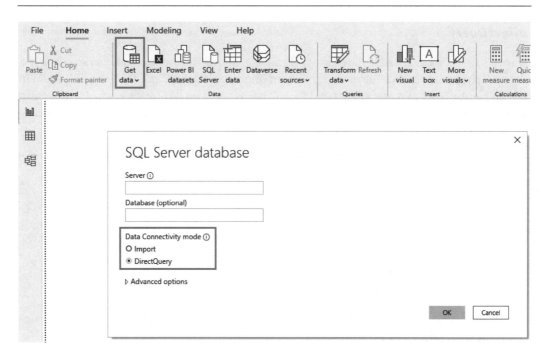

Figure 12.1 – Screenshot of the connection window when a user is trying to connect to a SQL Server database, with the options highlighted to select the Data Connectivity mode

It's important to note that you are able to switch between these modes but only in one direction. So you would be able to switch a DirectQuery table to an imported table but not the other way around.

Dimensional modeling

As discussed in *Chapter 5, Importing Data into Power BI*, dimensional modeling is a technique used to design databases with a focus on organizing data for easy querying and reporting. It emphasizes the separation of data into dimension tables and fact tables to provide a clear structure for analytical purposes:

- **Dimension tables** can be characterized as tables that store descriptive attributes about business entities (for example, products and customers) and provide context for the measures in the fact tables
- **Fact tables** can be characterized as tables that contain quantitative data or measures (for example, sales and revenue) and typically have foreign key relationships with dimension tables

The star schema that we introduced is a specific form of dimensional modeling where a central fact table is surrounded by dimension tables. It simplifies queries by minimizing the number of joins required to retrieve information.

Consider the example that was used in *Chapter 5, Importing Data into Power BI*, for a sales data scenario. You might have a mixture of the following tables to form a model:

- Dimension tables: `Products`, `Customers`, `Date`
- Fact table: `Sales`

The `Sales` table identified as the fact table would typically include foreign keys linking to the `Products`, `Customers`, and `Date` tables.

Now, it can be very common for people who are new to tools such as Power BI to simply think about creating one large table with no relationships, which, again, as highlighted in previous chapters, is fine when using a small set of data but is not best practice or scalable. To help you understand this further, let's go through a summary of the pros and cons of dimension modeling within Power BI.

Here are the pros:

- **Simplifies querying**: The separation of data into dimensions and fact tables simplifies the querying process, making it easier for users to retrieve and analyze data
- **Enhances performance**: Optimized for analytical queries, dimensional modeling typically results in improved performance due to reduced complexity
- **Simplified model**: With fewer tables and joins, the star schema simplifies query development, making it more intuitive and efficient
- **Intuitive design**: The structure is intuitive for users to understand, facilitating ease of use in reporting and analysis

Here are the cons:

- **Normalization challenges**: In transactional systems, where normalization is a priority, dimensional modeling may lead to challenges in maintaining normalized data structures
- **Redundancy risk**: While the star schema simplifies queries, it may introduce redundancy in dimension tables, potentially impacting storage efficiency

Snowflake schema

Snowflake schemas (aptly named because of their resemblance to the shape of a snowflake) consist of dimension tables that connect to further dimension tables. In a snowflake schema, fact tables form the core, connecting information from dimension tables that radiate outward, similar to a star schema. The distinctive feature is that dimension tables in a snowflake schema are split into multiple tables, creating a snowflake pattern. This can be seen in the following screenshot relating to the AdventureWorks store.

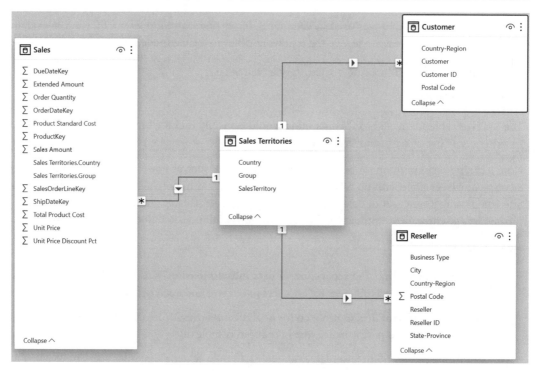

Figure 12.2 – Screenshot providing an example of snowflaking in the model view of Power BI

Through a process called **snowflaking**, the snowflake schema normalizes connected dimension tables by eliminating "low cardinality" attributes and breaking dimension tables into multiple tables until complete normalization is achieved. This complexity results in intricate data relationships, allowing child tables to have multiple parent tables.

Snowflake schemas offer benefits such as compatibility with many OLAP database modeling tools and significant savings on data storage requirements. Normalizing data and converting non-numerical information into numerical keys results in a substantial reduction in disk space. This should be considered if you're preparing the data in Power Query to then be used as part of a snowflake model.

However, snowflake schemas come with challenges, including complex data schemas leading to more intricate source query joins. Although processing technology advancements have improved snowflake schema query performance, there may still be performance declines. Snowflake schemas may also be slower at processing cube data compared to star schemas. While they offer greater normalization and lower risks of data corruption, they do not provide the same level of transactional assurance as highly normalized database structures.

Careful consideration and quality checks are crucial when loading data into a snowflake schema. Before jumping into building a snowflake schema, please consider the following pros and cons.

Pros:

- **Reduced redundancy**: The snowflake schema addresses redundancy concerns by normalizing dimension tables, leading to more efficient use of storage in Power BI
- **Storage efficiency**: Power BI can benefit from a reduction in storage requirements due to the normalized structure

Cons:

- **Complex joins**: Snowflake schemas may involve more complex joins, potentially impacting query performance in Power BI
- **User complexity**: Users may find snowflake schemas less intuitive compared to star schemas

Intermediate tables

In the context of a star schema, intermediate tables are typically used to establish many-to-many relationships (which you will learn more about in the *Understanding what's the right cardinality* section of this chapter) between two dimension tables. When dealing with many-to-many relationships in a star schema, intermediate tables act as junction or bridge tables to link the dimensions.

Consider a scenario where you have a star schema with a central fact table called `Sales` and two dimension tables, `Products` and `Categories`. Now, if each product can belong to multiple categories, and each category can include multiple products, you have a many-to-many relationship between `Products` and `Categories`. To resolve this, you might introduce an intermediate table, say `ProductCategories`, that connects the `Products` and `Categories` tables.

This might create the following structure for your model:

- `Sales` (fact table)
- `Products` (dimension table)
- `Customers` (dimension table)
- `ProductCategories` (intermediate table)

Circular dependencies issue

The introduction of intermediate tables can potentially lead to circular dependencies (discussed later in this chapter, in *the Avoiding circular references section*) in the data model. In short, a circular dependency occurs when the relationships between tables form a loop, making it challenging for the model to determine the correct direction for evaluation during query execution.

In the previous example, if relationships are not properly managed, the model might encounter difficulties understanding the flow of relationships when querying data involving multiple tables. Circular dependencies can impact the performance and accuracy of calculations in the model.

Calendars and date tables

Creating dedicated date tables is a common practice in Power BI to facilitate time-based analysis. It includes various date-related attributes for comprehensive date analysis. Of course, best practice would suggest creating this in a source system, but this can often also be created within Power BI itself using Power Query or DAX in some cases. This is why it's important to highlight this as part of the basics as it might factor into your data-cleaning steps.

Adding calendars and date tables has been made a common practice for several reasons, which are highlighted as follows:

- **Consistency in time intervals**: A dedicated date table ensures that you have a consistent set of time intervals, such as days, months, quarters, and years. This consistency is crucial for aggregating and comparing data over time.

- **Efficient filtering**: Having a separate date table allows you to efficiently filter and slice data based on time. Instead of extracting date information from each individual data record, you can use relationships and filters from the date table, making queries and calculations more efficient.

- **Custom columns and hierarchies**: A dedicated date table enables the creation of custom columns and hierarchies specific to date-related attributes. For example, you can create columns for the day of the week, month names, fiscal periods, and so on. These columns enhance the flexibility of analysis.

- **Time intelligence functions**: Power BI includes time intelligence functions that work seamlessly with dedicated date tables. Functions such as TOTALYTD, TOTALQTD, TOTALMTD, and others simplify calculations such as year-to-date, quarter-to-date, and month-to-date, thus making time-based analysis more straightforward.

- **Seasonality and trend analysis**: Dedicated date tables make it easier to analyze seasonality and trends in your data. You can easily compare performance over different time periods, identify patterns, and make informed decisions based on historical data.

- **Consistent date formatting**: A dedicated date table allows you to control the formatting of dates consistently throughout your reports. This ensures a cohesive and professional look and feel in your visualizations.

- **Handling non-standard fiscal calendars**: If your organization follows a fiscal calendar that doesn't align with the standard calendar year, a dedicated date table allows you to customize the calendar according to your organization's fiscal periods.

- **Enhanced data modeling**: Separating date-related information into its own table adheres to good data modeling practices, promoting a more modular and maintainable structure. It also helps in keeping the model organized and reduces redundancy.

It goes without saying, but by not creating or including a date dimension table in your model, you might encounter challenges with some of the highlighted benefits or actions listed. Due to the nature of the data we are often analyzing, there is usually more than one date we need to include within our analysis, which leads us nicely on to another key consideration when preparing your data for analysis.

Role-playing dimensions

Don't be alarmed – you've not stepped into a game. In Power BI, there are such things as role-playing dimensions. However, it's important to note that this is not just a Power BI thing; it's a universal data modeling technique that's used in the Kimball methodology we introduced in *Chapter 5, Importing Data into Power BI*. Of course, you could dive quite deeply into this topic, so we will provide a brief overview to help you establish a basic understanding.

Role-playing dimensions occur when a single dimension table is used in multiple roles within the same fact table. This is common when the same entity has different relationships within the same context. This is actually quite common particularly when working with data that includes dates. For example, let's imagine you're working with sales data that includes a number of dates such as order date, ship date, delivery date, and others.

One approach to modeling this could be to create separate copies of the same date dimension table for each role, establishing relationships with each of the corresponding date fields in the fact table. This allows for easy incorporation of new role-playing dimensions in a small model, and it simplifies the slicing and dicing of measures by different dimension roles. However, in larger models, the downside includes the inefficiency of importing identical dimension tables multiple times, leading to increased memory usage and potential confusion for end users.

An alternative method involves using one date dimension and establishing multiple relationships with the fact table. Power BI permits only one active relationship between two tables, so additional relationships are marked with dotted lines. To differentiate between these relationships in calculations, the DAX USERELATIONSHIP function is employed. This method offers benefits such as a more memory-efficient, cleaner data model, but it requires creating multiple measures to support different roles, which may be time-consuming and challenging to maintain in large models. The following method is an example highlighting the active relationships:

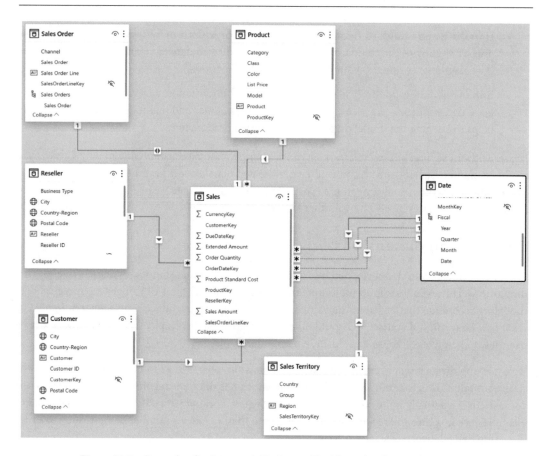

Figure 12.3 – Example of a data model in Power BI with a role-playing dimension

In conclusion, the choice between how you approach this depends on the specific use case. Generally speaking, using the "one date dimension and establishing multiple relationships with the fact table" approach is recommended for its advantages in efficiency and cleanliness, although careful evaluation is necessary based on the model's size and requirements.

Aggregating tables

Aggregation in Power BI involves summarizing and pre-calculating data at a higher level to improve query performance. By creating aggregated tables, you reduce the amount of data that needs to be processed when generating reports or dashboards, leading to faster response times. Highlighted next are some pros and cons of using aggregations that should be considered:

Pros:

- **Performance improvement**: Aggregating data reduces the amount of data that needs to be processed, resulting in faster report generation
- **Reduced resource usage**: Since pre-aggregated tables require less computational power, it reduces the strain on your data source and improves overall system efficiency

Cons:

- **Storage overhead**: Aggregated tables consume additional storage space, as you are storing both the detailed and aggregated versions of the data
- **Maintenance**: You need to manage the update process for aggregated tables whenever the underlying data changes, ensuring that the aggregated values remain accurate

If you're planning to use aggregated tables in your Power BI model, then you should consider the following points while preparing or cleaning your data:

- **Data quality assurance**: Make sure your data is clean and free from errors before creating the aggregated table. These errors could lead to inaccurate aggregated results.
- **Identify aggregation level**: Understand the reporting requirements and identify the appropriate aggregation levels. Then decide which dimensions and measures are essential for summarization and which can be removed to reduce the size/storage.
- **Handling missing data**: Decide on a strategy for handling missing or null values in your data, whether that is to remove these values entirely or return them as zero, for example. Aggregations can be affected if there are gaps in your data, so address missing values appropriately.

In this chapter, we will not be walking through how you go about creating aggregations, but you can refine your practical skills in this area by following the recommended material highlighted at the end of this chapter.

Incremental refreshes

An incremental refresh in Power BI allows you to refresh only the portion of your dataset that has changed since the last refresh. This is particularly useful when dealing with large datasets, as it reduces the amount of data that needs to be refreshed, saving time and resources.

Consider a scenario where you have a dataset that grows daily, but your reports only need the most recent data. With an incremental refresh, you can configure Power BI to refresh only the data that is new or has been updated since the last refresh, minimizing the refresh time.

Pros:

- **Time and resource savings**: An incremental refresh reduces the time and resources required for refreshing data, especially in scenarios where only a portion of the data changes regularly

- **Efficient data handling**: It allows you to handle large datasets more efficiently by focusing on the changes rather than refreshing the entire dataset

Cons:

- **Configuration complexity**: Setting up and configuring an incremental refresh requires careful consideration of your data and may add complexity to your Power BI model

- **Initial setup overhead**: The initial setup to enable an incremental refresh may require additional time and effort compared to a simple full refresh

Similar to aggregations, there are a number of considerations you should factor in when preparing your data if it's to be used with incremental refreshing. These are summarized as follows:

- **Define incremental refresh criteria**: Clearly define the criteria that determine which data should be considered for incremental refresh. This could include date ranges, unique identifiers, or other relevant factors.

- **Create timestamps or versioning**: Include timestamp columns or implement versioning mechanisms in your data to track when records were last modified. This is crucial for identifying changes during incremental refresh.

- **Address data dependencies**: Identify and address any dependencies between tables or data elements to ensure that incremental refresh doesn't introduce inconsistencies.

Top tip

To set up incremental refresh in Power BI Desktop, start by establishing two Power Query date/time parameters named `RangeStart` and `RangeEnd`. These parameters, with case-sensitive names, should be created through the **Manage Parameters** dialog in Power Query Editor. Initially, they serve to filter the data loaded into the Power BI Desktop model table, ensuring only rows within the specified date/time range are included. Once the model is published to the service, the service takes over and automatically overrides `RangeStart` and `RangeEnd`. It utilizes these parameters to query data based on the refresh period defined in the incremental refresh policy settings.

As this chapter focuses on the high-level overview introduction of the features and techniques to help prepare data for analysis, you will find resources under *Further reading* at the end of the chapter to expand your practical skills in actually configuring techniques such as incremental refresh.

Using bidirectional cross-filtering

Data relationships are a fundamental component of Power BI, allowing you to link tables and perform complex data analysis. One feature that enhances the capabilities of relationships is **bidirectional cross-filtering** (**BDCF**). However, wielding this double-edged sword effectively is crucial, as it can lead to unexpected errors and performance bottlenecks. In this chapter, we'll explore this in depth, learning how to harness its power without compromising data cleanliness. You can identify a join that has BDCF enabled because of the box with two arrows, as seen in the following screenshot:

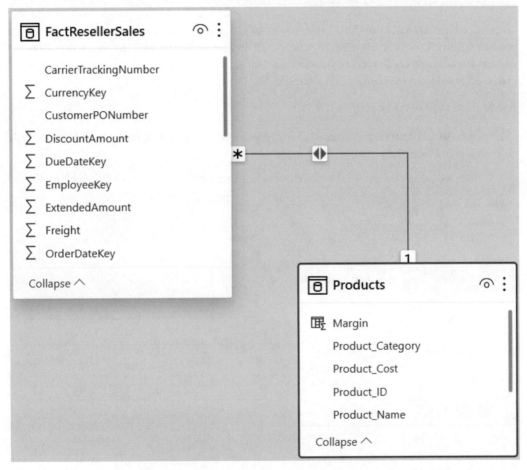

Figure 12.4 – Screenshot showing a BDCF relationship in Power BI

In the next section, you will learn more about what exactly BDCF is.

What is bidirectional cross-filtering?

Bidirectional cross-filtering is a feature that enables tables in Power BI to filter each other in both directions, allowing for more complex and interactive reporting. While bidirectional cross-filtering can be a valuable asset in your data model, it comes with some caveats. You will learn to identify potential issues that may arise from the usage and understand how to address them effectively. We'll delve into scenarios where bidirectional cross-filtering can lead to errors, such as circular dependencies, and how to mitigate them. Additionally, we'll discuss best practices for utilizing bidirectional cross-filtering in a way that ensures a clean and efficient data model.

To create a bidirectional cross-filter relationship, let's look at an example so you can gain first-hand product skills on how to adjust the relationships. To do this, we will be working on a Power BI model that has already been created, called `Cleaning Data With Power BI - BDCF.pbix`, which can be accessed from the book's GitHub repo.

Follow these steps to create your own BDCF:

1. Open the `Cleaning Data With Power BI - BDCF.pbix` file and select **Model View** in Power BI.

    Here, we can see the snowflake model, including four tables, shown in the following screenshot:

Figure 12.5 – Screenshot of the snowflake model in the file listed previously

This example represents financial transactions in accounts that can have one or more customers associated. This can be complex and require a snowflake because the relationship between sales transactions and customers would likely result in a many-to-many relationship. One customer could have many transactions. In reverse, a transaction could also have multiple customers attached. Currently, the model works by allowing us to see the relationships between the tables; however, let's try to do some analysis on this.

2. Select **Report View**.

3. Now let's imagine we would like to see the sum of sales by our customers. Select the checkbox next to **Sales Amount** from **Sales Transactions Table** in the field pane on the right-hand side. This will present us with a card visual showing the sum amount of sales.

4. Let's change this from a card to a table visual in the ribbon toolbar by selecting the visual labeled **Table**.

5. Now we are going to add customers to the table to see how much each customer has spent. Select the checkbox on the **Customer** field from the **Customer** table. As you will see from the output (*Figure 12.6*), Power BI has not been able to determine the relationship between customers and the transactions, so it has repeated the sum total amount for each customer. To calculate the sum amount for each individual customer, we must sort through the entries in the Transaction table corresponding to each customer. However, this process becomes problematic because the tabular model lacks the capability to sort the transaction table by customers.

Customer	Sum of Sales Amount
[Not Applicable]	29,358,677.89
Aaron Adams	29,358,677.89
Aaron Alexander	29,358,677.89
Aaron Allen	29,358,677.89
Aaron Baker	29,358,677.89
Aaron Bryant	29,358,677.89
Aaron Butler	29,358,677.89
Aaron Campbell	29,358,677.89
Aaron Carter	29,358,677.89
Aaron Chen	29,358,677.89
Aaron Coleman	29,358,677.89
Aaron Collins	29,358,677.89
Aaron Diaz	29,358,677.89
Aaron Edwards	29,358,677.89
Aaron Evans	29,358,677.89
Aaron Flores	29,358,677.89
Aaron Foster	29,358,677.89
Aaron Gonzales	29,358,677.89

Figure 12.6 – Screenshot of the results by selecting customer and sum amount

6. When you navigate to the Model View to inspect the relationships within the model, you'll see arrows denoting how tables are filtered. Notably, the arrow indicating the relationship between **AccountCustomer** and **Account** is pointing in the incorrect direction. By default, the model filters from the "1" side to the "Many" side of the relationship, which doesn't align with our objective of accessing transactions associated specifically with customer accounts. Now, there are two ways we can look to fix this, one of which is to use DAX measures and the other is to use BDCF. Let's explore how we would use this here. Select **Manage relationships** from the tabs. This will open the window to manage relationship. All existing relationships can be seen and adjusted here. Select the relationship from **Table AccountCustomer** to **Table Account**.

7. Select **Edit…**.

8. Adjust the **Cross filter direction** dropdown from **Single** to **Both**, as shown:

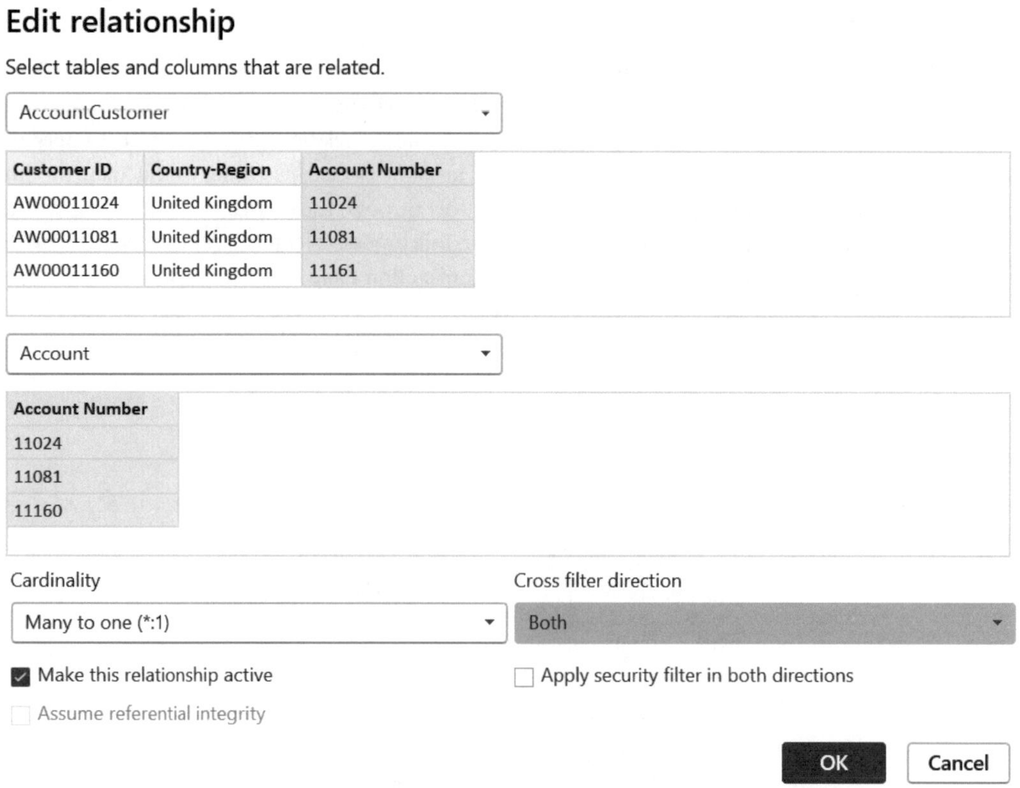

Edit relationship

Select tables and columns that are related.

AccountCustomer	▾

Customer ID	Country-Region	Account Number
AW00011024	United Kingdom	11024
AW00011081	United Kingdom	11081
AW00011160	United Kingdom	11161

Account	▾

Account Number
11024
11081
11160

Cardinality	Cross filter direction
Many to one (*:1) ▾	Both ▾

☑ Make this relationship active   ☐ Apply security filter in both directions

☐ Assume referential integrity

OK   **Cancel**

Figure 12.7 – Screenshot of the Edit relationship window within Power BI

9. Select **OK** to complete the relationship edit and select **Close** to exit the relationship manager.

10. Now navigate back to the Report View.

Here, you should see that the table has now been adjusted and we can see the values assigned to each of the customers we have, as shown:

Customer	Sum of Sales Amount
Aaron Adams	117.96
Aaron Alexander	69.99
Aaron Allen	3,399.99
Aaron Baker	1,750.98
Aaron Bryant	133.96
Aaron Butler	14.98
Aaron Campbell	1,155.48
Aaron Carter	39.98
Aaron Chen	39.98
Aaron Coleman	61.96
Aaron Collins	6,047.32

Figure 12.8 – Example results after applying BDCF to our model

We have been able to achieve the results because, with the help of BDCF, the model was able to push the filters to the **Account** table from the **Customer** table through **CustomerAccount**.

Here, you learned how to actually implement a bidirectional cross-filter within your model/semantic layer of Power BI. In the next section, you will explore more about the best practices when working with models that include these relationships.

Best practices for bidirectional cross-filtering

Mastering the basics of one-to-one, one-to-many, and many-to-one relationships lays the groundwork for effective data modeling. In this context, bidirectional cross-filtering should be approached with caution, serving as a tool in your arsenal rather than a default setting. This set of best practices aims to guide you through the judicious use of bidirectional cross-filtering and its potential challenges to ensure a robust and performant Power BI data model:

- **Understand the basics**: Before diving into bidirectional cross-filtering, ensure you have a strong grasp of Power BI relationships, including the basics of one-to-one, one-to-many, and many-to-one relationships. Understanding the underlying mechanics of relationships is crucial.

- **Use it sparingly**: Bidirectional cross-filtering should be used judiciously and only when necessary. Excessive use can lead to performance issues, so consider alternative relationship configurations before enabling it.

- **Identify potential issues**: Be vigilant for potential issues such as circular references. These can occur when bidirectional cross-filtering is not properly managed and can lead to data inconsistencies and performance problems. Utilize the **Manage Relationships** dialog to identify and resolve these issues.

- **Optimize for performance**: When working with bidirectional cross-filtering, be mindful of the performance implications. Large datasets and complex data models can suffer from slower query execution, so consider techniques such as summarization and aggregation to optimize performance.

- **Testing and validation**: Always thoroughly testing your data model when using this feature is critical. Check for errors and validate that your reporting remains accurate after implementing the feature. Implement test scenarios to ensure bidirectional cross-filtering doesn't introduce unexpected issues, particularly as you start building new measures or begin introducing new data.

In conclusion, while bidirectional cross-filtering offers a potent means to enhance the sophistication of your Power BI data models, a strategic and cautious approach is imperative. By understanding the foundational aspects of Power BI relationships, using bidirectional cross-filtering judiciously, identifying and resolving potential issues, optimizing for performance, and rigorously testing your data model, you can harness the full potential of this feature while mitigating challenges.

These best practices empower you to strike the right balance, ensuring that your data model not only meets your analytical needs but also maintains optimal performance and data integrity over time. As you navigate the complexities of bidirectional cross-filtering, adherence to these guidelines will pave the way for a robust and reliable Power BI reporting environment.

Now you have formed a foundational knowledge of what BDCF actually means when setting up relationships, in the next section, you will begin to learn about selecting the right cardinality for your data analysis.

Understanding what's the right cardinality

In the realm of Power BI data modeling, the concept of cardinality plays a pivotal role, influencing the dynamics of relationships between tables. Cardinality essentially defines how tables are interconnected, laying the groundwork for precise and efficient report generation. To grasp cardinality, imagine it as the rulebook that dictates how rows in one table relate to rows in another. A robust understanding of cardinality is fundamental for anyone creating a Power BI data model, as it underpins the accuracy and efficiency of subsequent reporting.

In this section, we'll explore what cardinality is, why it's essential, and how to make the right choices to ensure your data model is both accurate and high-performing. Let's start!

Understanding cardinality

Cardinality is all about defining the nature of the relationship between two tables. It answers questions such as *"For each row in Table A, how many corresponding rows exist in Table B?"* This understanding guides Power BI in navigating relationships when aggregating data, ensuring that the relationships are appropriately established to reflect the real-world connections in your dataset. There are four main types of cardinality:

- **One-to-one (1:1)**: In a one-to-one relationship, each row in the first table corresponds to one and only one row in the second table, and vice versa.

  - **Example scenario**: You have an `Order Lines` table where each row represents a line item in a sales order. Each order line pertains to one specific product.

  - **Usage**: In this case, you establish a many-to-one relationship between the `Order Lines` and `Products` tables. Each row in the `Order Lines` table can be associated with only one product (many order lines to one product). Conversely, a row in the `Products` table can be related to multiple rows in the `Order Lines` table, representing different instances of that product being sold.

- **One-to-many (1:N)**: In a one-to-many relationship, each row in the first table can correspond to multiple rows in the second table, but each row in the second table can correspond to only one row in the first table.

  - **Example scenario**: You have a `Categories` table and a `Products` table. Each product belongs to one specific category, but a category can have multiple products.

  - **Usage**: In this scenario, you establish a one-to-many relationship between the `Categories` table and the `Products` table. Each row in the `Categories` table can be related to multiple rows in the `Products` table (one to many products). On the other hand, each row in the `Products` table is associated with only one category, as each product belongs to a specific category (introducing many-to-one).

- **Many-to-one (N:1)**: Many-to-one is the reverse of one-to-many, where each row in the second table can relate to multiple rows in the first table, but each row in the first table relates to one row in the second table. It sounds confusing but which one you use really depends on how you build the schema in your model and where the data resides.

  - **Example scenario**: You have an `Order Lines` table where each row represents a line item in a sales order. Each order line pertains to one specific product.

  - **Usage**: In this case, you establish a many-to-one relationship between the `Order Lines` table and the `Products` table. Each row in the `Order Lines` table can be associated with only one product (many order lines to one product). Conversely, a row in the `Products` table can be related to multiple rows in the `Order Lines` table, representing different instances of that product being sold.

- **Many-to-Many (N:N)**: A many-to-many relationship is a type of relationship between two tables in your model where each record in one table can be related to multiple records in another table, and vice versa. In the context of Power BI or other data modeling tools, many-to-many relationships are often resolved using an intermediate or junction table.

  - **Example scenario**: You have a `Students` table and a `Courses` table, where each student can enroll in multiple courses, and each course can have multiple students.

  - **Usage**: In this scenario, you establish a many-to-many relationship between the `Students` and `Courses` tables. To implement this, you typically introduce an intermediate table, such as `Enrollments`, which contains records indicating which students are enrolled in which courses. This allows for flexibility in modeling complex relationships where many students can be associated with many courses.

Why cardinality matters

Cardinality is not just a technical detail; it has a significant impact on the accuracy and performance of your Power BI reports. Here's why it matters:

- **Data accuracy**: Choosing the correct cardinality ensures that your reports accurately represent the relationships in your data. Incorrect cardinality can lead to misinterpreted data and erroneous insights.

- **Performance**: Cardinality directly affects the performance of your queries and visualizations. An improper cardinality setting can slow down report generation, making it less responsive and efficient.

Choosing the right cardinality

Selecting the correct cardinality largely depends on the nature of your data and the relationships you're trying to represent. Here are some guidelines to help you choose the right cardinality:

- **Understand your data**: Before defining cardinality, thoroughly understand your data. Know the nature of the relationships between tables and how data is related. This understanding is essential for making informed choices.

- **Start with 1:N**: In most cases, one-to-many relationships are the safest choice. They cover scenarios where each item in one table can be related to multiple items in another table. If you're unsure, begin with 1:N and adjust as needed.

- **Use 1:1 sparingly**: One-to-one relationships should be employed only when it's crucial to restrict data. They are less common and should be used sparingly due to their potential to complicate the data model.

- **Be prepared to adjust**: The cardinality setting is not set in stone. As you work with your data and build reports, be ready to revisit and adjust the cardinality if necessary. Data models can evolve, and your initial assumptions may change.

  - For example, suppose you have a `Sales` fact table containing information about individual sales transactions, and a `Customer` dimension table providing details about each customer.

  - Initially, you might establish a relationship between the `Sales` table and the `Customer` table based on the `CustomerID` column in both tables. This creates a one-to-many relationship, as each customer can have multiple sales transactions. This setup is appropriate when you want to analyze sales data at the customer level and you have a direct relationship between each sale and a specific customer.

  - However, let's say you also want to analyze sales data at a regional level, and your `Customer` dimension table includes a `Region` column. In this case, you might want to aggregate the sales data at the regional level, treating each region as a single entity.

  - To achieve this, you could switch the cardinality of the relationship between the `Sales` table and the `Customer` table from one-to-many to many-to-one (or many-to-many). By doing so, you're indicating that each sale is associated with a specific region, and you want to aggregate the sales data based on the regions in the `Customer` dimension table.

  - Switching cardinality in this way allows you to change the granularity of your analysis. You can now analyze sales data at both the customer and regional levels, leveraging the flexibility of your data model to gain insights at different levels of detail.

- **Testing and validation**: Before finalizing your cardinality choices, thoroughly test your data model. Ensure that your queries provide accurate results and that the reports are performing well. Make adjustments based on your testing.

Choosing the right cardinality is a critical step in creating an effective Power BI data model. It impacts both the accuracy of your reports and the performance of your visualizations. By understanding your data, starting with 1:N relationships, evaluating the suitability of N:1 relationships, and being prepared to adjust as needed, you can create a data model that provides accurate insights and responsive reporting. Cardinality may seem like a technical detail, but it's the foundation of your Power BI success.

Remember, cardinality isn't a static setting but an evolving aspect of your data model, warranting thorough testing, validation, and continuous refinement. Through thoughtful consideration and strategic application of cardinality, you pave the way for a data model that not only mirrors the intricacies of your dataset but also empowers your reports with precision and efficiency.

In the following section, you will delve deeper into techniques you can take on while working on complex datasets within Power BI.

Handling large and complex datasets

Power BI is an excellent tool for data visualization and analysis, but what happens when you're dealing with big data?

When datasets become massive, challenges arise in terms of performance, data modeling, and query optimization.

In this section, we'll explore best practices for handling big data within Power BI, ensuring that you can still unlock valuable insights without compromising performance.

Understanding big data

Big data typically refers to datasets that are too large or complex for traditional data processing applications. These datasets often exceed the capacity of conventional software and may include various data types, such as structured, semi-structured, or unstructured data.

Challenges of working with big data in Power BI

When dealing with big data in Power BI, several challenges emerge:

- **Performance**: Large datasets can slow down report generation and visualization. Users expect responsive dashboards, which can be compromised with slow-performing queries.

- **Data modeling**: Designing a robust data model for big data can be complex. Poor data modeling can lead to inefficient queries and decreased report performance.

- **Data sources**: Big data often originates from various sources and may require data preparation, transformation, and integration before it's suitable for Power BI.

Best practices for handling big data

To help you work with big data in Power BI, I have provided a breakdown of tips focused on the key areas:

- **Data import strategies:**

  - **DirectQuery**: When dealing with big data, consider using DirectQuery, which connects to data sources in real time, avoiding data duplication. This approach minimizes data storage and allows for fresher data.

  - **Incremental loading**: If using Power Query to load data, implement incremental loading strategies. This involves loading only new or modified data, reducing the amount of data processed during refresh.

- **Data modeling:**

  - **Optimize relationships:** Ensure relationships between tables are well defined and optimized for performance. Use appropriate cardinality and active or inactive relationships.

  - **Use aggregations:** For large datasets, leverage aggregations to pre-calculate summarized data. Aggregations can significantly improve query performance by reducing the amount of data scanned.

  - **Star schema:** Organize your data model into a star schema, where a central fact table connects to dimension tables. This structure is efficient for query performance.

- **Query optimization:**

  - **Use query folding:** Encourage query folding, where Power Query pushes as much processing as possible back to the data source. This minimizes data transferred to Power BI.

  - **Filter and trim data:** Apply filters early in your queries to reduce the amount of data loaded. Trim unused columns to optimize memory usage.

  - **Table.Buffer:** Implement the `Table.Buffer` function in Power Query to load data into memory efficiently, especially when working with big data. As highlighted in the previous chapter, this should be judiciously used due to its impact on memory usage.

- **Data source specifics:**

  - **Data source tuning:** Depending on your data source, investigate tuning options that improve query performance, for example, indexing in databases. This is a huge topic, so if you're interested, you can learn more about this and what it entails from the link labeled data tuning in the *Further reading* section.

- **Monitoring and testing:**

  - **Performance monitoring:** Continuously monitor the performance of your Power BI reports. Identify and address any bottlenecks or slowdowns.

  - **Load testing:** Perform load testing to simulate heavy user traffic and identify how your reports perform under pressure. While this isn't a native feature within Power BI, there are third-party tools that can help with this. There is a link in *Further reading* to understand more on how to configure this.

- **Regular maintenance:**

  - **Scheduled refresh:** Plan your data refresh schedule carefully to avoid performance disruptions during business hours.

  - **Data archiving:** Consider archiving older data that is less frequently accessed using incremental refresh. This can reduce the dataset size and improve performance.

Big data presents unique challenges when working with Power BI, but with the right strategies and best practices, you can harness its potential. By optimizing data import strategies, carefully designing your data model, focusing on query optimization, and staying vigilant with performance monitoring and testing, you can create Power BI reports that provide valuable insights even when dealing with large and complex datasets. Handling big data within Power BI requires a combination of thoughtful design and continuous optimization to strike the balance between performance and data richness.

Again, the resources in *Further reading* and examples of data tuning and load testing can be found at the end of the chapter.

Avoiding circular references

Circular references in Power BI models can be a perplexing issue that hinders effective data analysis. They occur when there's a loop in the relationships between tables, creating ambiguity in calculations.

In this section, we'll delve into best practices for identifying and avoiding circular references in your Power BI models, ensuring data clarity and smooth report generation.

Understanding circular references

Circular references arise when there is an ambiguous or recursive relationship between two or more tables in your Power BI model. This ambiguity can lead to incorrect results in calculations, and Power BI attempts to address it by disallowing circular references by default.

Let's walk through an example of when this might happen:

1. Open the `Adventure Works Sales Data (Clean Star Schema).pbix` file and select **Model View** in Power BI.

2. Let's create a new table that contains all the products we own that are part of our clothing line. The reasoning is that this category of product will soon be discontinued so we want to create a separate table for that. To do this, select **New table** from the **Calculations** group within the ribbon.

3. To define the new table, enter the following code in the formula bar:

    ```
    Clothing Products =
    FILTER(
            VALUES('Product'),
            'Product'[Category]="Clothing"
    )
    ```

4. Press *Enter* – this will create a table that has all your clothing products listed.

5. To create the relationship between the tables, try selecting ProductKey from the **Clothing Products** table and dragging it onto the **ProductKey** field in the **Product** table. This will cause the following error message to appear:

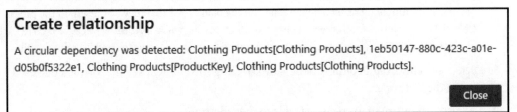

Create relationship

A circular dependency was detected: Clothing Products[Clothing Products], 1eb50147-880c-423c-a01e-d05b0f5322e1, Clothing Products[ProductKey], Clothing Products[Clothing Products].

Close

Figure 12.9 – Error caused by creating a relationship that would cause a circular dependency

6. Note that if we were to create a relationship by dragging **ProductKey** from the **Product** table to the **ProductKey** field in the new **Clothing Product** table, that would be fine. It would create a one-to-one relationship with BDCF enabled.

Edit relationship

Select tables and columns that are related.

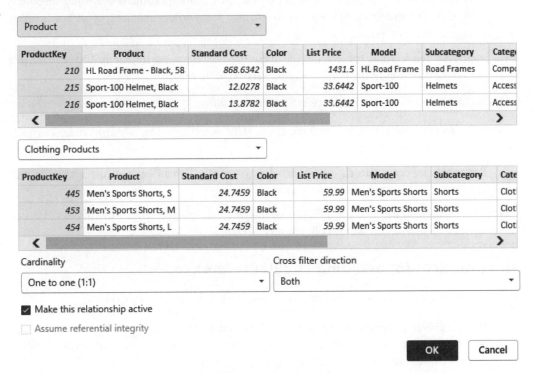

Product ▾

ProductKey	Product	Standard Cost	Color	List Price	Model	Subcategory	Categ
210	HL Road Frame - Black, 58	868.6342	Black	1431.5	HL Road Frame	Road Frames	Compc
215	Sport-100 Helmet, Black	12.0278	Black	33.6442	Sport-100	Helmets	Access
216	Sport-100 Helmet, Black	13.8782	Black	33.6442	Sport-100	Helmets	Access

Clothing Products ▾

ProductKey	Product	Standard Cost	Color	List Price	Model	Subcategory	Cate
445	Men's Sports Shorts, S	24.7459	Black	59.99	Men's Sports Shorts	Shorts	Clot
453	Men's Sports Shorts, M	24.7459	Black	59.99	Men's Sports Shorts	Shorts	Clot
454	Men's Sports Shorts, L	24.7459	Black	59.99	Men's Sports Shorts	Shorts	Clot

Cardinality

One to one (1:1) ▾

Cross filter direction

Both ▾

☑ Make this relationship active

☐ Assume referential integrity

OK   Cancel

Figure 12.10 – Example of the relationship between product tables
using a one-to-one relationship and with BDCF enabled

7. However, try selecting **ProductKey** from the **Clothing Products** table and dragging it onto the **ProductKey** field in the **Product** table.

   The main reason you are seeing this error is we created the new table using the VALUES function. The VALUES function creates a dependency on the blank rows that may be present in the product table. A better solution for this would be to use functions such as ALLNOBLANKROW or DISTINCT in place of VALUES. These functions would not add any blank rows for invalid relationships.

8. Select the **Clothing Products** table – by selecting this, we will see the formula bar used to create the table open.

9. Adjust the DAX used to create the table to the following:

```
Clothing Products =
FILTER(
        ALLNOBLANKROW('Product'),
        'Product'[Category]="Clothing"
    )
```

10. Press *Enter*.

    Now you will be able to create relationships from the **Clothing Products** table to the **Products** table, including the option to use a one-to-many or many-to-one relationship without causing a circular reference error.

If you're interested in learning more about the difference between these functions, I have attached a link to the relevant articles in the *Further reading* section of this chapter.

Common scenarios leading to circular references are as follows:

- **Many-to-many relationships**: Complex relationships, especially many-to-many, can inadvertently lead to circular references

- **Bidirectional cross-filtering (BDCF)**: The use of BDCF, while powerful, can sometimes introduce circular references if not managed correctly

- **Intermediate tables**: The introduction of intermediate tables in your data model can create intricate relationships that result in circular references

Best practices for avoiding circular references

Identify and resolve circular references early by using the following best practices:

- **Use the Power BI Relationship view**: The **Relationship view** is a powerful tool to visualize relationships in your model. It can help you identify circular references by highlighting tables that are part of the loop.

- **Inspect error messages**: If you encounter circular reference issues, carefully review error messages provided by Power BI. They often indicate the tables involved.

- **Use BDCF with caution**: Bidirectional cross-filtering can introduce circular references if not used judiciously. Be mindful of where you enable it and ensure it's essential for your analysis.

- **Opt for single-direction filtering**: Where possible, use single-direction filtering to reduce the complexity of relationships and mitigate the risk of circular references.

- **Intermediate tables and role-playing dimensions**: Evaluate the need for intermediate tables and role-playing dimensions. Simplify your data model where you can reduce the chances of circular references.

- **Avoid auto-detect relationships**: Be cautious with auto-detect relationships, as they can introduce circular references. For those not familiar, when you load data into Power BI for the first time, or when you add to an existing model, if you have two tables with common fields between them, Power BI will try to automatically create a relationship between the two tables. Instead, consider creating additional columns or tables that fulfill the same purpose.

- **Review many-to-many relationships**: Examine your many-to-many relationships. Simplify them by creating bridge tables or summarizing data before joining tables, rather than creating complex direct relationships.

- **Use DAX measures and functions**: Implement DAX measures and functions for calculations. Functions such as `AllExcept` help to bypass circular references by breaking down complex calculations into manageable steps.

- **Documentation and naming conventions**: Maintain documentation on your data model, relationships, and table structures. Naming conventions can provide clarity and help avoid accidental circular references.

- **Test and validate your model**: Regularly test your data model by creating reports and running calculations. Validating the results can help you uncover and resolve circular reference issues.

Circular references can complicate Power BI models and affect the accuracy of your data analysis. By following these best practices and staying vigilant about your data model's structure, you can avoid circular references and ensure a clean, reliable foundation for your Power BI reports.

While Power BI offers a robust set of features for data analysis, the responsibility of creating well-structured, non-circular models lies with the data modeler. Avoiding circular references is an essential step in achieving accurate and trustworthy insights from your data.

Summary

In this chapter, we delved into the intricate world of data modeling and managing relationships within Power BI. It provided a brief overview of and introduction to the pivotal role well-structured data modeling plays in ensuring clean and reliable data for informed decision-making.

We started by exploring/recapping the basics of dimension modeling in Power BI, bidirectional cross-filtering, understanding its power, identifying potential errors and bottlenecks, and adopting best practices to use it effectively. We also comprehensively covered the concept of cardinality with an emphasis on its impact on data cleanliness and performance.

Later, we learned how to make the right choices to create accurate and high-performing data models, with insights into challenges and best practices for optimizing performance and managing vast data. Lastly, we explored the complexities of avoiding circular references, gaining strategies and best practices to ensure data clarity.

In the next chapter, you will learn about essential strategies for maintaining data quality and consistency throughout the transformation process. It will cover topics such as evaluating whether Power BI is the right platform, creating a transformation plan, maintaining consistent naming conventions, and documenting changes.

Questions

1. What is the primary focus of managing relationships in Power BI?

    A. Writing efficient code

    B. Visualizing data

    C. Data modeling

    D. Advanced analytics

2. Why is **bidirectional cross-filtering (BDCF)** considered a double-edged sword in Power BI?

    A. It is too complicated to implement

    B. It can enhance capabilities but may lead to errors and performance issues

    C. It is only suitable for small datasets

    D. It is a default setting for all relationships

3. What is bidirectional cross-filtering, and how does it enhance data analysis in Power BI?

    A. A tool for data duplication

    B. A feature allowing tables to filter each other in both directions

    C. A method to create circular references

    D. A default setting for relationships

4. Why is understanding cardinality crucial in Power BI data modeling?

    A. It is a technical detail without any impact

    B. It defines the nature of relationships between tables

C. It only influences data visualization

D. It is essential for writing efficient code

5. What does one-to-one (1:1) cardinality mean in Power BI relationships?

A. Each row in one table corresponds to one row in another, and vice versa

B. Each row in the first table can correspond to multiple rows in the second table

C. Many rows in one table correspond to one row in another

D. Each row in one table corresponds to one and only one row in the second table

6. What impact does choosing the correct cardinality have on Power BI reports?

A. It doesn't affect reports

B. It directly influences data accuracy and performance

C. It only affects data modeling complexity

D. It slows down report generation

7. When dealing with big data in Power BI, what are the common challenges mentioned in the chapter?

A. Slow internet connection

B. Data cleaning issues

C. Performance, data modeling, and query optimization challenges

D. Lack of visualization options

8. What is one of the best techniques for handling big data in Power BI, particularly when importing data?

A. Use DirectQuery for all scenarios

B. Avoid incremental loading strategies

C. Optimize relationships by using any cardinality

D. Implement incremental loading to load only new or modified data

9. What role do DAX measures and functions play in avoiding circular references?

A. They introduce circular references

B. They complicate calculations

C. They help bypass circular references by breaking down complex calculations

D. They are not relevant to circular references

Further reading

Here is a list of great articles for further learning and development of practical skills on the topics we covered in this chapter:

- Modeling data: `https://learn.microsoft.com/en-us/power-bi/transform-model/desktop-relationships-understand`

- DirectQuery, Import, and Composite:

  - `https://learn.microsoft.com/en-us/power-bi/connect-data/desktop-directquery-about`

    - `https://learn.microsoft.com/en-us/power-bi/transform-model/desktop-composite-models`

- Aggregated Tables:

  - `https://lytix.be/power-bi-aggregations/#:~:text=NOTE%3A%20when%20the%20detail%20columns,and%20the%20detail%20table%20match!`

  - `https://learn.microsoft.com/en-us/power-bi/transform-model/aggregations-advanced`

- Incremental Refresh: `https://learn.microsoft.com/en-us/power-bi/connect-data/incremental-refresh-configure`

- Cardinality: `https://powerbidocs.com/2021/02/15/cardinality-of-relationship-in-power-bi/`

- BDCF: `https://learn.microsoft.com/en-us/power-bi/transform-model/desktop-bidirectional-filtering`

- Auto-Detect Relationships: `https://radacad.com/power-bi-design-tip-disable-the-auto-detect-relationship`

- Circular dependencies:

  - `https://www.antmanbi.com/post/circular-dependency-between-calculated-columns-in-a-table`

  - `https://www.sqlbi.com/articles/avoiding-circular-dependency-errors-in-dax/`

  - Fixing calculated columns example: `https://www.youtube.com/watch?v=CQH-cZFk7pXc`

- DAX functions:

  - `https://learn.microsoft.com/en-us/dax/values-function-dax`

  - `https://learn.microsoft.com/en-us/dax/distinct-function-dax`

  - `https://learn.microsoft.com/en-us/dax/allnoblankrow-function-dax`

- Optimization:

  - Data source tuning:

    - `https://learn.microsoft.com/en-us/power-bi/guidance/power-bi-optimization`

    - `https://www.sqlgene.com/2019/09/27/a-comprehensive-guide-to-power-bi-performance-tuning/`

  - Load testing:

    - `https://blog.crossjoin.co.uk/2023/04/23/why-load-testing-power-bi-is-important/`

Part 4 – Paginated Reports, Automations, and OpenAI

In this last part of the book, you will explore paginated reports, automation through Power Automate, and the transformative potential of OpenAI. You will learn how to prepare data for paginated reporting in Power BI and leverage Power Automate as a powerful ally in data cleaning tasks. Later, you will discover how OpenAI technologies, such as ChatGPT, are revolutionizing data work, providing insights into simplifying tasks and staying ahead in the dynamic landscape of data management. This part serves as a bridge between traditional data practices and cutting-edge technologies, offering a holistic understanding of the evolving landscape of data management.

This part has the following chapters:

- *Chapter 13, Preparing Data for Paginated Reporting*
- *Chapter 14, Automating Data Cleaning Tasks with Power Automate*
- *Chapter 15, Making Life Easier with OpenAI*

13

Preparing Data for Paginated Reporting

Across this book, we have learned about a number of best practices on how to leverage Power BI to clean and prepare your data for analysis. In this chapter, we will delve into how we can take that knowledge in using Power BI Report Builder to connect, prepare, and report on data with paginated reports. Power BI Report Builder is a powerful authoring tool within the Microsoft Power BI suite designed for creating paginated reports. Unlike the traditional Power BI reports that are interactive and dynamic, paginated reports are highly formatted, pixel-perfect, and optimized for printing or generating PDFs. This part of the platform allows users to design and generate paginated reports with precision.

This introductory chapter will provide insight into how you should clean, prepare, and connect to your data if you wish to use that data for paginated reporting in the future.

Some of the key features of Report Builder include the following:

- **Pixel-perfect reporting**: Users can create reports with precise layouts and formatting to meet specific business requirements. This is particularly important for industries where regulatory or compliance standards necessitate exact reporting formats.

- **Rich data visuals**: While paginated reports are more focused on tables and matrices, Report Builder still provides a range of ways to enhance the presentation of information.

- **Versatile data source connectivity**: Power BI Report Builder supports various data sources including relational databases, multidimensional sources, Power BI semantic models, and more.

- **Advanced expressions and calculations**: Users can leverage powerful expressions and calculations to derive insights from the data and create custom fields.

While the learnings in the book will take you far, having the complete knowledge, including paginated reports, will leave you more experienced than many in the industry. Although based on slightly more legacy technology, paginated reports are still widely used across many industries and are now very much integrated into the Fabric platform.

In this chapter, you will learn about the following:

- Understanding the importance of paginated reports
- Connecting to data sources within Power BI Report Builder
- Data preparation
- Using filters and parameters
- Using row groups/column groups

By the end of this chapter, you will feel confident in approaching and using Power BI Report Builder to prepare data for use in paginated reports.

Technical requirements

To follow along in this chapter, please ensure that you download and install Power BI Report Builder. You can get more details from `https://www.microsoft.com/en-us/download/details.aspx?id=58158`.

Later in the chapter, we will connect to a published semantic model. As such, please ensure that you have published this semantic model to your Power BI web service: `https://github.com/PacktPublishing/Data-Cleaning-with-Power-BI/blob/main/AdventureWorks%20Sales.pbix`.

Ensure that you also download the following file to be used in the report: `https://github.com/PacktPublishing/Data-Cleaning-with-Power-BI/blob/main/AdventureWorksLogo.jpg`.

Understanding the importance of paginated reports

The importance of connecting, preparing, and analyzing data for paginated reports is vital for accuracy and consistency.

When bringing data into Power BI Report Builder, it's essential to consider the following:

- **Data accuracy and consistency**: Ensure data sources are reliable to maintain accuracy and uniformity in reports
- **Customization and user interaction**: Utilize dynamic data sources and parameters for creating customizable reports with interactive features
- **Compliance and formatting**: Adhere to specific formatting requirements to meet regulatory obligations and mitigate risks
- **Efficient communication**: Use precise formatting options to facilitate effective communication of critical information within and outside the organization

When you first open Power BI Report Builder, you'll immediately notice that, although there are some similarities to Power BI, it is for the most part vastly different. It is often termed as having a more wizard-like feel to the creation of the reports. The following screenshot will help you get your bearings around the Power BI Report Builder UI as well as provide a summary of what each section does:

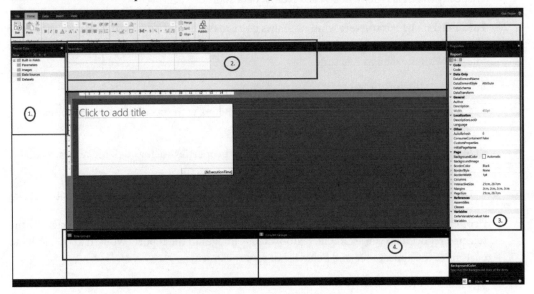

Figure 13.1 – The Power BI Report Builder UI

Important tip

If you are not seeing the boxes as shown, simply navigate to the **View** ribbon and ensure all the boxes are checked.

Let's review the components of Report Builder:

1. **Report Data**: The **Report Data** window is a crucial panel in Power BI Report Builder that provides an organized view of the datasets, parameters, and images used in the report. It acts as a central hub for managing and navigating through the various elements of the report.

    Let's look at its functionality:

    - **Built-in Fields**: Lists a series of data fields that are available for use in any report, such as page number and execution time (which can be useful for adding context about when the report was run).

    - **Parameters**: Displays the parameters defined in the report, enabling users to incorporate interactive elements and dynamic data.

    - **Images**: Lists any images imported or embedded in the report.

- **Data Sources**: Allows you to configure and manage connections to selected data sources. To bring data into your dataset or even report, you need to establish a data source.

- **Datasets**: Once a connection is established, datasets include the query commands that specify the fields that will be used from a data source.

2. **Parameters**: The **Parameters** window allows users to define and manage parameters within the report. Parameters are user-defined values that can be used to filter, customize, or otherwise interact with the data in real time.

Let's look at the functionality:

- **Create parameters**: Users can define new parameters with specific data types (for example, text, date, and integer)

- **Set properties**: Users can configure parameter properties such as default values, available values, and visibility options

- **Use in expressions**: Parameters can be used in expressions to create dynamic and flexible reports

3. **Properties**: The **Properties** window is a dynamic panel that displays the properties of the selected report item (for example, textbox, table, image) in the report layout. It allows users to customize the appearance and behavior of report elements.

Let's look at the functionality:

- **Formatting**: Adjust font, color, alignment, and other formatting options

- **Data binding**: Configure data source, dataset fields, and expressions

- **Interaction**: Set up interactive features, such as drill-through actions and hyperlinks

- **Visibility**: Control the visibility of report items based on conditions

4. **Row Groups/Column Groups**: The **Row Groups/Column Groups** window is primarily associated with tabular or matrix-style reports. It allows users to define and manage groups of rows or columns based on specified criteria.

Here is the functionality:

- **Grouping levels**: Create nested groups to organize data hierarchically

- **Aggregations**: Define aggregations within groups to perform calculations at different levels

- **Visibility**: Control the visibility of groupings to create collapsible sections

In the next section, we will dive deeper into how you actually go about connecting to data from within Power BI Report Builder.

Connecting to data sources within Power BI Report Builder

Power BI Report Builder offers a variety of data source options to meet the diverse needs of its users – whether that is connecting directly to the data source or connecting to a data source that has already been curated and published to the Power BI service. Here is an example screenshot of the connection types available when creating a data source with Power BI Report Builder:

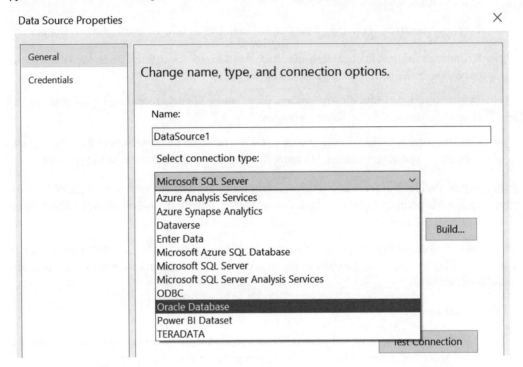

Figure 13.2 – Data Source Properties showing connection types available

This includes the following connectors:

- **SQL Server**: Connect to Microsoft SQL Server databases, allowing users to pull in data directly from relational databases

- **ODBC**: Can be used to access data from Excel workbooks, enabling users to incorporate spreadsheet data into their paginated reports

- **Power BI datasets**: Connect to semantic models in Power BI to integrate published data into paginated reports

- **Other databases**: Power BI Report Builder supports a wide range of other databases, such as Oracle, TERADATA, and more, extending compatibility to different database management systems

- **Azure data sources**: Utilize Azure data services, such as Azure SQL Database or Azure Analysis Services, to connect to cloud-based data sources seamlessly

- **Multidimensional sources**: Connect to multidimensional data sources, including **SQL Server Analysis Services** (**SSAS**) cubes, for complex analytical reporting

Generally, there are not as many data connectors within Report Builder; as such, it is recommended to publish your data model to the Power BI service using Power BI Desktop if the data source is not included in the list of supported connectors.

Beyond mere connectivity, leveraging a data model in Power BI offers a number of advantages:

- It eliminates the need to duplicate business logic within reports, enabling centralized management of business rules within the data model itself

- By structuring data into dimensions and facts, Power BI's data modeling capabilities facilitate clearer insights and more effective analysis

- Features such as **Object-Level Security** (**OLS**) and **Row-Level Security** (**RLS**) bolster data governance and access control, ensuring that sensitive information remains protected

While Report Builder can serve as a quick solution for direct data retrieval into paginated reports, investing in a comprehensive data model is crucial for maximizing analytical potential and ensuring data integrity in the long run.

Connecting to data within Report Builder consists of two parts: firstly, we must specify the **data source** and then we must add **datasets** to reports. The two serve distinct roles within the platform, as summarized here:

- **Data sources**:

  - A data source in Power BI Report Builder represents the connection to the external data repository or system from which the report retrieves its information

  - It defines the location and type of the data, such as a SQL Server database, an Excel workbook, or a Power BI dataset

  - A data source contains the necessary information to establish a connection, such as server details, database names, and authentication credentials

  - Power BI Report Builder allows users to create multiple data sources within a report, enabling the integration of data from diverse locations

- **Datasets**:

  - A dataset is a specific subset of data that is retrieved from a data source for use in a report

  - It is essentially the result of a query or set of queries applied to the data source to extract the relevant information needed for the report

- Datasets can be seen as virtual tables that store the selected data in a format that is optimized for reporting

- Users define queries and filters within a dataset to shape the data according to their reporting requirements

- Multiple datasets can be created within a report, each pulling data from a different data source or applying unique transformations to the same data source

In summary, while a data source establishes the connection to the external data, a dataset represents a refined and structured subset of that data, tailored for use in a specific report. Here is an example view of a **Dataset Properties** window when configuring a new dataset:

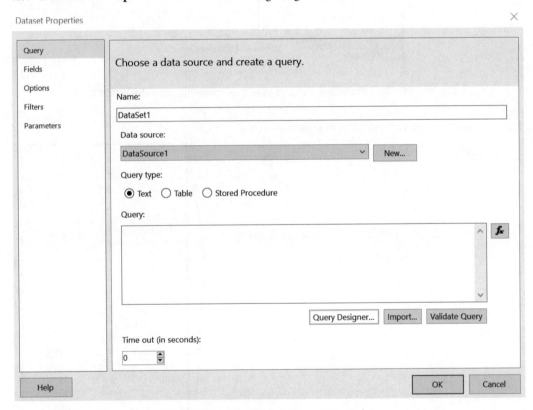

Figure 13.3 – The Dataset Properties window

The separation of these concepts allows for flexibility and efficiency in designing reports, as users can connect to various data sources and then shape the data as needed through different datasets within the same report.

To create a new data source, follow these steps:

1. First, open Power BI Report Builder.

2. Navigate to the **Report Data** window.

3. Right-click on **Data Sources** and select one of the following options, depending on which source your data is coming from:

   - Connect to a Power BI published dataset:

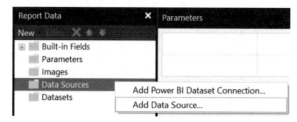

Figure 13.4 – The data source properties where connections can be established

   - Alternatively, connect to a new data source:

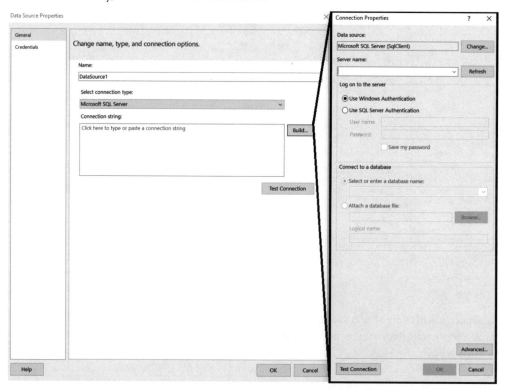

Figure 13.5 – The data source properties where connections can be established

For this example, we are actually going to connect to a Power BI data source. To follow along in this section, please ensure you have published the file highlighted in the *Technical requirements* section to your own workspace within the Power BI service.

4. Select **Add Power BI Dataset Connection…** from the menu. This should open a window where you can sign in to your Power BI service and specify which workspace/dataset you would like to connect to, as seen in the following figure:

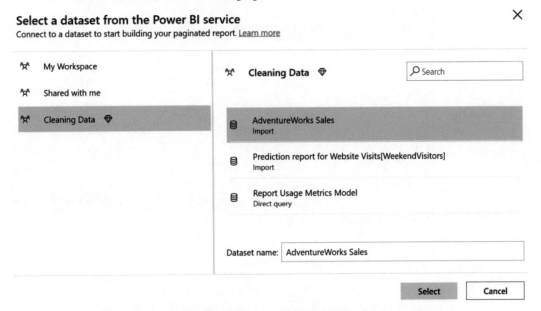

Figure 13.6 – The configuration window to select the workspace and dataset
from the Power BI service you would like to establish a connection to

5. Select **AdventureWorks Sales** and then click **Select** to complete the data source connection.

6. You'll see this appear under the `Data Sources` folder of the **Report Data** window. To rename, right-click on the data source and rename this to `DS_AdventureWorksSales`.

Data preparation

Now that we have connected to our data source, we are ready to begin preparing and creating datasets ready for our analysis. To do so, create a new dataset by right-clicking in the **Report Data** window and selecting **Add Dataset**.

This will open a new window labeled **Dataset Properties** (*Figure 13.7*). Here, we can select a table or write a query to define what data we want to include in the dataset:

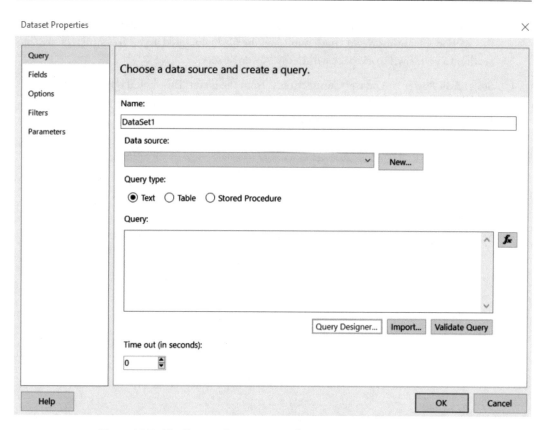

Figure 13.7 – The Dataset Properties window in Power BI Report Builder

Before going ahead, let's review what each property tab controls within the dataset.

Query

The **Query** section of **Dataset Properties** is responsible for defining the data source and specifying the query that retrieves data from that source. This is where users configure the connection details and write or generate DAX queries, MDX queries for multidimensional sources, or other query types, depending on the data source.

Here are the key components:

- **Data source**: Specifies the details of the data source, including server name, database name, and authentication method.

- **Query**: Allows users to input or edit the query that fetches data from the data source.

- **Query Designer…**: Helps with creating a dataset without manually typing out a DAX or MDX query. This works by selecting the dimensions/KPIs/measures for the list of available fields and dragging this into the table to add to the query. As you're getting started, I would highly recommend using this and then reverting to see and understand the query it creates for you.

- **Time out**: Specifies the maximum time allowed for the query to execute before timing out.

Fields

The **Fields** section is responsible for managing and organizing the fields or columns retrieved from the data source. When you create a dataset using Query Designer, you'll find that the fields here automatically populate with the ones you selected in the designer. The names might not always be easy to understand, as characters such as spaces or symbols would have been replaced by underscores.

Here are the key features:

- **Field Name**: Displays a list of all field names assigned to the fields you've selected from the data source.

- **Field Source**: Specifies where the field is being pulled from – that is, the table name and field name. If it's a measure, it will appear without a table name.

- **Add Fields**: You can add or delete query fields here as well as add your own calculated fields for any measures that are not available in your dataset already.

> **Important tip**
>
> Make sure to check the field names here before getting started. Any changes you make to the field names later will not be pushed through to the locations in the report where the field names are used, which can be very time-consuming to then replace, as you will need to go and manually change them in every place they are used.

Options

The **Options** section allows users to configure various settings related to the dataset's behavior and performance. It includes settings for **Collation**, and other aspects of dataset behavior, such as case sensitivity. It's important to note this might show different options depending on the type of data you're connecting to.

Filters

The **Filters** section enables users to apply filters to the dataset, limiting the data retrieved based on specified conditions. The following screenshot shows an example of a filter created for an example dataset. As you can see, the filter is looking to filter the [Segment] column to equal SALES. Expressions can be used here in order to create more complex filtering options.

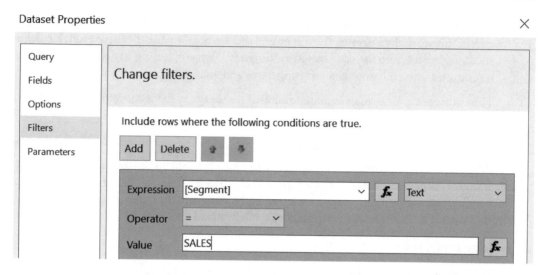

Figure 13.8 – Screenshot of the Filters view from within Dataset Properties in Power BI Report Builder

Filters help in refining the dataset to include only the relevant information for the report. It's important to point out that filters are applied locally after data has been retrieved from the source. In other words, the filter is not pushed down to the data source, the way query folding would do in Power Query. This can have some important performance implications if users are not aware. For this reason, it is often better to add parameters/filters directly to the query rather than use the **Filters** feature from within **Dataset Properties**.

Here are the key features:

- **Filter conditions**: Users can define filter conditions based on field values, expressions, and operators
- **Multiple filters**: Allows the user to add multiple filters to further refine the dataset

Parameters

The **Parameters** section is where users define and manage parameters associated with the dataset. Parameters allow for dynamic and interactive elements in the report, enabling users to input values at runtime or through other specified means.

Here are the key features:

- **Parameter definition**: Users can create parameters and set properties such as data type, available values, and default values
- **Parameterized queries**: Parameters can then be used within the query text to make the dataset more flexible and adaptable

Creating a dataset example

In this example, we will look at building a dataset to be used within Report Builder:

1. To create a new dataset, right-click on the `Datasets` folder and select **Add dataset**. Alternatively, navigate to the **Data** ribbon and select **New** under the **Dataset** group. This will open the **Dataset Properties** window.

2. Let's connect to the data source we specified in the previous section of this chapter. Notice in the following example how you can also create a data source from this step by selecting **New...**:

Choose a data source and create a query.

Name:

DS_AdventureWorksTestDataset

Data source:

DS_AdventureWorksSales   ⌄   New...
DS_AdventureWorksSales

Query type:

◉ Text   ◯ Table   ◯ Stored Procedure

Figure 13.9 – Dataset properties in Power BI Report Builder for specifying the data
source to connect to or create a new data source connection entirely

3. Next, we have the option to either manually create our own query expression or use **Query Designer** to build the query. The following figure details where this is visible in **Dataset Properties**:

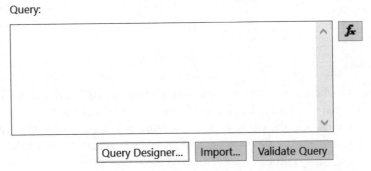

Query:

Query Designer...   Import...   Validate Query

Figure 13.10 – The Query section within Dataset Properties in Power BI Report Builder

This is where you can add your own query or use **Query Designer** to help with this.

4.   Select **Query Designer...**, which will bring the following window:

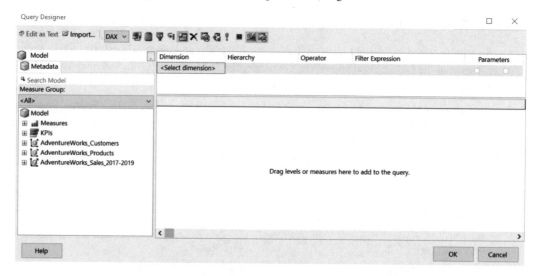

Figure 13.11 – Query Designer from within Power BI Report Builder

5.   Now, we can begin to build our query by visually dragging and dropping the columns or measures we need from this dataset.

6.   For this example, drag in the following:

A.   `AdventureWorks_Sales_2017-2019`:

- `Model Name`
- `OrderNumber`
- `OrderDate`

B.   `Measures`:

- `Total Order Price`
- `Total Order Cost`

7.   Add a filter to the query at the top of the window. Here, you will specify what filter you would like. In this example, let's add a filter on `OrderDate` as we would like to see all orders for a particular date. Add the relevant values for **Dimension**, **Hierarchy**, **Operator**, and **Filter Expression**, so it mirrors the following configuration. Ensure that you tick the **Parameter** box so this automatically creates a parameter to be used in the report:

Dimension	Hierarchy	Operator	Filter Expression	Parame...
AdventureWorks_Sales_2017-2019	OrderDate	Equal	{ 01/01/2019 }	☑ ☐
<Select dimension>				☐ ☐

Figure 13.12 – The filter being applied within Query Designer in Power BI Report Builder

8. Select **OK** to save the selection:

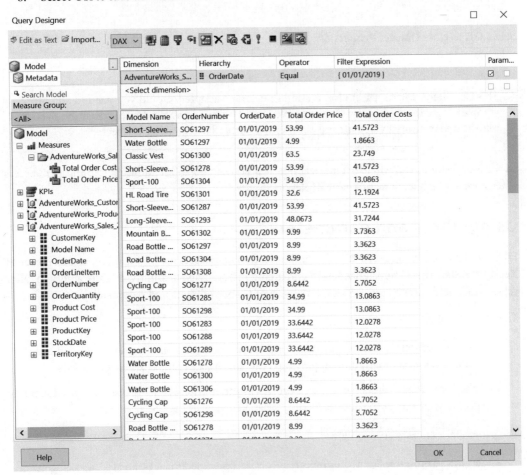

Figure 13.13 – Query Designer with my selected items

Now that we have saved our selection, you will see that Query Designer has actually generated the following query expression for our desired dataset. This simple query specifies where to find our selected dimensions and measures within our selected data source:

```
EVALUATE SUMMARIZECOLUMNS('AdventureWorks_Sales_2017-
2019'[Model Name], 'AdventureWorks_Sales_2017-2019'[OrderNumber],
'AdventureWorks_Sales_2017-2019'[OrderDate], RSCustomDaxFilter(@
AdventureWorksSales20172019OrderDate,EqualToCondition,[AdventureWorks_
Sales_2017-2019].[OrderDate],String), "Total Order Price", [Total
Order Price], "Total Order Costs", [Total Order Costs])
```

Select **OK** to close **Dataset Properties**.

> **Note**
>
> This can often provide a great foundation that can be adapted should you need to add more complex logic to your query. One example would be to add an `if` logic so that the dataset returns one measure by default and another if a particular parameter is selected.

In the next section, you will learn more about how you can go about adding filters and parameters when connecting to data from Power BI Report Builder.

Using filters and parameters

Filters and parameters play crucial roles in the creation of datasets for paginated reports in Power BI Report Builder. Their importance lies in enhancing interactivity, flexibility, and the ability to tailor reports to specific user needs. Let's explore the significance of filters and parameters.

The use cases of filters are as follows:

- **Date range filters**: Filtering data based on a specific date range allows users to view information within a selected timeframe, supporting trend analysis or comparison over periods
- **Category filters**: Filters based on categories or other criteria enable users to drill down into specific segments of the data, providing a detailed view of particular subsets

The parameter use cases are as follows:

- **Region parameter**: For a sales report, a `Region` parameter can be created, allowing users to select a specific region to analyze sales performance for that region
- **Top N parameter**: A `Top N` parameter can be applied to show the top *N* items or categories based on sales, providing users with the flexibility to focus on the most significant data points

- **KPI or currency selection**: Often, parameters can help the user switch the type of report or KPIs they're looking at – whether that's switching a KPI depending on which parameters are selected or switching to another currency if you have a measure field in a different currency

Let's build upon this by looking at how we can add further parameters and filter logic to our query. To refine which data we bring into our report, perform the following steps:

1. Start by selecting and right-clicking on the `Parameters` folder.

2. Select **Add parameters…** to open the **Report Parameter** properties. By default, it will open on the **General** tab on the left-hand side.

3. Here, we will define the name of our parameter as well as the prompt. Rename this to `P_KPI_Selector`.

4. Leave the other boxes unchecked and the parameter visibility set to **Visible**.

5. Select **Available Values**. Here, the parameter will currently be set to **None**. Adjust this by selecting the **Specify Values** radial. This will cause the **Add** button to appear, allowing us to manually add values.

Important tip

If you are looking to create a parameter from a field in your data, you should look to create a dataset that only pulls in that field or column. Then, you can select **Get values from a query**. This then pulls available values for your parameter directly from your data. Be careful not to select a column with thousands of values as this could affect your performance.

---

6. Click on **Add**.

7. Adjust the label and value to **Revenue**.

8. Repeat this process to add another field with the label and value set to **Cost**.

9. Select the **Default values** tab. Here, you can specify which value you would like to be set by default when the report is run.

10. Adjust the **Default value** configuration to **Specify values**. Then, select **Add** and select **Revenue** from the dropdown.

11. Click on **OK** to close the **Report Parameter** properties window. You'll now see your parameter appear in the `Parameters` folder.

12. Right-click on the dataset you created called `DS_AdventureWorksTestDataset` and select **Dataset Properties**.

> **Important tip**
>
> Be advised that if you begin adjusting the query that was created by Query Designer, you won't be able to access Query Designer after.

13. Reformat the query for simpler reading, as shown next. Be sure to add = " at the beginning as Query Designer doesn't add this originally:

```
="
EVALUATE SUMMARIZECOLUMNS (
'AdventureWorks_Sales_2017-2019'[Model Name],
'AdventureWorks_Sales_2017-2019'[OrderNumber],
'AdventureWorks_Sales_2017-2019'[OrderDate],
RSCustomDaxFilter(@AdventureWorksSales20172019OrderDate,EqualTo-
Condition,[AdventureWorks_Sales_2017-2019].[OrderDate],String),
"Total Order Price", [Total Order Price],
"Total Order Costs", [Total Order Costs]
)
```

14. Now, remove the last three rows, which include our highlighted measure:

```
"Total Order Price", [Total Order Price],
"Total Order Costs", [Total Order Costs]
)
```

15. Replace this with the following code:

```
""Sales/Cost"",
" + IIF (Parameters!P_KPI_Selector.Value="Revenue","[Total Order
Price]","[Total Order Costs]") + "
)"
```

16. Review the screen as shown to confirm you have entered the same code as shown in the previous step and select **Validate Query** to have Report Builder check your query. Notice that **Query Designer...** has now been grayed out:

Query:

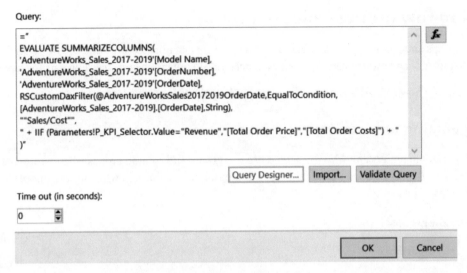

```
="
EVALUATE SUMMARIZECOLUMNS(
'AdventureWorks_Sales_2017-2019'[Model Name],
'AdventureWorks_Sales_2017-2019'[OrderNumber],
'AdventureWorks_Sales_2017-2019'[OrderDate],
RSCustomDaxFilter(@AdventureWorksSales20172019OrderDate,EqualToCondition,
[AdventureWorks_Sales_2017-2019].[OrderDate],String),
""Sales/Cost"",
" + IIF (Parameters!P_KPI_Selector.Value="Revenue","[Total Order Price]","[Total Order Costs]") + "
)"
```

Query Designer...   Import...   Validate Query

Time out (in seconds):

0

OK   Cancel

Figure 13.14 – Dataset query

17. Before clicking on **OK**, we need to change the fields to ensure we are pulling through the new dynamic field we created. Select the **Field** tab on the left of the **Properties** window.

18. Then, remove the previous two fields and add the following values:

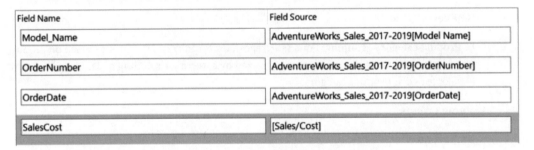

Field Name	Field Source
Model_Name	AdventureWorks_Sales_2017-2019[Model Name]
OrderNumber	AdventureWorks_Sales_2017-2019[OrderNumber]
OrderDate	AdventureWorks_Sales_2017-2019[OrderDate]
SalesCost	[Sales/Cost]

Figure 13.15 – Fields within Dataset Properties

19. Click on **OK**.

You have just created a new parameterized field in your dataset that can be used in our report to dynamically switch the data we pull into our query.

To conclude, filters and parameters are integral components when creating datasets for paginated reports in Power BI Report Builder. They empower users to refine data, focus on relevant information, and customize reports dynamically. The ability to interact with and tailor reports based on specific criteria enhances the value and usability of paginated reports in diverse business scenarios. In the next section, you will learn more about key features when creating and connecting to a dataset within Power BI Report Builder, called **row groups** and **column groups**.

Using row groups/column groups

Row groups and column groups in paginated reports are essential features that provide a structured way to organize and present data. They play a crucial role in preparing and analyzing data for reporting.

Let's explore how row groups and column groups help users in this process.

Organizing and structuring data

It's important to understand why you should use row groups and column groups when creating reports in Power BI Report Builder. Let's dive deeper into more information on why they are important and the use cases for them:

- **Row groups**:

  - **Importance**:

    - **Hierarchical structure**: Row groups allow users to create a hierarchical structure in the report based on the values in a specific column. This is particularly useful for representing data in a nested or grouped manner.

    - **Logical organization**: By grouping rows based on certain criteria (for example, category and date range), users can logically organize data, making it easier to understand and analyze.

  - **Use cases**:

    - **Product category grouping**: For a sales report, users can create row groups based on product categories. This results in a report organized by category, providing a clear breakdown of sales for each product category.

- **Column groups**:

  - **Importance**:

    - **Cross-tabular presentation**: Column groups allow users to present data in a cross-tabular format. This is valuable when users need to view data across multiple dimensions simultaneously.

    - **Comparative analysis**: Users can use column groups to compare data across different categories, periods, or other dimensions, facilitating comparative analysis.

  - **Use cases**:

    - **Quarterly revenue comparison**: In a financial report, column groups can be created to represent revenue figures for each quarter horizontally. This enables users to compare revenue performance across different quarters.

Enhancing readability and presentation

Row and column groups can be used in Power BI Report Builder to enhance the readability and structure of the report. Here are some examples of the importance they play in doing this:

- **Structured presentation**: Both row groups and column groups contribute to a structured and organized presentation of data in the report, enhancing readability

- **Reduced clutter**: Grouping allows users to present complex data in a more readable and concise format by reducing clutter and focusing on key information

Overall, row groups and column groups provide the following:

- **Analytical flexibility**: Row groups and column groups provide users with the flexibility to organize and analyze data in multiple ways, adapting the report to specific analytical needs

- **Improved decision-making**: The structured presentation and aggregated analysis facilitated by row groups and column groups contribute to more informed decision-making by providing a comprehensive view of the data

Let's put this knowledge to the test and begin creating a report that utilizes row and column groups:

1. **Adding a title**: Now that we have created a dataset in earlier sections, we are ready to begin creating the report. As a first step, let's begin by adding a title to the top of the report. Select the title area at the top of the report and type `Sales/Cost Report`.

2. **Adding an image**: Often, paginated reports need branding with a company logo, for example. In order to add an image, we first need to add this to the report data by following these steps:

   I.   Select and right-click on the `Images` folder, as shown:

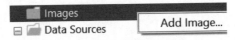

Figure 13.16 – The Images folder within the report data window of Power BI Report Builder

   II. Navigate to the file named `AdventureWorksLogo`, which you downloaded from the GitHub repo.

   III. You will see the file appear under the `Images` folder. Simply select that file and drag this into the report. Alternatively, select **Insert image** from the toolbar. This will open the **Image Property** window.

   IV. Rename the image and select **OK**.

   V.   Then, reposition the image by selecting it and dragging it to the top-right corner of the report, as shown. The image can be resized by clicking and dragging the corners in:

Figure 13.17 – The report preview in Power BI Report Builder

3. **Inserting a table**: Now that we have added the title and company logo, it's time to build the report. We are going to create a simple table that provides a summary of our orders using **Row Groups/Column Groups** to help organize the report. To do this, follow these steps:

I.   Select the **Insert** tab on the toolbar.

II.   Select **Table**, and from the dropdown that appears, select **Table Wizard**.

III.   Choose **Dataset**, select our dataset named `DS_AdventureWorksTestDataset`, and then select **Next**.

IV.   This will take you to the **Arrange fields** window, as shown. This is really useful as you can add row groups right from the start. Add the following items by dragging them from the **Available fields** section to the respective sections to mirror the configuration in the following figure. Make sure to set the aggregation for `SalesCost` to **Sum**. Then, click on **Next**.

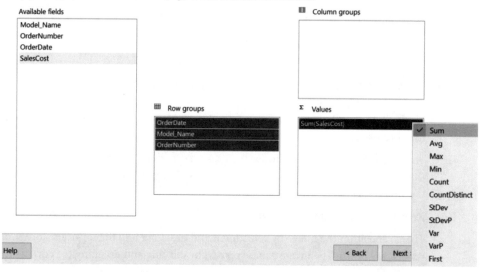

Figure 13.18 – Screenshot of the Arrange fields window within Table Wizard

V.   On the **Choose the layout** screen, leave the configuration as it is. Leaving **Expand/ collapse groups** selected will enable the reader to interact and expand these sections of the report. Select **Next**.

Choose the layout

If you choose to show subtotals and grand totals, you can place them above or below the group. Stepped reports show hierarchical structure with indented groups in the same column.

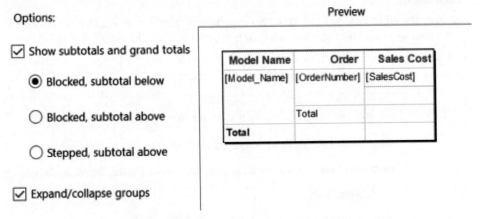

Figure 13.19 – The table layout configuration within Table Wizard

VI.   This will bring up the preview of the report item before it is then added to the report.

VII.   Select **Finish** after viewing the preview, which will insert the table into the report.

VIII. Now, move the table you created into a better space on the report (as it may have been inserted on top of the title) by selecting the table and dragging it into position. Alternatively, you can do this by selecting the table. This should open the Tablix properties on the right-hand side. Scroll to the bottom and you should see the Position property folder shown. Here, you can specify the coordinates of where you would like the top left of the table to be located.

Position	
Location	**2.5mm, 20mm**
Left	**2.5mm**
Top	**20mm**
Size	**149.86mm, 24mm**

Figure 13.20 – The Properties window zoomed in on the Position properties

> **Important note**
> In Power BI Report Builder, tables and matrices are collectively called tablix.

4. **Cosmetic changes**: Now we have the table within the report, we need to apply some changes to ensure the report will show correctly when we run it. To do this, follow these steps:

I.   Select the cell containing the column header for Model_Name. This will be labeled something like Textbox1. Selecting this cell will show the **Textbox** properties in the right-hand view.

> **Important tip**
>
> Selecting the middle of the textbox within a tablix will cause you to select/edit the content of the textbox and thus will show the **Selected text** properties on the right-hand side.
>
> To ensure you select the textbox itself and thus avoid showing the textbox properties, either select the edge of the textbox or select it by right-clicking instead of left-clicking.

II.   You will now adjust the following properties to ensure this is showing nicely:

• **Alignment | Text Align**: Switch this to **Left**

• **Position | Size**: Adjust the size of the textbox to **70mm, 6mm**, as shown:

∨ **Position**	
＞ Location	0mm, 0mm
∨ Size	**70mm, 6mm**
Width	**70mm**
Height	**6mm**

Figure 13.21 – The Properties window zoomed in on the Position properties

III. Select the textbox containing the column header for OrderNumber. Then, delete the contents of this textbox as we don't want to see this when order numbers aren't visible.

IV.   Next we will remove padding. Select all the cells within the table, as shown. To do this, select the box with Model Name (ensuring that you select the edges of the box), hold down the *Shift* button, and select the bottom-right box. This will then show group properties for all the selected cells on the right.

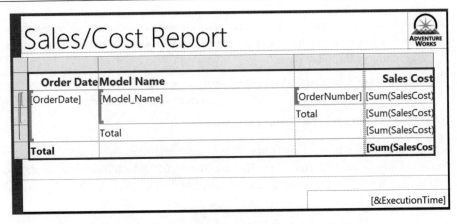

Figure 13.22 – The report being created and its layout

V. Adjust **Padding** from **2pt** to **0pt**, as shown. This will remove the padding applied around each cell's edges, which might obstruct the view.

Padding	0pt, 0pt, 0pt, 0pt
Left	0pt
Right	0pt
Top	0pt
Bottom	0pt

Figure 13.23 – The Properties window zoomed in on the padding properties

VI. Add a dynamic column header for `Sales_Cost` so that it dynamically changes depending on what the viewer has selected in the parameter. To do this, select the textbox containing the header. Right-click on the box and select **Expression**.

VII. Replace the existing test with the following and select **OK**:

```
=IIF(Parameters!P_KPI_Selector.Value="Revenue",
"Revenues","Costs")
```

VIII. Add currency formatting to ensure that price and cost are output in the correct format. To do this, we will start by selecting the cells that contain values for `Price` and `Costs`.

IX. Then, in the properties window to the right, select **Number** and then select **Format**. Enter the following format in this property box. This will ensure that values show with a currency of £ and that negative values are shown in brackets:

```
£#,#;(£#,#)
```

X. Adjust the visibility of **Row Group**. If you were to run your report now, it'd be great; however, you would have to adjust the grouping toggles as this is currently set to hide for your grouping called `Model_Name`. To adjust this, select the row group called `Model_Name`.

XI.   Right-click and select **Group Properties**. This will open the **Group Properties** window similar to the **Group by** function in Power Query, which shows you the details on the grouping of the data.

XII. To adjust visibility, select the **Visibility** tab on the left-hand side. Now, adjust the toggle by selecting **Show**. This will result in the Model Name column being visible when you run the report.

XIII. Select **OK** to close the **Group Properties** window.

5. Save your report, navigate to the **Home** ribbon, and select **Run**. This will run your report with the parameter already selected of **OrderDate 01/01/2019**. The following example shows the output from the report. Expand the dates by selecting the plus toggle to the left of the date field.

OrderDate 01/01/2019	P_KPI_Selector Revenue		View Report

Sales/Cost Report

Order Date	Model Name		Revenues
01/01/2019	Bike Wash	Total	£8
	Classic Vest	Total	£64
	Cycling Cap	Total	£35
	Fender Set - Mountain	Total	£88
	Hitch Rack - 4-Bike	Total	£120
	HL Mountain Tire	Total	£35
	HL Road Tire	Total	£65
	LL Road Tire	Total	£86
	Long-Sleeve Logo Jersey	Total	£96
	ML Mountain Tire	Total	£90
	ML Road Tire	Total	£25
	Mountain Bottle Cage	Total	£50
	Mountain Tire Tube	Total	£30
	Mountain-200	Total	£6,170
	Mountain-500	Total	£565
	Patch kit	Total	£11
	Road Bottle Cage	Total	£54
	Road Tire Tube	Total	£12
	Road-250	Total	£4,363
	Road-350-W	Total	£6,804
	Road-750	Total	£1,080
	Short-Sleeve Classic Jersey	Total	£270
	Sport-100	Total	£409
	Touring Tire	Total	£29
	Touring Tire Tube	Total	£10
	Touring-1000	Total	£2,384
	Touring-2000	Total	£1,215
	Touring-3000	Total	£742
	Water Bottle	Total	£65
	Women's Mountain Shorts	Total	£70
	Total		£25,044
Total			**£25,044**

Figure 13.24 – The output after running the report

Overall, by leveraging row groups, we have been able to aggregate our data into the report. These row/column groups are powerful tools in paginated reports that help users organize, analyze, and present data in a structured and meaningful way. They contribute to the clarity of information, support aggregated analysis, and enhance the overall effectiveness of paginated reports for data preparation and analysis in a similar way that the **Group By** function works in Power Query.

Summary

In this chapter, you were introduced to Power BI Report Builder to prepare your data for building paginated reports.

Your journey unfolded with insights into the significance of paginated reports, connecting to data sources, utilizing Query Designer, parameters, and filters. Navigating the user interface, you discovered the functionalities of **Report Data**, **Parameters**, **Properties**, and **row groups** and **column groups** as well as how to create parameterized fields to refine your dataset queries. Finally, using an example, you began building your report to aggregate and group data by the row groups you created when building the tablix.

This chapter served as just an introduction to the world of Power BI Report Builder and how you can prepare and report on data using paginated reports. I hope a key takeaway from this chapter is that, even if the data you're working with is clean in your Power BI model or upstream databases, you will still need to do some level of data preparation to connect to that data and build paginated reports from it.

The next chapter promises to elevate your expertise by exploring other Power Platform technologies to automate data preparation for analysis in Power BI. Your journey in mastering the Power BI landscape continues.

Questions

1. What is the primary purpose of Power BI Report Builder in creating paginated reports?

    A. Dynamic and interactive reporting

    B. Pixel-perfect, highly formatted reporting

    C. Creating relational databases

    D. Multidimensional source connectivity

2. What role do row groups and column groups play in paginated reports?

    A. Enhancing user interactivity

    B. Structuring and organizing data

    C. Creating rich data visuals

    D. Facilitating data preparation

3. Why are filters and parameters important in paginated reporting?

    A. To add pixel-perfect formatting

    B. To enhance user experience and efficiency

    C. To create hierarchical structures

    D. To organize and present data

4. How does Power BI Report Builder contribute to meeting compliance standards in industries with stringent regulations?

    A. By providing versatile data source connectivity

    B. By creating rich data visuals

    C. By offering advanced expressions and calculations

    D. By generating paginated reports with precise formatting

14

Automating Data Cleaning Tasks with Power Automate

In the dynamic landscape of data analytics, the synergy between Power BI and Power Automate opens new horizons for efficient data preparation.

Power Automate, Microsoft's workflow automation tool, seamlessly integrates with Power BI, offering a powerful duo for automating and enhancing your data cleaning processes.

Power Automate is a cloud-based service that allows you to automate workflows between your favorite applications and services. It provides a user-friendly interface for creating automated processes, known as flows, without the need for extensive coding. With a wide array of connectors for various applications, Power Automate enables seamless integration and automation across different platforms. Power Automate is a great tool and ally in the power tools kitbag for Power BI.

In this chapter, we'll delve into what Power Automate is and explore how it can be strategically employed to streamline and automate the cleaning and preparation of data, ensuring that your Power BI reports are not just visually compelling but also built on a foundation of consistently clean and updated data.

We will cover the following topics:

- Handling triggers for automation
- Automating notifications
- Automating refreshing of data
- Best practices with Power Automate

By the end of this chapter, you will have an understanding of how Power Automate can be used to clean and prepare data and how it can automate the process, and also gain hands-on experience creating your own flows to prepare data.

Technical requirements

In this chapter, you will require access to Power Automate either via cloud or desktop. This will then also need to be linked to your Power BI subscription, which we will highlight in walkthrough examples.

In this example, we will be connecting to the Power BI service and using a prebuilt workbook that should be published on the Power BI web service. This `store sales` files can be located at `https://github.com/PacktPublishing/Data-Cleaning-with-Power-BI/blob/main/Store%20Sales.pbix`.

Handling triggers for automation

Automation begins with triggers, and Power Automate offers a variety of triggers that can initiate workflows based on specific events. In the context of data cleaning for Power BI, triggers can be designed to activate when new data is added or modified or when certain conditions are met.

For instance, you can set up a trigger that initiates a data cleaning process whenever new data is ingested into your data source. This ensures that your data is consistently cleaned and prepared whenever there are updates, saving you time and ensuring the reliability of your reports.

Here's a screenshot showing the type of triggers available specifically for Power BI within Power Automate:

Power BI

Power BI is a suite of business analytics tools to analyze data and share insights. Connect to get easy access to the data in your Power BI dashboards, reports and datasets. Read less

When a data driven alert is triggered		In App	Trigger ⓘ
When a data refresh for a goal fails	Preview	In App	Trigger ⓘ
When a goal changes	Preview	In App	Trigger ⓘ
When current value of a goal changes	Preview	In App	Trigger ⓘ
When someone adds or edits a goal check-in	Preview	In App	Trigger ⓘ
When someone assigns a new owner to a goal	Preview	In App	Trigger ⓘ
When status of a goal changes	Preview	In App	Trigger ⓘ

Figure 14.1 – Screenshot of the triggers available within Power Automate to be used with Power BI

Having understood how triggers can be used and leveraged to kickstart the action flows within Power Automate, you're now ready to move on to the next section, where we will learn more about what you can do once a flow is triggered.

Automating notifications

Effective communication is key when implementing data and analytics across your business, especially when dealing with automated processes. Power Automate allows you to integrate notifications seamlessly into your data cleaning workflows.

For instance, you can set up notifications to be sent to relevant stakeholders or team members when a data-cleaning process is completed. This ensures that everyone is informed about the status of the data and any potential issues that may require attention. Integrating notifications into your automated processes enhances transparency and collaboration within your data preparation pipeline.

Setting up a notification for a Power BI refresh using Power Automate involves creating a flow that monitors the refresh status and sends a notification when it completes. It's worth noting that you can also set up refresh notifications for dataflows in Power BI, but this will only be to alert you when it's failed. Here are step-by-step instructions on how to set this up:

1. Create a new flow as follows:

    A. Go to the Power Automate portal (`https://flow.microsoft.com/`).

    B. Click on **Create** in the top navigation bar and choose **Automated cloud flow** – under **Start from blank** to create a new flow from scratch. This will help us select a trigger that will start our flow. The following is an example:

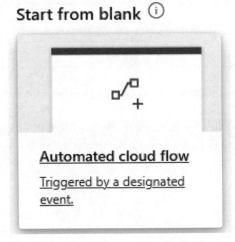

Figure 14.2 – Screenshot of the Start from blank selection within Power Automate

2. Name your flow `SequencedRefreshes` and select **Trigger for Power BI Dataflow Refresh**:

    A. Search for dataflow within the triggers search.

    B. Choose the **When a dataflow refresh completes** trigger event.

    C. Select **Create**.

3. Configure Power BI Trigger:

    A. Sign in with your Power BI account if you haven't already.

    B. Set the group type as **Workspace** and choose the group you'd like to connect to. In this case, it will be the workspace you published your datasets in previously.

    C. Select the dataflow to connect to. In this example, we are connecting to the **Online Visitors** dataflow we published previously in *Chapter 9, Advanced Data Cleaning Techniques*:

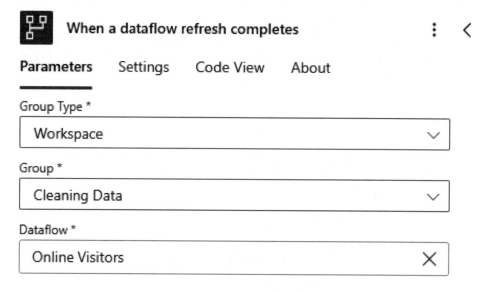

Figure 14.3 – Screenshot of the Power Query trigger from within the Power Query UI

    D. You will also have the option to configure how often this trigger polls to check whether a refresh has occurred. Continue with the trigger set to 3-minute intervals and specify the time zone as shown:

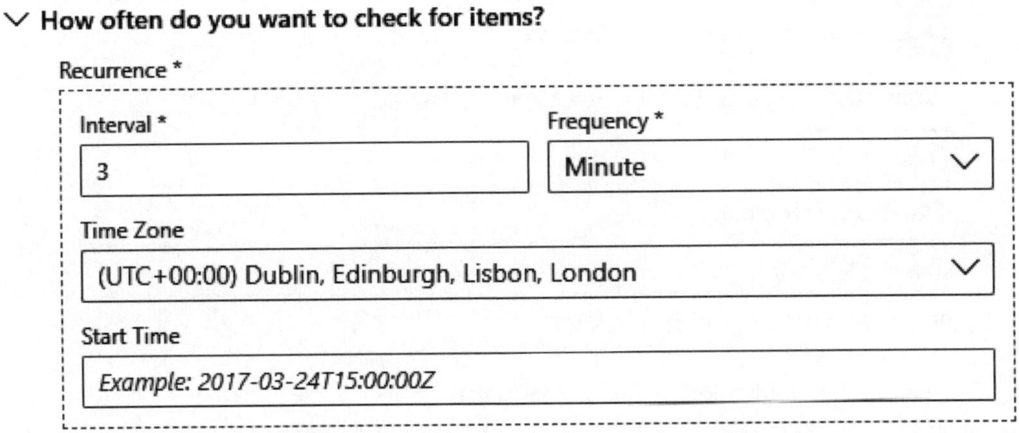

How often do you want to check for items?
Recurrence *
Interval *
Frequency *
3
Minute
Time Zone
(UTC+00:00) Dublin, Edinburgh, Lisbon, London
Start Time
Example: 2017-03-24T15:00:00Z

Figure 14.4 – Screenshot of the Power Query trigger from within the Power Query UI where you can specify the recurrence intervals

4. Add a notification action:

   A. Add an action by clicking on the + icon below the trigger as shown:

When a dataflow refresh completes
Add an action

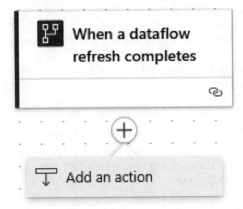

Figure 14.5 – Screenshot of the trigger created in the previous step with the option to add an action

   B. Search for and select the **Notifications** connector. Choose an action that suits your needs, for example, **Notifications – Send me an email notification**.

5. Configure the notification:

   A. Configure the notification action with the necessary details. This may include the subject, the message body, and other relevant information:

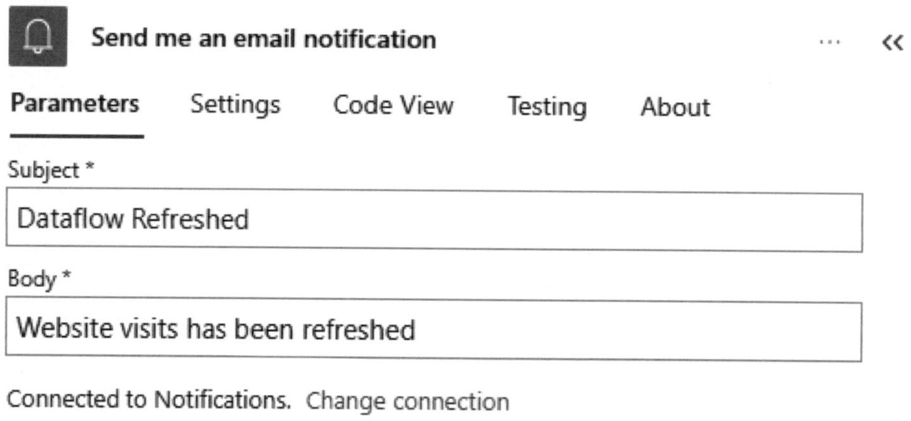

Figure 14.6 – Screenshot of the notifications action within the Power Automate UI

B.   Save your flow.

C.   Click on the back arrow in the top-left corner to go to the overview page of your flow.

6.   Turn on the flow:

A.   Once you've configured your flow, turn it on by clicking on the **Turn on** button. This should be located in the toolbar underneath the search bar when on the overview page for your flow.

7.   Return to your Power BI workspace where the dataflow is stored and select **Refresh Dataflow** to test the action/alert.

Now, whenever the Power BI dataflow refresh is completed for the specified dataflow, you will receive a notification through the chosen channel (for example, email notification). This is a great introduction to using Power Automate with Power BI, as you build upon the capabilities directly available within Power BI. This trigger is also really useful in the future when you want to trigger other refreshes or actions once the data has been updated.

Automating refreshing of data

Data in Power BI needs to be refreshed regularly to ensure that your reports reflect the most recent information. Power Automate can be instrumental in automating the data refresh process. By setting up a workflow that triggers a data refresh at scheduled intervals or in response to specific events, you can ensure that your Power BI reports are always up to date. This is particularly useful when dealing with dynamic datasets that undergo frequent changes. Automating the data refresh not only saves time but also ensures the accuracy and relevance of your analyses.

In addition to these advantages, refreshing data works really well when you're building complex models that leverage a number of dataflows. Instead of having to manually refresh dataflows, wait for them to complete, and then action the refresh of the semantic model; you can simply build this into a Power Automate flow. Of course, you could just schedule refreshes in Power BI, but the challenge here is that you can sequence these refreshes from within the Power BI service itself.

Here is how we can create/automate a flow to sequence your refreshes:

1. Within the same flow you created in the previous step, select **Edit** in the toolbar:

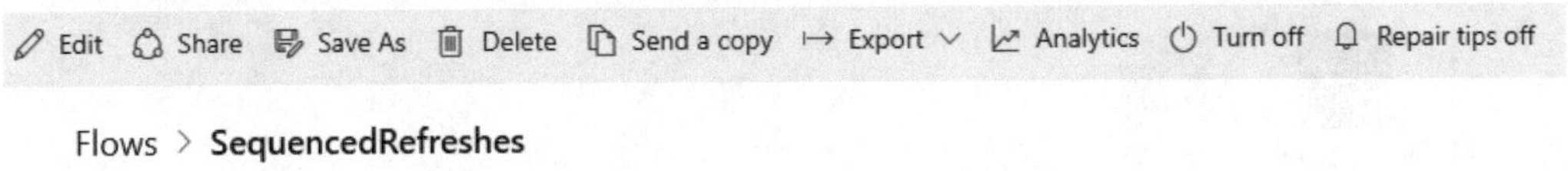

Figure 14.7 – Screenshot of the flow overview page in Power Automate

2. Now that we have created the trigger in the previous example (where the trigger was a dataflow refresh completing), we can select **Add an action** and use the **Refresh a dataflow** action to determine which dataflow should be refreshed next in our sequence. In this example, let's select the named `mtcars` dataflow you created in *Chapter 9, Advanced Data Cleaning Techniques*:

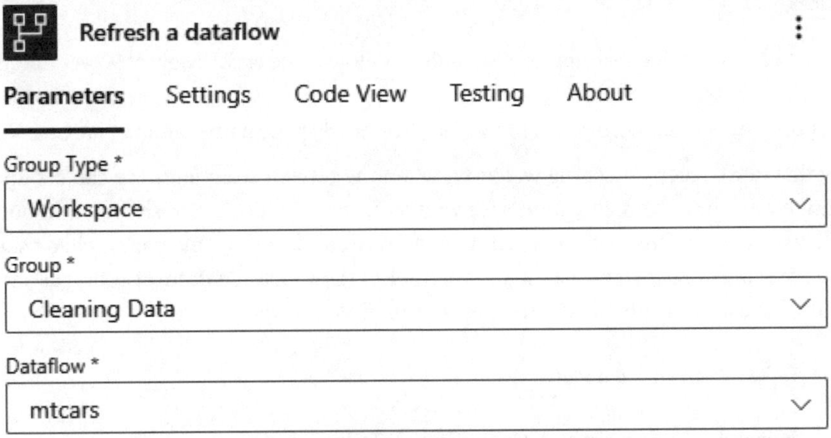

Figure 14.8 – Screenshot of the Refresh a dataflow window in Power Automate

3. To avoid actioning a refresh of the semantic model while the dataflow is still refreshing, we need the next action to wait until the previous data flow has refreshed (which is actually our initial trigger). If you try to add this in the new designer view, though, it won't work, as you won't be able to find triggers. To switch back to the classic view, click on the toggle in the top-right corner of the Power Automate page. This will request that you save your flow before switching. Click on **Save and Switch**.

4. Select **New Step**, then enter `dataflow` into the search bar, and select the **Triggers** tab as shown:

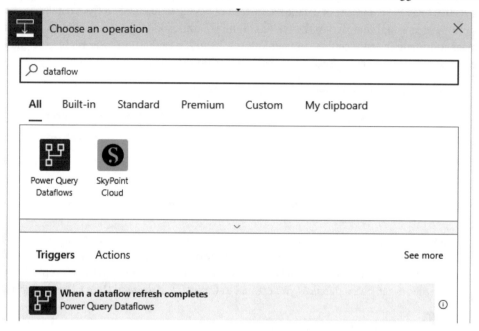

Figure 14.9 – Screenshot of the new step configuration window in the classic view of Power Automate flow

5. Select this trigger and then select the workspace, workspace name, and the `mtcars` dataflow.

6. Now that our trigger is keeping watch on when the refresh completes, we can set up the next action to refresh the semantic model we would like to sequence a refresh of within our selected workspace. Select This option is given as "**New Step**" at top of this page - check screen text option and make casing consistent and then select the **Refresh a dataset** action as shown (you can also save and switch back to the new designer if you wish):

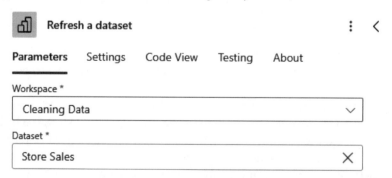

Figure 14.10 – Screenshot of the Refresh a dataset action used in Power Automate flow

7. Save your flow.

Having now learned how you can create automated and sequenced refreshes using Power Automate flows, this will prove very useful as you look to automate some of the actions within your service. In the next section, you will explore techniques for creating snapshots or temporary tables within Power BI.

Creating snapshots (temporary tables) of cleaned data

This is extremely useful when it comes to creating and cleaning snapshots of a particular data model. Snapshots of data can be particularly useful when looking to create temporary table views of data. This is a step in data preparation (creating temporary tables) that isn't easily done from within the Power BI service alone.

Let's go through some examples of reasons why you might need to create snapshots of data:

- **Complex calculations:**

  - **Scenario**: You need to perform intricate calculations that involve multiple steps, conditions, or aggregations.

  - **Use of temporary table**: Create a temporary table to break down the complex calculation into manageable stages. Store intermediate results in the temporary table before deriving the final output.

- **Data segmentation:**

  - **Scenario**: You want to segment your data based on specific criteria for focused analysis.

  - **Use of temporary table**: Generate temporary tables to filter and segment data subsets based on predefined conditions. Each temporary table represents a distinct segment, allowing for more targeted analysis.

- **Performance optimization:**

  - **Scenario**: Your dataset is extensive, and complex queries are slowing down report generation.

  - **Use of temporary table**: Create summary or aggregated temporary tables to pre-calculate and store key metrics. Use these precomputed values in your reports to significantly improve query performance.

- **Historical analysis:**

  - **Scenario**: You need to analyze data changes over time or compare historical trends.

  - **Use of temporary table**: Generate temporary tables to capture historical snapshots of your data at specific points in time. This enables you to perform historical analyses without altering your main dataset.

- **Scenario analysis:**

  - **Scenario:** You want to explore various hypothetical scenarios without affecting your original data.

  - **Use of temporary table:** Create temporary tables to duplicate your dataset and apply changes or adjustments for scenario analysis. This allows you to assess the potential impact of different scenarios without modifying the original data.

- **Data enrichment:**

  - **Scenario:** You have additional data sources that can enrich your existing dataset.

  - **Use of temporary table:** Merge or append temporary tables with supplemental data to enhance the richness of your analysis. This approach keeps your original dataset intact while providing a more comprehensive view.

- **Intermediate results storage:**

  - **Scenario:** Your analysis involves multiple iterative steps and you want to store intermediate results.

  - **Use of temporary table:** Create temporary tables to store intermediate results during each step of your analysis. This aids in troubleshooting and validation and facilitates the ability to pick up the analysis from specific points.

- **Security and sensitivity:**

  - **Scenario:** You are working with sensitive data and want to restrict access to specific subsets.

  - **Use of temporary table:** Generate temporary tables to filter and store subsets of data with restricted access. This ensures that only authorized users can access sensitive information within the temporary table.

- **Custom aggregations:**

  - **Scenario:** You need to perform custom aggregations or derive specialized metrics.

  - **Use of temporary table:** Create temporary tables to store the results of custom aggregations or calculated metrics. This simplifies the integration of these specialized metrics into your reports.

- **Data transformation iterations:**

  - **Scenario:** Your data requires multiple transformations and you want to iterate through various scenarios.

  - **Use of temporary table:** Use temporary tables to store data at different stages of transformation. This facilitates iterative development and allows you to refine the transformation steps without affecting the original dataset.

With an understanding of where temporary tables could be used, let's now go through an example to see them in action.

Example – creating a snapshot of yesterday's data

In this example, we will walk through a scenario where you might need to leverage the Power Platform to create snapshots of your data. This is particularly useful if your data can change but you have no method of tracking the variances.

Step one – recurrence

In the first step, you are going to set up the trigger for your flow as a **Recurrence** action. This will typically be set up to run at the end or beginning of the day to get a snapshot of yesterday's data. However, this can change depending on how often your data is updated.

In this example, we have set up the trigger to reoccur once every day at 00:30. This can be seen and confirmed in the following preview:

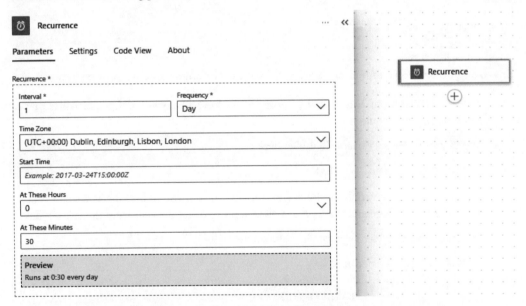

Figure 14.11 – Screenshot of the Recurrence function within Power Automate

Step two – query the dataset

Next, we will set an action to query the dataset/semantic model in Power BI. This will use DAX language to query our model and return a subset of data that will be used for the snapshot. To do this, we start by selecting the **Run a query against a dataset** function. First, we will select the workspace and dataset we will be using within the wizard window.

Then we can begin by adding the following code:

```
DEFINE
VAR CurrentYear = YEAR(TODAY())
VAR DateFilterTable =
FILTER(
All('FiscalDate'[Date]),
YEAR('FiscalDate'[Date])= CurrentYear
)
VAR SnapshotTable=
SUMMARIZECOLUMNS(
'FiscalDate'[Date], 'Store'[StoreNumber],Sales[Category],
Sales[SubCategory], Sales[OrderNumber], District[DM],
DateFilterTable,
"Sales Order Value", 'Sales'[Total Sales],
"Average Order Value", 'Sales'[Avg $ / Unit]
)

EVALUATE
SnapshotTable
```

This code is broken down into three parts, which have been summarized for your reference:

- The DEFINE section: This is the beginning of the DAX query and defines variables that can be used later in the query.

- The CurrentYear variable is shown here:

  ```
  VAR CurrentYear = YEAR(TODAY())
  ```

  The CurrentYear variable is defined to store the current year. It uses the TODAY() function to get the current date and the YEAR() function to extract the year from the current date.

- The DateFilterTable variable is shown here:

  ```
  VAR DateFilterTable =
      FILTER(
          ALL('FiscalDate'[Date]),
          YEAR('FiscalDate'[Date]) = CurrentYear
      )
  ```

The DateFilterTable variable is defined to filter FiscalDate' [Date] based on the condition that the year should be equal to the CurrentYear value. The FILTER function is used to filter the dates, and ALL('FiscalDate'[Date]) removes any existing filters on the 'FiscalDate'[Date] column.

- The SnapshotTable variable is shown here:

```
VAR SnapshotTable =
    SUMMARIZECOLUMNS (
        'FiscalDate'[Date],
        'Store'[StoreNumber],
        Sales[Category],
        Sales[SubCategory],
        Sales[OrderNumber],
        District[DM],
        DateFilterTable,
        "Sales Order Value", 'Sales'[Total Sales],
        "Average Order Value", 'Sales'[Avg $ / Unit]
    )
```

The SnapshotTable variable uses the SUMMARIZECOLUMNS function to create a summarized table. It includes various columns, such as 'FiscalDate'[Date], 'Store'[StoreNumber], Sales[Category], and so on.

The DateFilterTable variable is used as one of the filters for the summarized table. The resulting table contains aggregated values, such as Sales Order Value and Average Order Value, based on the specified columns.

- The EVALUATE section is shown here:

```
EVALUATE
    SnapshotTable
```

The EVALUATE statement is used to display the result of the SnapshotTable variable. It returns the summarized table with the applied filters, showing the sales order values and average order values for the specified columns in the current fiscal year:

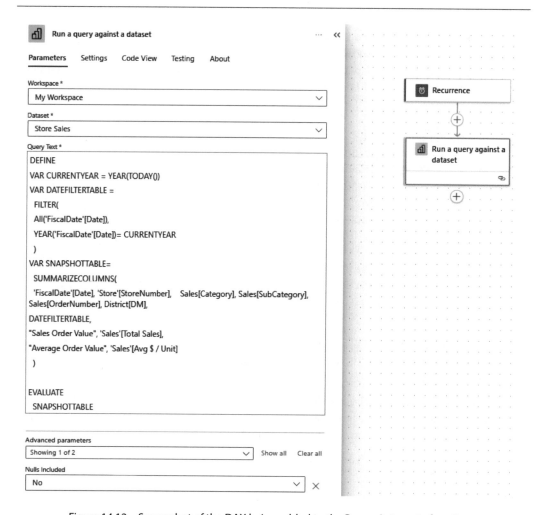

Figure 14.12 – Screenshot of the DAX being added to the Power Automate function

Step three – create the file

In the last step, we will take the output of the previous step, which was the returned query, and generate a file to store the query result in. In this example, we will use the Create File function from the SharePoint actions to generate a CSV file to store the returned data.

To do this, you will need to specify the site address and folder path for the SharePoint site in which you'd like the CSVs stored. As this will be running on a daily basis, it's important that we give these files a dynamic naming convention, so we can identify the files when we need to pull them into Power BI after. This is best done by using an expression within our file name. To do so, we can add the following expression within the file name (if you're in the new designer view, then you will need to select the **fx** button that appears at the end of the file name box – this will cause the expression box to appear on the right side):

```
formatDateTime(addDays(utcNow(), -1), 'dd-MM-yyyy')
```

Select **Add** or **Update** depending on which view you're in.

This now means that every time the flow is run, it will save the file with yesterday's date.

Then, by adding `.csv` to the end of the file name, we can ensure that the file will be saved as a CSV file as shown:

Figure 14.13 – Screenshot of the Create file function within Power Automate

Lastly, we determine the file content, which is where we select the outputs from the previous step using dynamic content. To select the output of the previous step, select the box under **File Content** and then select the output from the dynamic content menu (under the dynamic content from the last step). If you are using the new designer, you will need to select the lightning bolt button at the end of the box to open this view. Save and test your flow.

To summarize, in this comprehensive section, you have been able to create a flow that provides you with a snapshot view of a particular set of data. This will be extremely beneficial if you're looking at doing a variance analysis across a time series.

> **Important note**
>
> Using Power Automate to save a CSV file based on a DAX query does have some important limitations that could impact the data you're trying to save. The limit is that a maximum of 100,000 rows or 1,000,000 values can be retrieved in your query, or 15 MB of data (whichever is hit first). Keep this in mind as you may need to filter the query to within these limitations or use aggregations in your query to reduce the amount of data loaded to within the limits. If you need to create temporary tables of large datasets, then you might find it better to use other data or analytics services from within Azure, for example.
>
> More information on these limitations can be found here: `https://learn.microsoft.com/en-us/rest/api/power-bi/datasets/execute-queries`

You have covered a lot in the past sections, so as we transition to the next section, you will learn some best practices to keep in mind as you explore and use Power Automate.

Best practices with Power Automate

Some of the best practices to be aware of for data cleaning in Power Automate:

- **Workflow planning**: Before diving into automation, carefully plan your data cleaning workflow. Identify the key steps that require automation and the triggers that will initiate the processes.

- **Error handling**: Implement robust error-handling mechanisms within your automated workflows. This includes adding notifications for failed processes, enabling quick identification, and resolving issues. One example would be to check the flow checker from within your flow. To do this, select **Flow check** in the top right corner of the Power Automate toolbar.

- Flow check will then provide details of any errors or warnings identified within your flow.

- **Testing and validation**: Thoroughly test your automated data cleaning workflows in different scenarios. Validate the results to ensure that the automated processes align with your data quality standards.

- **Security considerations**: When automating data processes, prioritize security. Ensure that sensitive data is handled securely and that only authorized personnel have access to critical automation components. The following explains how to review or add authorized personnel to your flow:

  I.   Navigate to the overview page of your created flow.

  II.   Select **Edit** in the **Co-owners** section to open the view as shown:

Co-owners

Adding an owner gives them full control of this flow, so make sure you only share with people you trust. They'll be able to add or remove other users as owners, access the run history, and can update, edit or delete this flow.

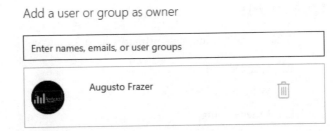

Figure 14.14 – Screenshot showing the Co-owners section

III.   Here you can give **full access** to others as well as manage the **connections** used within your flow to other services, such as Power BI.

• **Documentation**: Maintain comprehensive documentation for your automated data cleaning workflows. This documentation should include details about triggers, processes, and any custom scripts or expressions used in the automation.

With these best practices, you fortify your approach to data cleaning in Power Automate, ensuring not just efficiency but also reliability in your processes. By embracing these best practices, you not only enhance the efficiency of your data cleaning processes but also future-proof your Power Automate endeavors with a foundation of meticulous planning, resilience, security, and knowledge accessibility.

Summary

Incorporating Power Automate into your data cleaning workflows for Power BI can significantly enhance efficiency and reliability. By automating triggers, notifications, and data refresh processes, you not only save time but also ensure that your data is consistently prepared for impactful analyses. Following best practices in planning, testing, security, and documentation will further contribute to the success of your automated data cleaning endeavors.

In this chapter, you learned how to use Power Automate to automate or sequence your refreshes, how to create alerts or notifications, and how to use the actions to create snapshot files of your data in CSVs. The automation of Power BI data refresh processes, either through scheduled refreshes or event-based triggers, was explored to ensure up-to-date reports for dynamic datasets. We concluded with some best practices for utilizing Power Automate, encompassing workflow planning, error handling, testing, security considerations, and documentation.

Embracing the power of automation can help you elevate your data preparation practices and unlock the full potential of your Power BI reports. In the next and final chapter, you will learn how to begin using new and trending technologies, such as OpenAI and ChatGPT, to help you prepare and analyze data. Given how much of a storm this technology has caused already, learning how this can be used to clean your data will most definitely help you and your business get ahead.

Questions

1. What is Power Automate primarily used for in conjunction with Power BI?

    A. Graphic design

    B. Workflow automation

    C. Video editing

    D. Social media management

2. Which of the following is NOT a trigger mentioned in the chapter for initiating workflows in Power Automate?

    A. Data addition

    B. Data modification

    C. Weather change

    D. Specific conditions met

3. What is the purpose of setting up notifications in Power Automate for data cleaning workflows?

    A. To enhance data security

    B. To communicate workflow failures

    C. To generate additional data

    D. To automate data refresh

4. How can you schedule data refreshes in Power BI using Power Automate?

    A. Use a manual trigger

    B. Set up a recurrence action

    C. Wait for external requests

    D. Use conditional statements

Further reading

*   Use the Power BI button to trigger a Power Automate Flow:

    *   https://powerautomate.microsoft.com/en-us/blog/trigger-flows-from-power-bi-reports/

- Schedule a refresh of a dataflow from within the Power BI service:

  - `https://learn.microsoft.com/en-us/power-bi/connect-data/refresh-scheduled-refresh`

  - `https://learn.microsoft.com/en-us/power-bi/transform-model/dataflows/dataflows-understand-optimize-refresh`

- Add expression in flow actions and dynamic content:

  - `https://powerautomate.microsoft.com/en-us/blog/use-expressions-in-actions/`

  - `https://digitalmill.net/2023/07/31/using-dynamic-content-in-power-automate/`

15

Making Life Easier with OpenAI

OpenAI is taking over the world, with senior stakeholders across industries asking how it can be integrated into their businesses. Many teams also worry about whether this technology will make their roles obsolete. This chapter provides context and insight as to how OpenAI will only help and make life easier when it comes to cleaning data in Power BI.

This chapter delves into the significance of data cleaning, addressing challenges such as inconsistent data formats, missing values, and outliers. The discussion emphasizes the pivotal role that sophisticated tools play in elevating data quality to meet the demands of modern analytics.

ChatGPT, powered by the GPT architecture, is a cutting-edge language model that excels in natural language understanding and generation. Its ability to comprehend and respond to user inputs in a conversational manner opens innovative possibilities for data cleaning and preparation.

Through this chapter, we will cover the following topics:

- Optimizing efficiency with OpenAI, ChatGPT, and DAX
- Using OpenAI for M queries
- Using Microsoft Copilot
- Tackling challenges with AI

By the end of this chapter, you will have built upon your knowledge of the latest trending technology and how it might be used within your workflows to clean, prepare, and analyze data using Power BI.

Optimizing efficiency with OpenAI, ChatGPT, and DAX

Azure OpenAI is a cutting-edge natural language processing service that empowers applications to understand, generate, and interact with human-like text. For those not familiar with Azure, Azure is a cloud computing platform and set of services provided by Microsoft. It offers a wide range of services for computing, analytics, storage, and networking, allowing businesses to build, deploy, and manage applications and services through Microsoft-managed data centers.

Its ability to comprehend contextual nuances makes it an ideal companion for data cleaning in Power BI. OpenAI's impressive AI features are an excellent addition to the plethora of AI services already available within Azure, as highlighted in the following screenshot:

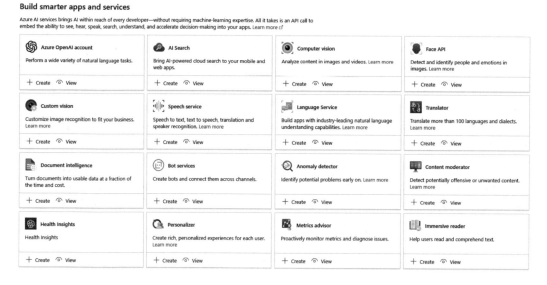

Figure 15.1 – Screenshot of the Azure AI services within the Azure portal

When we begin looking at use cases for where OpenAI can begin to assist us in preparing data, we see that there are three key areas:

- **Cleaning textual data**: Azure OpenAI shines in parsing and normalizing textual data. Whether it's standardizing product names or cleaning unstructured text, the language model's contextual understanding enhances the efficiency of text-related transformations in Power BI.

- **Identifying anomalies and outliers**: Leveraging Azure OpenAI's natural language processing, Power BI users can develop anomaly detection models that understand the context of data points. This goes beyond statistical methods, enabling the identification of anomalies based on contextual relevance.

- **Data imputation strategies**: Azure OpenAI's language capabilities extend to intelligent data imputation. By analyzing surrounding data points, the model can intelligently predict and fill in missing values, contributing to more robust datasets for Power BI analysis.

As we progress through some examples in the next section, you might wish to follow along within your own instance. Before doing this though, you will need to create your own Azure OpenAI instance. To do this, follow the next steps (alternatively, if you already have access to an Azure portal, then skip to *step 3*):

1. To get started with Azure, go to `https://azure.microsoft.com/en-in/free/` to create an Azure account. This will give you access to free usage of popular Azure services. More details are available at the preceding link. Once you're ready to sign up, select **PayAsYouGo** (note that you won't be able to access Azure OpenAI on the free account service, and your account will be given $200 worth of credit on getting started).

2. You will then be asked to log in with your Microsoft account. If you don't have one already, create an account following the onscreen instructions.

3. Once you have logged in, you'll be able to log in to your Azure portal account. Note that if this is the first time logging in to the Azure portal, you can use the next link to find a series of on-demand demos of how to navigate the portal and deploy common services: `https://azure.microsoft.com/en-GB/get-started/on-demand/`.

4. When you log in (for the first time), you will by default be taken to the Quickstart Center, where you can go through a checklist to ensure you have set up your Azure portal correctly. Select the search bar at the top of the screen.

5. Type in `Azure OpenAI` and select the service in the dropdown that appears. This will take you to the Azure OpenAI services window within the Azure portal. Here you will be able to see all the AI services available on the left-hand side. From here, you can create and manage Azure OpenAI resources.

6. Next, click on **Create Azure OpenAI** in the middle of the page or on the button labeled **Create +** in the toolbar.

7. If this is the first time you are accessing Azure, you will need to set up a resource group. In order to proceed, click on **Create new** below the **Resource group** dropdown as shown:

Create Azure OpenAI   ...

1 Basics   ② Network   ③ Tags   ④ Review + submit

Enable new business solutions with OpenAI's language generation capabilities powered by GPT-3 models. These models have been pretrained with trillions of words and can easily adapt to your scenario with a few short examples provided at inference. Apply them to numerous scenarios, from summarization to content and code generation.

Learn more

Project Details

Subscription * ⓘ

| Azure subscription 1 | ∨ |

Resource group * ⓘ

| (New) CleaningDataWithPowerBI | ∨ |

Create new

Figure 15.2 – Screenshot of the Azure OpenAI services setup within the Azure portal

8. Then, to proceed with creating an Azure OpenAI service, you will need to complete the application form in the configuration window.

9. Once approved, you will be able to complete the configuration by clicking on **Next** and then **Review + Submit** to create your OpenAI service.

10. Once configured, you will be brought to the OpenAI service window as shown. Now this will have details on your new service as well as the configurations that you can apply, such as access controls, encryptions, monitoring, and more. There are some useful links in the *Further reading* section if you wish to learn more about these features.

Figure 15.3 – The Get Started options from Azure OpenAI services within the Azure portal

11. Click on **Go to Azure Open AI Studio** to get started with creating some AI models.

This section opened your eyes to how Azure OpenAI models can be used to innovate; the next section aims to build on that with ideas about how it can be used to optimize your coding in M.

Using OpenAI for M queries

Azure OpenAI, with ChatGPT functionality within it, can be a helpful tool for generating M queries in Power BI by providing suggestions, helping with syntax, and offering insights into data transformation tasks. In the following example, you will learn about how you can leverage the chat playground within OpenAI to improve your productivity and efficiency when writing M queries. We will do this by asking a series of questions directly within Azure OpenAI.

Complete the next steps to follow along with the example in your own environment:

1. Click on **Deployment** on the left-hand side and then select **Create new deployment** to get started.

2. Select a model from the base models, in this case, select **gpt-35-turbo**, and then name your deployment. In this example, name it `CleaningDataOpenAI`.

3. Select **Chat playground** from the Azure OpenAI Studio home screen or from the **Playground** tab on the left of your screen. This should open the following view:

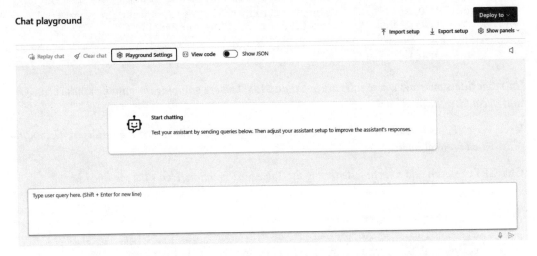

Figure 15.4 – Screenshot of the chat playground from within Azure OpenAI

Now that you have set up an instance of OpenAI, here's an example conversation taken from OpenAI, where the chat functionality has been used to assist with writing M queries in Power BI:

User: *Hi, I'm working on a Power BI project, and I need to transform some data using M queries. I have a table with sales data, and I want to calculate the total sales for each product category. Can you help me with the M query for that?*

ChatGPT: *Of course! To calculate the total sales for each product category, you can use the Group By transformation in Power BI's Power Query Editor. Here's a sample M snippet for your scenario:*

```
let
    Source = YourDataSource,
```

```
        GroupedTable = Table.Group(Source, {"ProductCategory"},
    {{"TotalSales", each List.Sum([Sales]), type number}})
    in
        GroupedTable
```

Replace `YourDataSource` *with the actual name of your data source. This code groups the data by the* `ProductCategory` *column and calculates the total sales for each group.*

User: *Thanks! That's a great starting point. What if I want to filter out products with sales less than $1,000 before calculating the total sales?*

ChatGPT: *You can add a filtering step before the Group By transformation. Here's an updated version of the M:*

```
    let
        Source = YourDataSource,
        FilteredTable = Table.SelectRows(Source, each [Sales] >= 1000),
        GroupedTable = Table.Group(FilteredTable, {"ProductCategory"},
    {{"TotalSales", each List.Sum([Sales]), type number}})
    in
        GroupedTable
```

This code filters out rows where sales are less than $1,000 before grouping the data by product category and calculating the total sales.

User: *Perfect! This is really helpful. One more thing – what if I want to sort the results in descending order based on total sales?*

ChatGPT: *You can add a sorting step using the Table.Sort function. Here's the modified M:*

```
    let
        Source = YourDataSource,
        FilteredTable = Table.SelectRows(Source, each [Sales] >= 1000),
        GroupedTable = Table.Group(FilteredTable, {"ProductCategory"},
    {{"TotalSales", each List.Sum([Sales]), type number}}),
        SortedTable = Table.Sort(GroupedTable,{{"TotalSales", Order.
    Descending}})
    in
        SortedTable
```

This code sorts the grouped table in descending order based on the "TotalSales" column.

This interaction represents a simple example of how those who can leverage the power of tools such as OpenAI and ChatGPT will be able to quickly upskill in areas such as coding. It has to be said, though, that while this is still in its infancy, it's important to always test and validate the answers provided before implementing them in production. Also, ensure that you take precautions when using the publicly available ChatGPT model to avoid sharing sensitive data publicly. If you would like to use sensitive data or you want to ensure that requests are given within a secured governed environment, make sure to use the ChatGPT model within your own Azure OpenAI instance.

In more complex examples, optimizing Power Query transformations could involve efficient interaction with Azure OpenAI. This includes streamlining API calls, managing large datasets, and incorporating caching mechanisms for repetitive queries, ensuring a seamless and performant data cleaning process.

As we begin to explore the use cases where this technology can be most effective, there are a number of clear early winners:

- **Optimizing query plans**: ChatGPT's natural language understanding can assist in formulating more efficient Power Query plans. By describing the desired transformations in natural language, users can interact with ChatGPT to generate optimized query plans. This involves selecting the most suitable Power Query functions and structuring transformations for performance gains.

- **Caching strategies for repetitive queries**: ChatGPT can guide users in devising effective caching strategies. By understanding the context of data transformations, it can recommend where to implement caching mechanisms to store and reuse intermediate results, minimizing redundant API calls and computations. The following is an example of just this, where I have asked Azure OpenAI to verify and optimize my query from the Power Query Advanced Editor. The model suggested I use the `Table.Buffer` function to help cache the table in memory and optimize the query.

Could you help me by optimizing the below m-query from power bi advanced editor?

```
let
    Source = YourDataSource,
    // Step 1: Filter out inactive customers
    FilteredTable = Table.SelectRows(Source, each [Status] = "Active"),
    // Step 2: Rename columns for clarity
    RenamedColumns = Table.RenameColumns(FilteredTable,
{{"CustomerName", "Name"}, {"OrderAmount", "Spending"}}),
    // Step 3: Group by customer and calculate total spending
    GroupedTable = Table.Group(RenamedColumns, {"CustomerID",
"Name"}, {{"TotalSpending", each List.Sum([Spending]), type number}}),
    // Step 4: Sort the results by total spending in descending order
    SortedTable = Table.Sort(GroupedTable, {{"TotalSpending",
Order.Descending}})
in
    SortedTable
```

Figure 15.5 – An example request to OpenAI to help optimize my query for Power Query

This m-query looks well optimized and efficient. However, if you want to further optimize it, you can try the following:

1. Use Table.Buffer function to cache the table in memory, which can improve performance when working with large datasets.
2. Use the "each" keyword sparingly, as it can slow down query performance. Instead, use the "=>" syntax to create lambda expressions.
3. Use the "let" statement to define intermediate steps and break down complex queries into smaller, more manageable parts.

Here is an optimized version of your m-query:

```
let
Source = YourDataSource,
// Filter out inactive customers and cache the table in memory
FilteredTable = Table.Buffer(Table.SelectRows(Source, each [Status] = "Active")),
// Rename columns for clarity
RenamedColumns = Table.RenameColumns(FilteredTable,{{"CustomerName", "Name"},
{"OrderAmount", "Spending"}}),
// Group by customer and calculate total spending
GroupedTable = Table.Group(RenamedColumns, {"CustomerID", "Name"},
{{"TotalSpending", each List.Sum([Spending]), type number}}),
// Sort the results by total spending in descending order
SortedTable = Table.Sort(GroupedTable, {{"TotalSpending", Order.Descending}})
in
SortedTable
```

Figure 15.6 – An example response from OpenAI to help optimize my query for Power Query

Now as we highlighted in *Chapter 11, M Query Optimization*, Table.Buffer can indeed improve the performance of your queries and refreshes, but this really depends on the data you are working with. In the previous example, the model doesn't take the characteristics, size, or complexity of your data into consideration as it isn't plugged into your data at this stage. Also linking back to the example you walked through in *Chapter 11*, the placement of where you add Table.Buffer can really impact how your query performs. In the previous example, if you were connecting to a small dataset, you would likely cause it to run slower by adding the Table.Buffer function as the second variable in the query.

Lastly, it's worth mentioning that how you prompt these models is crucially important. In the previous example, we didn't specify what type of data source we were using in our query. As such, the model hasn't provided an insight or overview that using Table.Buffer on a data source supporting query folding will cause it to break the fold. Again, this is not so much of a problem if Table.Buffer is placed at the end of your query for smaller datasets, but it is a problem if you add it nearer to the beginning of the query, like in the previous example.

- **Handling large datasets**: Dealing with large datasets often poses a challenge in Power Query. OpenAI models, including ChatGPT, can provide insights into dividing and conquering large datasets. This includes strategies for parallel processing, filtering data early in the transformation pipeline, and using aggregations to reduce computational load.

- **Dynamic query adjustments**: ChatGPT's interactive nature allows users to dynamically adjust queries based on evolving requirements. It can assist in crafting queries that adapt to changing data scenarios, ensuring that Power Query transformations remain flexible and responsive to varied datasets.

- **Guidance on complex transformations**: Power Query often involves intricate transformations. ChatGPT can act as a virtual assistant, guiding users through the process of complex transformations. It can suggest optimal function compositions, advise on conditional logic placement, and assist in structuring transformations to enhance efficiency. The best example of this can be seen in the following two screenshots of an active use case seen in many businesses. The example begins with a user asking the model for a description of what the query is doing. OpenAI then provides a breakdown of what the query is doing in each step to help the user interpret the code. It helps to break down the barriers to coding and also helps to decipher code that has not been documented well by previous employees.

Can you help me understand what the below query from power query advanced editor is trying to do?

```
let
    Source1 = YourDataSource1,
    Source2 = YourDataSource2,

    MergedTable = Table.NestedJoin(Source1, {"CustomerID"}, Source2, {"CustomerID"},
"MergedData"),

    ExpandedTable = Table.ExpandTableColumn(MergedTable, "MergedData", {"CustomerName",
"OrderDate", "ProductID", "Quantity"}),

    FilteredTable = Table.SelectColumns(ExpandedTable, {"CustomerID", "CustomerName",
"OrderDate", "ProductID", "Quantity"}),

    GroupedTable = Table.Group(FilteredTable, {"CustomerID", "CustomerName"},
{{"TotalQuantity", each List.Sum([Quantity]), type number}}),

    SortedTable = Table.Sort(GroupedTable, {{"TotalQuantity", Order.Descending}}),

    CalculatedColumn = Table.AddColumn(SortedTable, "AverageQuantity", each [TotalQuantity] /
Table.RowCount(SortedTable), type number),

    FinalTable = Table.RemoveColumns(CalculatedColumn, {"OrderDate"})
in
    FinalTable
```

Figure 15.7 – An example request to OpenAI to help translate my query

This Power Query script is performing a series of data transformation steps on two data sources (Source1 and Source2) to merge them, expand them, filter them, group them, sort them, and calculate a new column. The resulting table is the FinalTable.

Here is a breakdown of the individual steps:
1. Define the data sources as Source1 and Source2.
2. Merge the two data sources based on the common column "CustomerID" using a nested join and create a new column called "MergedData".
3. Expand the "MergedData" column to show the columns "CustomerName", "OrderDate", "ProductID", and "Quantity".
4. Select only the columns "CustomerID", "CustomerName", "OrderDate", "ProductID", and "Quantity" from the expanded table.
5. Group the table by "CustomerID" and "CustomerName" and calculate the total quantity for each group.
6. Sort the table based on the total quantity in descending order.
7. Calculate a new column called "AverageQuantity" by dividing the total quantity by the number of rows in the sorted table.
8. Remove the "OrderDate" column from the calculated table to obtain the final table.

Figure 15.8 – An example response from OpenAI to help describe my query

- **Error handling strategies**: Optimizing Power Query also entails robust error handling. ChatGPT can provide recommendations for anticipating and handling errors gracefully within a query. This includes strategies for logging errors, implementing fallback mechanisms, and ensuring the stability of the overall data preparation process.

In this section, you learned how to optimize Power Query transformations with Azure OpenAI efficiently. Key takeaways include using ChatGPT for natural-language-based query planning and effective caching strategies. Insights include handling large datasets through parallel processing, early filtering, and aggregations. This knowledge equips you to streamline and enhance your Power Query processes effectively.

In the next section, you will learn about Microsoft Copilot, how to set up a Power BI instance with Copilot activated, and also how you can use this new AI technology to help clean and prepare your data.

Using Microsoft Copilot

For those who have never heard of Microsoft Copilot, it is a new technology that Microsoft has released across a number of its platforms that combines generative AI with your data to enhance productivity. Copilot for Power BI harnesses cutting-edge generative AI alongside your dataset, revolutionizing the process of uncovering and disseminating insights with unprecedented speed. Seamlessly integrated into your workflow, Copilot offers an array of functionalities aimed at streamlining your reporting experience.

When it comes to report creation, Copilot streamlines the process by allowing users to effortlessly generate reports by articulating the insights they seek or posing questions regarding their dataset using NLP. Copilot then analyzes the data, pulling together relevant information to craft visually striking reports, thereby transforming raw data into actionable insights instantaneously. Moreover, Copilot has the ability to read your data and suggest the best position to begin your analysis, which can then be tailored to suit the direction you want to take the analysis in.

This is great, but how can it help you clean and prepare data for analysis? Well, Copilot can be leveraged on multiple data tools from within the Microsoft Fabric platform. For those who are not aware, Power BI has now become part of the Fabric platform. Depending on what type of license you have for Power BI, you might already have access to this. Any customers with Premium capacity licensing for the Power BI service would have automatically been given access to Microsoft Fabric, and more importantly, Copilot.

That being said, currently, Copilot has only been made available to customers with a P1 (or above) Premium capacity or a Fabric license of F64 (or above), which is the equivalent licensing available directly from the Azure portal.

If you would like to follow along with the next example, you will need to set up a Fabric capacity within your Azure portal. Don't worry, you can pause this service when it's not being used to ensure you are only charged for the time you're using it. Alternatively, follow the steps to see the outcome:

1. Log in to the Azure portal that you set up in the previous section of this chapter.

2. Select the search bar at the top of the page and type in `Microsoft Fabric`. Select the service in the menu that appears below the search bar, which should take you to the page where you can manage your capacities.

3. Select **Create a Fabric capacity**. Note that you will need to use an organizational account in order to create a Fabric capacity as opposed to a personal account. You can sign up for a Microsoft Fabric trial for your organization within the window. Further details on how to do this are provided here: `https://learn.microsoft.com/en-us/power-bi/enterprise/service-admin-signing-up-for-power-bi-with-a-new-office-365-trial`.

4. Select the subscription and resource group you would like to use for this Fabric capacity.

5. Then, under capacity details, you can enter your capacity name. In this example, you can call it `cleaningdata`.

6. The **Region** field should populate with the region of your tenant, but you can change this if you like. However, this may have implications on performance, which it should warn you about with a message.

7. Set the capacity to `F64`.

8. Then, click on select **Review + create**.

9. Review the terms and then click on **Create**, which will begin the deployment of your capacity.

10. Once deployed, select **Go to resource** to view your Fabric capacity. Take note that this will be active once deployed. Make sure to return here after testing to pause or delete your Fabric capacity to prevent yourself from getting charged for this service.

    Now you will need to ensure you have activated the Copilot settings from within your Fabric capacity. To do this, go to `https://app.powerbi.com/admin-portal/` to log in and access the admin portal.

Important tip

If you can't see the **Tenant settings** tab, then you will need to ensure you have been set up as an admin within your Microsoft 365 admin center. If you have just created a new account, then you will need to set this up. Follow the next links to assign roles:

- `https://learn.microsoft.com/en-us/microsoft-365/admin/add-users/assign-admin-roles`

- `https://learn.microsoft.com/en-us/fabric/admin/microsoft-fabric-admin`

---

11. Scroll to the bottom of **Tenant settings** until you see the **Copilot and Azure OpenAI service (preview)** section as shown:

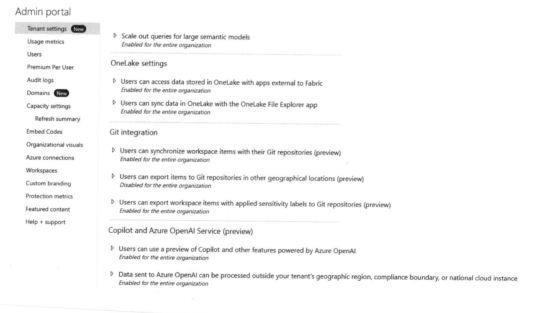

Figure 15.9 – The tenant settings from within Power BI

12. Ensure both settings are set to **Enabled** and then click on **Apply**.

Now that you have created your Fabric capacity, let's jump into an example of how we can use Copilot to help with the cleaning of data. As we have created a new capacity, you will have to create a new workspace that uses this new capacity:

1. Navigate back to **Workspaces** using the left navigation bar. Then, select **New Workspace**.

2. Name your workspace `CleaningData(Copilot)`, then select the dropdown for advanced configuration settings.

3. Ensure you have selected Fabric capacity in the license mode, which in turn will have selected your capacity below, and then select **Apply**. You have now created your capacity!

4. Now let's use Fabric to create a new dataflow using the latest update of Dataflow Gen2. Select **New** from within the workspace and then select **More options**.

5. This will navigate you to a page with all the possible actions to create items within your Fabric workspace. Under **Data Factory**, select **Dataflow Gen2**.

6. This will load a Dataflow Gen2 instance called **Dataflow 1**. On the top row, you should now see the Copilot logo within the **Home** ribbon as highlighted:

Figure 15.10 – The ribbon within a Dataflow Gen2 instance

7. Select Copilot to open the Copilot window on the right-hand side of the page. As you have not connected to any data, it will prompt you to select get data.

8. Select **Text/CSV** and then enter the following into the **File path or URL** box:

    ```
    https://raw.githubusercontent.com/PacktPublishing/Data-Cleaning-
    with-Power-BI/main/Retail%20Store%20Sales%20Data.csv
    ```

9. Leave the rest of the settings as their defaults and click on **Next**.

10. This will then open a preview of the file data. Click on **Create** to load this data into your Dataflow Gen2 instance. You will see that the Copilot window will have now changed to prompt you as to what you would like to do (if it hasn't, then simply close the Copilot window and reopen):

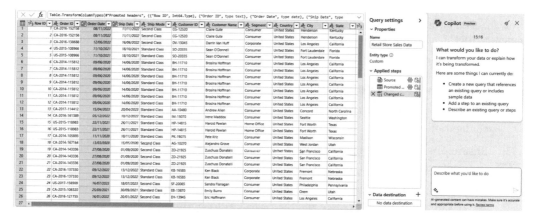

Figure 15.11 – Data loaded into Dataflow Gen2

11. In this example, we can see that the data includes a column called **Order Date** but we don't have a field for the fiscal year. Enter the following prompt to ask Copilot to help with the transformation:

    There's a column in the data named Order Date, which shows when an order was placed. However, I need to create a new column from this that shows the Fiscal Year. Can you extract the year from the date and call this Fiscal Year? Set this new column to type number also.

12. Proceed using the arrow key or press *Enter*. Copilot will then begin working on your request. As you will see in the resulting output, the model has added a function (or step) called **Custom** to the query that we had selected.

13. Scroll to the far side and you will see that this has added a new column called **Fiscal Year**.

14. Now add the following prompt to narrow down our data and press *Enter*:

    Can you now remove all columns leaving me with just Order ID, Order Date, Fiscal year, category, and Sales?

15. This will then add another function or step called **Choose columns**. Finally, add the following prompt to aggregate this data and press *Enter*:

    Can you now group this data by Category, Fiscal year, and aggregated by Sum of Sales?

    As you can see, Copilot has now added another function called **Custom 1** to the applied steps in this query, resulting in this table:

🔢	A♭C 🔑 Cat... ▼	1²3 🔑 Fisca... ▼	1.2 Sum of Sales ▼
1	Homeware	2022	198901.436
2	Office	2022	183939.982
3	Homeware	2021	170518.237
4	Office	2021	137233.463
5	Homeware	2020	157192.8531
6	Office	2020	151776.412
7	Technology	2020	175278.233
8	Office	2023	246097.175
9	Homeware	2023	215387.2692
10	Technology	2022	226364.18
11	Technology	2021	162780.809
12	Technology	2023	271730.811

Figure 15.12 – The results from asking Copilot to transform the data

To view the M query that Copilot has added, select **Advanced editor**, which will show the functions that Copilot has added for you:

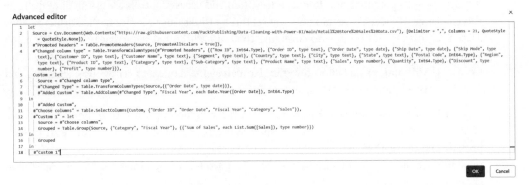

Figure 15.13 – The resulting M query created by Copilot to carry
out the request transformations to clean the data

In this example, you explored the new technologies available with Copilot and how they help to transform the data using tools such as Dataflow Gen2.

While it's great to understand the amazing possibilities AI brings to data, it's also crucially important that you understand the challenges it presents. In the next section, we will learn more about the challenges and risks associated with technology such as OpenAI/ChatGPT. Additionally, Copilot can leverage its intelligent model to provide narrative visuals that provide a summary of findings within the data you have selected.

Tackling challenges with AI

While Azure OpenAI opens new avenues for data cleaning in Power BI, challenges such as API rate limits and cost considerations should be navigated. Robust error handling, caching strategies, and efficient resource management are crucial aspects to address potential roadblocks.

While considering how these technologies can be leveraged, you should consider the following challenges:

- **Risk of incorrect information**: One of the primary concerns when leveraging technologies such as OpenAI for data cleaning is the risk of generating incorrect information. Misinterpretation of user queries or inadequate context understanding can lead to suboptimal data transformations, potentially impacting the reliability of insights derived from Power BI reports.

- **Complexity of natural language understanding**: Natural language understanding, a key feature of technologies such as ChatGPT, is inherently complex. Data cleaning instructions provided in natural language may have nuances that are challenging for models to grasp accurately. Ambiguities in language can result in unintended transformations, emphasizing the need for careful validation.

- **Ensuring query security and confidentiality**: As users interact with AI models to optimize Power Query, ensuring the security and confidentiality of queries becomes paramount. Sensitive information embedded in queries, especially when dealing with proprietary or confidential datasets, poses a potential risk. Robust encryption and access controls are essential to mitigate this challenge. We won't dive into how you set this up (links can be found in the *Further reading* section of this chapter on how to configure this) but additional security can be added using controls such as **role-based access controls** (**RBAC**) from within your Azure service's Access Control (IAM) options that allow for granular management of user permissions, ensuring that only authorized individuals can access sensitive queries.

- **Dynamic nature of data requirements**: Data cleaning and optimization requirements are often dynamic, influenced by changing business needs or evolving datasets. While AI models provide assistance, they may struggle to adapt quickly to shifting requirements. Practitioners must balance the benefits of automation with the need for manual intervention in response to changing data contexts.

- **Over-reliance on AI recommendations**: A potential pitfall is the over-reliance on AI recommendations without critical scrutiny. Users might be tempted to blindly accept suggestions, assuming they are optimal for their specific use case. This can lead to suboptimal transformations if users don't exercise due diligence in validating AI-generated recommendations.

- **Interpreting and addressing ambiguous queries**: Ambiguity in user queries can be challenging for AI models to handle effectively. Practitioners may inadvertently provide ambiguous instructions, leading to unintended outcomes. Establishing clear communication and refining queries for precision is crucial in overcoming this challenge.

- **Integration with existing workflows**: Integrating AI-powered optimization seamlessly into existing Power BI workflows is a technical challenge. Ensuring a smooth user experience, real-time interaction, and compatibility with Power Query's user interface requires thoughtful design and development efforts. Microsoft has also now released Copilot, which is an incredible piece of technological innovation, bringing these AI services into the Power BI service and other technologies we've discussed in this book (Power Automate and Azure services such as Fabric).

- **Ethical considerations and bias**: The potential introduction of bias in AI-generated recommendations raises ethical considerations. AI models may inadvertently perpetuate biases present in training data, influencing data cleaning decisions. Practitioners must be vigilant in identifying and rectifying biased outcomes.

- **Model explainability**: Understanding and explaining the rationale behind AI-generated recommendations is essential. A lack of model explainability can hinder user trust and confidence. Efforts should be made to enhance transparency and provide users with insights into how AI models arrive at specific optimization suggestions.

- **Data governance and compliance**: Adhering to data governance standards and compliance regulations is an ongoing challenge. The use of AI in data cleaning introduces additional complexities in ensuring that automated transformations align with organizational data governance policies and regulatory requirements.

Addressing the complexities of utilizing technologies such as Azure OpenAI and ChatGPT for data cleaning in Power BI will help you establish yourself as a subject expert. What will add further value, though, is implementing effective workarounds to overcome these challenges.

Robust error handling and careful validation of natural language instructions address the risk of incorrect information, fortifying the reliability of insights. In order to address security and confidentiality concerns, implement stringent measures such as access controls on who can use this technology. Clear communication and refined instructions are key to overcoming the challenge of interpreting ambiguous queries.

This section was just an introduction to the high-level challenges I've seen in the short time that OpenAI has been around. However, if you're interested in learning more about these challenges and how to overcome them, then I highly recommend taking a look at the articles added to the *Further reading* section of this chapter.

By incorporating these workarounds, you can navigate the complexities of data cleaning and preparation, maximizing the potential of innovative technologies while mitigating potential pitfalls in your data-driven journey.

Summary

In this final chapter, we focused on how OpenAI, particularly ChatGPT, powered by the GPT architecture, can enhance data cleaning in Power BI, making processes more efficient and insightful.

The significance of data cleaning was emphasized. We showed you how to begin leveraging OpenAI and Copilot's capabilities when enhancing the data cleaning processes, whether that was through query optimization in the chat playground or the use of Copilot within Dataflow Gen2. The chapter then introduced the concepts of natural language processing for identifying anomalies and outliers in your data.

We also explored specific use cases where OpenAI can be effective, including optimizing query plans, caching strategies, handling large datasets, dynamic query adjustments, guidance on complex transformations, and error handling strategies.

Lastly, you learned about some challenges associated with leveraging OpenAI in Power BI, including the risk of incorrect information, the complexity of natural language understanding, query security, and more. You also learned how to approach and overcome these challenges.

In summary, the key lessons from this chapter include the potential benefits of integrating OpenAI into Power BI for data cleaning, the specific use cases where it can be most effective, and the challenges that need to be navigated for successful implementation. You now know how to optimize Power Query transformations, handle large datasets, and address ethical and compliance considerations. These lessons are crucial for practitioners seeking to enhance data cleaning processes and analytics in Power BI.

Questions

1. What are the three key areas where Azure OpenAI can assist in preparing data?

    A. Optimizing query plans, handling large datasets, and dynamic query adjustments

    B. Cleaning textual data, identifying anomalies and outliers, and data imputation strategies

    C. Error handling strategies, guidance on complex transformations, and caching strategies

    D. Security and confidentiality, integration with existing workflows, and model explainability

2. In the example M code conversation between a user and ChatGPT, what step was taken to filter out products with sales less than $1,000?

    A. The `Table.Buffer` function

    B. A group by transformation

    C. A filtering step before a group by transformation

    D. A sorting step using the `Table.Sort` function

3. What challenge is associated with the dynamic nature of data requirements when using AI models for data cleaning?

    A. Model explainability

    B. Over-reliance on AI recommendations

    C. Ensuring query security and confidentiality

    D. Adapting quickly to shifting requirements

4. What is one of the potential pitfalls when using AI recommendations without critical scrutiny?

    A. Over-reliance on AI recommendations

    B. Lack of model explainability

    C. Ensuring query security and confidentiality

    D. Handling large datasets

Further reading

- *Role-based access control for Azure OpenAI Service*: `https://learn.microsoft.com/en-us/azure/ai-services/openai/how-to/role-based-access-control`

- *Azure monitoring REST API walkthrough*: `https://learn.microsoft.com/en-us/azure/azure-monitor/essentials/rest-api-walkthrough?tabs=portal`

- *Encryption within Azure OpenAI*: `https://learn.microsoft.com/en-gb/azure/ai-services/encryption/cognitive-services-encryption-keys-portal`

- *Monitoring Azure OpenAI*: `https://learn.microsoft.com/en-us/azure/ai-services/openai/how-to/monitoring`

- *Copilot tenant settings (preview)*: `https://learn.microsoft.com/en-us/fabric/admin/service-admin-portal-copilot`

- *Getting started with Copilot*: `https://learn.microsoft.com/en-us/power-bi/create-reports/copilot-create-report`

Putting it together

As you reach the end of this book, it's important to reflect on the journey you have been on since the first chapter. You've embarked on a transformative journey through the intricate realm of cleaning and preparing data with Power BI.

Consider this not as an endpoint, but a stepping stone into a vast landscape of possibilities. The techniques and insights you've learned in this book will serve as the foundation for your ongoing exploration into the dynamic world of data analytics.

Throughout this book, you were introduced to a number of transformation concepts as well as functions that can be used to clean and prepare data. You were introduced to theory on how to approach data preparation, how to bring data into Power BI, and how to prepare that data. Within the chapters, you found links to resources to continue growing your knowledge. Outside of this book, though, I'd recommend you build upon this foundation by focusing on the following topics:

- **DAX**: With DAX being such a critical part of Power BI, I recommend building upon your knowledge of how to leverage DAX to build your measures and more. *Hands-On Business Intelligence with DAX* (`https://www.packtpub.com/product/hands-on-business-intelligence-with-dax/9781838824303`) can help you build upon this.

- **M**: As we have highlighted many times in this book, Power Query and M are critical when it comes to data cleaning and preparation in Power BI. This book has introduced you to lots of concepts, so I'd recommend building on this with a book such as *The Definitive Guide to Power Query (M)* (`https://www.packtpub.com/product/the-definitive-guide-to-power-query-m/9781835089729`).

- **Data modeling**: This book introduced data modeling as a key factor to consider when you're cleaning and preparing your data. Build upon the concepts you were introduced to in *Chapter 12, Data Modeling and Managing Relationships*, with a book such as *Expert Data Modeling with Power BI – Second Edition* (`https://www.packtpub.com/product/expert-data-modeling-with-power-bi-second-edition/9781803246246`).

- **Leveraging R and Python**: We introduced some basics on how you can shape and enhance your data by using R and Python. A book such as *Expert Data Modeling with Power BI – Second Edition* (`https://www.packtpub.com/product/expert-data-modeling-with-power-bi-second-edition/9781803246246`) could help you grow this knowledge with further examples and use cases.

- **Power BI management**: I'd recommend learning more about the management of Power BI deployment with a book such as *Mastering Microsoft Power BI – Second Edition* (`https://www.packtpub.com/product/mastering-microsoft-power-bi-second-edition/9781801811484`).

This book finished with an introduction to how new technologies and innovations in AI are helping people like you become more productive when it comes to cleaning, preparing, and gaining insights from their data. With these topics, I'd continue to keep in mind how innovations with AI will affect these topics specifically.

Remember, learning is a perpetual voyage, and each challenge surmounted is an opportunity for growth. Please continue to hone your skills, apply the knowledge gained, and let this book be a companion on your journey toward mastery.

The world of data awaits your exploration, and with the tools acquired here, you are well equipped to navigate its depths and extract meaningful insights.

Safe travels on your data-driven adventure!

Assessments

Chapter 1 – Introduction to Power BI Data Cleaning

1. B – 50-80%
2. D – Power Query, data modeling, DAX formulas
3. C – Data transformation and preparation
4. C – As a formula language for creating calculations and measures
5. B – To bridge the gap between relational databases and spreadsheet tools
6. D – It can be used for both calculations and querying within Power BI
7. B – It enhances clarity and reduces ambiguity

Chapter 2 – Understanding Data Quality and Why Data Cleaning is Important

1. A – The extent to which data represents true values and attributes
2. D – Human errors during data entry
3. B – Data completeness
4. B – It helps maintain data integrity and accuracy
5. B – A culture of data stewardship
6. A – Proactively identifying and addressing data quality issues
7. C – Criteria for data accuracy, completeness, consistency, validity, and timeliness
8. A – Minimizing human errors
9. B – They automate the data cleaning process

Chapter 3 – Data Cleaning Fundamentals and Principles

1. B – Transforming data into a masterpiece – The aim of data cleaning in the data preparation process is to refine and enhance raw data, ensuring it is accurate, consistent, and high-quality for effective analysis

2.   B – To prevent a cycle of perpetual data cleaning – While the other answers may have some truth to them, they do not describe why it is essential to establish a framework and principles for data cleaning efforts

3.   B – Data assessment, data profiling, data validation, data cleaning strategies, data transformation, data quality assurance, and documentation– These processes together are involved in the data cleaning process

4.   A – Patterns, distributions, and outliers – Data profiling aids in recognizing patterns, understanding distributions, and identifying outliers, providing crucial insights for effective data cleaning and quality improvement

5.   C – It is crucial for tracking data governance and changes made to the data – Documenting the steps taken to clean data is crucial for tracking data governance and changes made to the data as it establishes a transparent and auditable record, ensuring accountability, facilitating reproducibility, and promoting compliance with data quality standards

6.   D – Prioritizing the accuracy, reliability, and consistency of data – Ensuring that the focus is on improving the overall quality rather than merely increasing the quantity of data

Chapter 4 – The Most Common Data Cleaning Operations

1.   B – To enhance data accuracy in the analysis – Removing duplicates is crucial to prevent inaccuracies in data analysis, especially when dealing with numerical values.

2.   C – Product Name, as the main identifier – In the provided example, the Product Name column is selected to remove duplicates, as it serves as the main identifier.

3.   B – Distorts analysis results – Missing data, or NULL values, can distort analysis results and visuals.

4.   C – To gain desired dimensions for analysis – for example, splitting a date field – Columns may need to be split to extract specific dimensions for analysis.

5.   C – **Split Columns by Delimiter**, based on data format – In the Date table example, the **By Delimiter** function is used to split the date column based on the / delimiter.

6.   C – Merging columns to format date data – Merging columns may be necessary to format data appropriately.

7.   A – Select the columns, click Merge Columns, choose a separator, and select Close & Apply – The **Merge Columns** function is used by selecting columns to merge and choosing a custom separator, such as / for dates.

8.   B – To standardize and correct data; scenarios include fixing errors and standardizing formats – Replacing values is important to correct errors or standardize data.

9.   C – **Using the Replace Values function** – In the product names example, the incorrect value Mono poly is replaced using the **Replace Values** function, accessible through either the right-click menu or the toolbar.

10. B – Measures are dynamic, columns are precalculated row by row – A calculated column in Power BI is a static column computed row by row in a table, while a measure is a dynamic, context-aware calculation applied to aggregated data in a visual or report.

11. D – Calculated columns for row-level context; measures for aggregations – Calculated columns are precalculated and consume more memory, whereas measures are dynamic and respond to user interactions, being memory-efficient. The choice depends on factors such as the need for row-level context or aggregation.

Chapter 5 – Importing Data into Power BI

1. C – Data completeness – Ensuring data completeness is essential for accurate analyses and reliable reporting in Power BI. By using data profiling techniques, users can identify columns with high percentages of missing values, such as the `ProductSize` column in the provided example. This allows for targeted attention to areas requiring data completion.

2. C – Conditional formatting – Conditional formatting in Power BI is a valuable tool for validating data accuracy. Users can define rules to highlight data points falling outside predefined accuracy ranges. This method, as showcased in this chapter, ensures that potential errors or outliers are flagged for further investigation, promoting trustworthy insights.

3. D – Calculated columns and measures – Power BI's DAX language empowers users to create calculated columns and measures, enforcing consistent data rules and business logic. This capability contributes to data consistency across reports by ensuring that calculations are standardized, as demonstrated in the provided example.

4. D – Utilizing data transformation capabilities – Data relevance is crucial for meaningful insights. Power BI's data transformation capabilities allow users to filter and transform data during the import process. By selectively including pertinent information, users can create focused datasets aligned with their analysis objectives. In the example, the removal of an irrelevant column enhances data relevance.

5. C – Data normalization – Data normalization, explored as a fundamental concept, is crucial for efficient data organization. Power BI's data modeling capabilities support normalization by establishing relationships between tables. By reducing data redundancy, normalization ensures consistent data updates across related tables, leading to streamlined and efficient data analyses, as illustrated in the provided example.

Chapter 6 – Cleaning Data with Query Editor

1. C – Power Query ribbon – The crucial components of the Query Editor interface include the Power Query ribbon, navigation pane, preview pane, and settings pane. However, the correct answer in the multiple-choice format is Preview Binoculars.

2. C – Translating high-level transformations into low-level SQL statements – Query folding is the process of translating high-level transformations into low-level SQL statements, optimizing query execution.

3. C – Adding columns – The technique that allows the creation of new data based on existing columns is adding calculated columns.

4. B – Join types – The factor that determines how records are matched between tables in merging queries is join types.

5. C – Loading, cleaning, and shaping data – Power Query is used for loading, cleaning, and shaping data.

Chapter 7 – Transforming Data with the M Language

1. B – Transforming entire columns or tables – M's purpose is transforming entire columns or tables

2. C – `let` – The keyword marking the beginning of an M variable declaration block is `let`

3. C – Using a variable, often named `Source` – A data source is typically connected using the `Source` function

4. B – A step/identifier that includes a space or special characters – The # symbol helps to identify steps or identifiers that include spaces or special characters within the name

5. B – `Number.From` – The function used to convert extracted text into a numeric value is `Number.From`

Chapter 8 – Using Data Profiling for Exploratory Data Analysis (EDA)

1. B – To summarize data characteristics and gain insights – EDA serves as a pivotal phase in the data analysis workflow, aiming to summarize data characteristics, identify patterns, detect outliers, and gain insights into data structure.

2. A – Identifying potential outliers – Benefits of a well-carried-out EDA include familiarizing analysts with the dataset, assessing data scope, identifying data quality issues, revealing patterns and trends, and aiding in the selection of appropriate modeling techniques.

3. C – Column Transformation – Power BI's data profiling capabilities include the following:

    - Column Quality Assessment
    - Column Distribution Analysis
    - Column Profile Views

4. B – Within Power Query, open the **View** tab – Data profile views can be accessed in Power Query by opening Power Query and selecting the **View** tab.

5. B – Histograms and statistics – The **Column distribution** view in Power BI allows exploration of the distribution of values within a specific column, providing visualizations such as histograms and statistics such as mean and median.

6. B – Validity, Error, and Empty percentages – The **Column quality** view assesses the quality of data in a specific column, representing Valid, Error, and Empty percentages, indicating data correctness, errors, and missing values, respectively.

7. D – All of the above – The **Column profile** view in Power BI combines data distribution and quality insights, presenting statistics such as count, error count, empty count, distinct count, unique count, NaN count, zero count, min, max, average, and standard deviation.

8. C – Removing duplicates – Based on the insights gained, actions can include data cleaning steps. For example, Power BI might recommend removing duplicates, which can be efficient but depends on the analysis.

9. C – By providing recommended actions in the interface – Power BI automates cleaning steps by providing recommended actions within the interface. For instance, selecting a recommended action, such as filtering to a specific value, results in the addition of a corresponding step in Power Query.

Chapter 9 – Advanced Data Cleaning Techniques

1. C – Fuzzy matching and fill down – They are the two essential techniques discussed in the chapter for cleaning and preparing data using the Query Editor in Power BI

2. C – Range from 0 to 1, indicating no to perfect similarity – In the context of fuzzy matching, the similarity score ranges from 0 to 1, indicating no to perfect similarity

3. D – When working with time series data and maintaining data continuity – The fill down technique in Power BI's Query Editor is particularly useful in this scenario

4. D – Regularly validate the results of data cleaning efforts and maintain documentation – This is a crucial best practice emphasized when working with fuzzy matching and fill down in Power BI

5. C – To extend the capabilities of Power BI by leveraging external ecosystems – This is the primary purpose of using custom data scripts in languages such as R and Python in Power BI

6. B – To write R scripts – The **Run R Script** option in the Power Query Editor from within Power BI Desktop is used to write R scripts

7. B – Integration with external data sources – This is the benefit of using R and Python scripts in Power BI for data preparation

8. C –Anomaly Detection – The Anomaly Detection built-in machine learning feature in Power BI is used for identifying and addressing outliers in data

9. B – Automated data preparation with machine learning suggestions – The purpose of AutoML in Power BI is to provide automated data preparation with machine learning models

10. C – Sentiment analysis, image recognition, and text analytics – They are some of the most common use cases for AI Insights in Power BI

Chapter 10 – Creating Custom Functions in Power Query

1. C – Defining the problem – The first step in planning for a custom function is to clearly define the problem that the function will solve.

2. C – Making functions flexible and adaptable – Parameters in custom functions allow flexibility by serving as variables that users can adjust, making the function applicable to various scenarios.

3. C – To improve the overall user experience – Default parameter values enhance user friendliness, allowing users to quickly understand and use the function without extensive configuration.

4. C – Choosing a descriptive name – Choosing a descriptive name is crucial for the structure of a custom function as it provides clarity about the function's purpose and use.

Chapter 11 – M Query Optimization

1. B – Filtering and reducing data, using native M functions, creating custom functions, optimizing memory usage – These are the four key tips to optimizing M queries

2. A – Parameters: table, weights, values; the weighted average is calculated by summing the weighted values and dividing by the total weight – The function takes three parameters (table, weights, values) and calculates the weighted average by summing the weighted values and dividing by the total weight.

3. C – It loads a table into memory once, reducing memory duplication – `Table.Buffer` is used to load a table into memory only once, reducing memory duplication and improving query speeds on subsequent steps. Note though that it can also have the reverse effect as the initial reading and loading of the data can cause your query to run more slowly.

4. B – Splits a table into smaller partitions for parallel processing – The `Table.Split` function divides a large table into small partitions, enabling parallel processing for faster query execution.

Chapter 12 – Data Modeling and Managing Relationships

1. C – Data modeling – The primary focus of managing relationships in Power BI is data modeling. This involves structuring data tables, creating relationships between them, and ensuring a proper foundation for analysis.

2. B – It can enhance capabilities but may lead to errors and performance issues – **Bidirectional cross-filtering (BDCF)** is considered a double-edged sword because while it can enhance analytical capabilities, it may introduce errors and performance issues if not used carefully.

3. B – A feature allowing tables to filter each other in both directions – Bidirectional cross-filtering is a feature in Power BI that allows tables to filter each other in both directions, providing more flexibility in data analysis.

4. B – It defines the nature of relationships between tables – Understanding cardinality is crucial in Power BI data modeling as it defines the nature of relationships between tables, influencing how data is related and queried.

5. D – Each row in one table corresponds to one and only one row in the second table – One-to-one (1:1) cardinality in Power BI relationships means each row in one table corresponds to one and only one row in the second table.

6. B – It directly influences data accuracy and performance – Choosing the correct cardinality in Power BI relationships influences data accuracy and performance in reports, ensuring the right relationships between tables. In many cases, Power BI will prevent you from selecting the wrong cardinality; however, it is possible to go from a many-to-one to a many-to-many relationship, which could cause problems.

7. C – Performance, data modeling, and query optimization challenges – When dealing with big data in Power BI, common challenges include performance issues, data modeling complexity, and query optimization challenges.

8. D – Implement incremental loading to load only new or modified data – One of the best techniques for handling big data in Power BI, particularly when importing data, is to implement incremental loading to load only new or modified data, optimizing the data loading process.

9. C – They help bypass circular references by breaking down complex calculations – DAX measures and functions play a crucial role in avoiding circular references by providing a way to break down complex calculations and avoid creating direct circular dependencies in the model.

Chapter 13 – Preparing Data for Paginated Reporting

1. B – Pixel-perfect, highly formatted reporting – Power BI Report Builder is designed for creating paginated reports that are highly formatted, pixel-perfect, and optimized for printing or generating PDFs

2. B – Structuring and organizing data – Row groups and column groups in paginated reports play a crucial role in organizing and structuring data, creating hierarchical structures, and facilitating aggregated analysis

3. B – To enhance user experience and efficiency – Filters and parameters are important in paginated reporting to enhance user experience and efficiency by providing dynamic interactivity and customization options

4. D – By generating paginated reports with precise formatting – Power BI Report Builder contributes to meeting compliance standards by allowing the creation of paginated reports with precise formatting, which is crucial in industries with stringent regulations

Chapter 14 – Automating Data Cleaning Tasks with Power Automate

1. B – Workflow automation – This is the primary purpose of Power Automate in conjunction with Power BI

2. C – Weather change – This is NOT a trigger mentioned in the chapter

3. B – To communicate workflow failures and successes – The notifications in Power Automate help in achieving this

4. B – Set up a recurrence action – Although you can use a manual trigger to refresh data, we set up a recurrence action in order to schedule the data refreshes

Chapter 15 – Making Life Easier with OpenAI

1. B – Cleaning textual data, identifying anomalies and outliers, and data imputation strategies – Azure OpenAI can assist in cleaning textual data, identifying anomalies and outliers, and implementing data imputation strategies

2. C – A filtering step before a group by transformation – The example conversation shows that to filter out products with sales less than $1,000, a filtering step is added before the group by transformation.

3. D – Adapting quickly to shifting requirements – Data cleaning and optimization requirements are often dynamic, and AI models may struggle to adapt quickly to shifting requirements

4. A – Over-reliance on AI recommendations – The chapter warned about the potential pitfall of over-reliance on AI recommendations without critical scrutiny, which may lead to suboptimal transformations

Index

A

aggregated tables
cons 207
considerations 207
pros 207
AI
challenges, tackling with 294, 295
AI insights
examples 146
analytics (BI) managers 21
anomaly detection
examples 134
automated machine learning (AutoML) 134
implementing 135-145
use cases 134
automation
triggers, handling 260, 261

B

**bidirectional cross-filtering
(BDCF) 125, 210, 222**
applying, results to model 213
best practices 213, 214
creating 210-212
using 209

big data 218
handling, best practices 218-220
working, challenges in Power BI 218
business intelligence (BI) 6, 21
business users 21

C

calculated columns 41
considerations 44
versus measures 41
Calculation group 43
calendars
adding, reasons 204, 205
cardinality 214, 215
need for 216
selecting 216, 217
cardinality, types
many-to-many (N:N) 216
many-to-one (N:1) 215
one-to-many (1:N) 215
one-to-one (1:1) 215
ChatGPT
efficiency, optimizing with 280-282
**Chief Analytics Officer (CAO)/
Chief Data Scientist 22**

Chief Compliance Officer (CCO) 22

Chief Data Officer (CDO) 22

Chief Executive Officer (CEO) 21

Chief Financial Officer (CFO) 22

Chief Information Officer (CIO) 21

Chief Information Security
    Officer (CISO) 22

Chief Risk Officer (CRO) 22

Chief Technology Officer (CTO) 22

circular dependencies issue 203

circular references 220-222

avoiding 220

avoiding, best practices 222, 223

scenarios, leading to 222

Column distribution 109

recommended actions on 113

column groups

importance 250

use cases 250

used, for enhancing presentation
    of report 251-257

used, for enhancing readability
    of report 251-257

using 250

Column profile 111, 112

Column quality 110

Empty percentage 111

Error percentage 111

Valid percentage 110

columns

merging 38

splitting 36-38

Comprehensive R Archive
    Network (CRAN) 121

C-suite executives 21

custom function

creating 163-170, 174-176

debugging 164

documentation 164

M code, writing 164

objectives, setting 154

parameters, identifying 154

planning for 153

problem, defining 154

structure, defining 163

testing 164

D

data

cleaning, in Power BI 4, 5

filtering 176-183

filtering and sorting, with M 87

organizing 250

process, initiating 9

reducing 176-183

structuring 250

transforming, with M 88, 89

data accuracy 12, 54

Data Analysis Expressions
    (DAX) 4, 6, 55, 78, 82

as formula language 6

as query language 7

column 8

efficiency, optimizing with 280-282

functions 8

measure 8

operators 8

table references 8

using, reasons by Power BI customers 7

data analysts 20

data cleaning

data assessment 23

data profiling 23, 24

data transformations 24

data validation 24

defining 20
documentation 25
process, building 22
quality assurance 24
quality importance, over quantity 25, 26
role, for improving data quality 13-15
roles, responsible for 20-22
strategies 24
data cleaning techniques 73
columns, adding 73, 74
data type conversions 74, 75
date/time functions 75
pivot/unpivot columns 75
query merging 76
rounding functions 75
data cleaning with anomaly detection 134
data completeness 12, 52-54
data consistency 12, 54
data enhancement with AI insights 146-149
Dataflow Gen1
Power Query Editor, using 122
data formatting
assessing 56-61
data in Power BI
refresh, automating 264-267
snapshots (temporary tables), creating
of cleaned data 267-269
data modeling 4
calendars and date tables 204, 205
dimensional modeling 200, 201
fundamentals 198
importing versus DirectQuery 198
incremental refresh 207, 208
intermediate tables 203
role-playing dimensions 205, 206
snowflake schema 201-203
tables, aggregating 207

data normalization 61
assessing 61-63
data preparation 239, 240
dataset example, creating 243-246
Fields section 241
Filters section 241, 242
Options section 241
Parameters section 242
Query section 240, 241
data preparation with AutoML 134
data profiles
turning, into high-quality data 113
data profiling features
exploring, in Power BI 108
data quality 12
best practices 15
data quality issues
sources 12, 13
data quality manager 21
data quality standards
establishing 15, 16
data relevance
assessing 55, 56
datasets 236
data sources 236
connecting, within Power BI
Report Builder 235-239
data sources, M language 83, 84, 90
data steward 20
data timeliness 12
data types 84, 85
data validity 12
date tables
adding, reasons 204, 205
denormalization
assessing 61-63
considerations 66
diagnostic tools 189

dimensional modeling 63, 64, 200, 201
  cons 201
  pros 201
dimension tables 200
  denormalized data 65, 66
DirectQuery 199, 200
  cons 199
  example scenario 199
  pros 199
  versus importing 198
drill-through context 44
duplicates
  removing 30-33

E

Exploratory Data Analysis (EDA) 23, 107
  benefits 108
extract, transform, and load (ETL) 5

F

fact tables 200
fill down 122, 126
  best practices 127, 128
  implementing, in Power BI 126
  use cases 126
filter context 44
filters
  use cases 246
  using 246-249
functions 84, 85
fuzzy matching 122
  best practices 127, 128
  implementing, in Power BI 123-125
  use cases 123

H

high-quality data
  data profiles, turning into 113

I

identifiers 82
importing 198
  cons 198
  example scenario 198
  pros 198
  versus DirectQuery 198
incremental refresh 207
  cons 208
  considerations 208
  pros 208
in expression 85
intermediate tables 203, 222
  circular dependencies issue 203
IT professionals 20

K

key performance indicators (KPIs) 4

L

large and complex datasets
  handling 218
let keyword 82
literals 85, 86

M

many-to-many (N:N) relationship 216, 222
  example scenario 216
  usage 216

many-to-one (N:1) relationship 215
  example scenario 215
  usage 215
market-leading visualization platform
  data cleaning with anomaly detection 134
  data enhancement with AI insights 146-149
  data preparation with AutoML 134
  using 133
measures 42
  considerations 44
  versus calculated columns 41
memory-efficient coding practices
  considering 185
memory usage
  optimizing 184, 185
Microsoft Copilot
  using 288-293
miles per gallon (mpg) 130
missing data
  removing 33-36
M language 81, 82, 164
  data, filtering and sorting 87
  data sources 90
  data, transforming with 88, 89
  structure 82
  use cases 86
M queries
  OpenAI, using for 283-288
multiple CSV files
  combining 98-103

N

native M functions
  using 183, 184
notifications
  automating 261-264

O

Object-Level Security (OLS) 236
one-to-many (1:N) relationship 215
  example scenario 215
  usage 215
one-to-one (1:1) relationship 215
  example scenario 215
  usage 215
OpenAI
  efficiency, optimizing with 280-282
  using, for M queries 283-288

P

page context 44
paginated reports
  components, reviewing 233, 234
  importance 232
parallel query execution 185, 186
  best practices 186
parameters
  best practices 163
  creating 90, 91
  defining 155
  Formula 1 wins example 155-163
  use cases 246, 247
  using 154, 246-249
  using, in SQL server connection 92-94
  using, to filter data and conditional
    data source selection 95-98
parameter types
  function parameters 155
  list parameters 155
  number parameters 154
  table parameters 155
  text parameters 154

Power Automate
  best practices 274, 275
Power BI
  data, cleaning 4, 5
  data profiling features, exploring 108
  Python scripts, using 129-133
  R scripts, using 129-133
Power BI Report Builder
  data sources, connecting within 235-239
  features 231
Power Query 5, 6
Power Query Editor 4, 77
  integration 79
  using, from Dataflow Gen1 122
  workflow 78
predictors 143
probability threshold 143
Python
  reference link 122
Python scripts
  benefits 129
  using 128
  using, in Power BI 129-133

Q

query
  creating 76
  merging 76
  merging options 76
Query Editor interface 69-72
query steps 84

R

relationship autodetect 63
role-based access controls (RBAC) 294
role-playing dimensions 205, 206

roles
  responsible, for data cleaning 20-22
row context 44
row groups
  importance 250
  use cases 250
  used, for enhancing presentation
    of report 251-257
  used, for enhancing readability
    of report 251-257
  using 250
Row-Level Security (RLS) 236
R Project
  reference link 121
R scripts
  benefits 129
  reference link 122
  using 128
  using, in Power BI 129-133

S

snapshots, of data
  creating, examples 267-274
snowflake schema 201-203
  cons 203
  pros 203
snowflaking 202
SQL Server Analysis Services (SSAS) 6, 236
SQL Server Integration Services (SSIS) 6
star schema 63, 64
  assessing 61-63
  benefits 65
structure, M language 82
  data source 83, 84
  data types 84, 85
  functions 84, 85
  identifiers 82

in expression 85
let keyword 82
literals 85, 86
query steps 84
subject matter experts 21

T

Table.Buffer
  using 187-194
tables
  aggregating 207
Table.Split
  using 187-194
tablix 253
Tabular Editor 43
  advantages 43
time intelligence (TI) 7

U

use cases, M language 86

V

value distribution 113-115
values
  replacing 38-40
  replacing, scenarios 39
variables
  creating 90

Subscribe to our online digital library for full access to over 7,000 books and videos, as well as industry leading tools to help you plan your personal development and advance your career. For more information, please visit our website.

Why subscribe?

- Spend less time learning and more time coding with practical eBooks and Videos from over 4,000 industry professionals

- Improve your learning with Skill Plans built especially for you

- Get a free eBook or video every month

- Fully searchable for easy access to vital information

- Copy and paste, print, and bookmark content

Did you know that Packt offers eBook versions of every book published, with PDF and ePub files available? You can upgrade to the eBook version at packtpub.com and as a print book customer, you are entitled to a discount on the eBook copy. Get in touch with us at customercare@packtpub.com for more details.

At www.packtpub.com, you can also read a collection of free technical articles, sign up for a range of free newsletters, and receive exclusive discounts and offers on Packt books and eBooks.

Other Books You May Enjoy

If you enjoyed this book, you may be interested in these other books by Packt:

Microsoft Power BI Performance Best Practices

Bhavik Merchant

ISBN: 978-1-80107-644-9

- Understand how to set realistic performance targets and address performance proactively
- Understand how architectural options and configuration affect performance
- Build efficient Power BI reports and data transformations
- Explore best practices for data modeling, DAX, and large datasets
- Understand the inner workings of Power BI Premium
- Explore options for extreme scale with Azure services
- Understand how to use tools that help identify and fix performance issues

Microsoft Power BI Data Analyst Certification Guide

Orrin Edenfield, Edward Corcoran

ISBN: 978-1-80323-856-2

- Connect to and prepare data from a variety of sources
- Clean, transform, and shape your data for analysis
- Create data models that enable insight creation
- Analyze data using Microsoft Power BI's capabilities
- Create visualizations to make analysis easier
- Discover how to deploy and manage Microsoft Power BI assets

Packt is searching for authors like you

If you're interested in becoming an author for Packt, please visit `authors.packtpub.com` and apply today. We have worked with thousands of developers and tech professionals, just like you, to help them share their insight with the global tech community. You can make a general application, apply for a specific hot topic that we are recruiting an author for, or submit your own idea.

Share Your Thoughts

Now you've finished *Data Cleaning with Power BI*, we'd love to hear your thoughts! Scan the QR code below to go straight to the Amazon review page for this book and share your feedback or leave a review on the site that you purchased it from.

`https://packt.link/r/1-805-12640-7`

Your review is important to us and the tech community and will help us make sure we're delivering excellent quality content.

Download a free PDF copy of this book

Thanks for purchasing this book!

Do you like to read on the go but are unable to carry your print books everywhere?

Is your eBook purchase not compatible with the device of your choice?

Don't worry, now with every Packt book you get a DRM-free PDF version of that book at no cost.

Read anywhere, any place, on any device. Search, copy, and paste code from your favorite technical books directly into your application.

The perks don't stop there, you can get exclusive access to discounts, newsletters, and great free content in your inbox daily

Follow these simple steps to get the benefits:

1. Scan the QR code or visit the link below

https://packt.link/free-ebook/9781805126409

2. Submit your proof of purchase

3. That's it! We'll send your free PDF and other benefits to your email directly

Made in the USA
Columbia, SC
19 May 2024

35900897R00187